Social Welfare Policy

Related books of interest

Advocacy Practice for Social Justice, Third Edition
Richard Hoefer

Policy, Politics, and Ethics: A Critical Approach, Third Edition
Thomas M. Meenaghan, Keith M. Kilty, Dennis D. Long, and
John G. McNutt

Caught in the Storm: Navigating Policy and Practice in the Welfare Reform Era
Miguel Ferguson, Heather Neuroth-Gatlin, and Stacey Borasky

The Dynamics of Family Policy
Alice K. Butterfield, Cynthia J. Rocha, and William H. Butterfield

New Perspectives on Poverty: Policies, Programs, and Practice
Elissa D. Giffords and Karen R. Garber

The Helping Professional's Guide to Ethics: A New Perspective
Valerie Bryan, Scott Sanders, and Laura E. Kaplan

Straight Talk about Professional Ethics, Second Edition
Kim Strom-Gottfried

Social Welfare Policy

Responding to a Changing World

JOHN G. McNUTT

University of Delaware

RICHARD HOEFER

The University of Texas
at Arlington

LYCEUM
BOOKS, INC.

5758 South Blackstone Avenue
Chicago, Illinois 60637

© 2016 by Lyceum Books, Inc.

Published by

LYCEUM BOOKS, INC.
5758 S. Blackstone Avenue
Chicago, Illinois 60637
773-643-1903 fax
773-643-1902 phone
lyceum@lyceumbooks.com
www.lyceumbooks.com

6 5 4 3 2 1   16 17 18 19 20

ISBN 978-1-933478-75-3

Printed in the United States of America.

Library of Congress Cataloging-in-Publication Data

McNutt, John G., 1951– author.
    Social welfare policy : responding to a changing world / John G. McNutt, Richard Hoefer.
        pages cm
    Includes bibliographical references.
    ISBN 978-1-933478-75-3 (alk. paper)
  1. Social service. 2. Social policy. 3. Public welfare. 4. Human services.
  5. Policy sciences. I. Hoefer, Richard, author. II. Title.
    HV40.M4486   2016
    361.6'1—dc23
                                                            2015026579

Contents

Preface

We practice social work in the real world, and the only constant about our world is the unhalting pace of change. At every moment we must be willing to consider, not only the past, but also the future in order to comprehend our current condition. The world today faces many challenges. Every day people are confronted with massive threats to their well-being—threats to economic welfare from an emerging global information economy, environmental threats that destroy health and safety, global political instability that has repercussions far beyond borders, and a rise of political, social, and cultural violence. People are suffering throughout the world, and although some aspects of this reality have always existed, much of this is new. At the same time, the possibilities for the realization of human potential are at a point that was never before possible or even thought about. Developments in medicine, communication, energy, social and behavioral sciences, and other fields are emerging every day.

Social policy, public policy, and social welfare policy encompass some of the most powerful tools for shaping and interacting with the world. Policy is an essential part of organizational and societal life, and properly developed, policies can protect human rights and health, assure the delivery of benefits, and create opportunities to address the growing inequalities in society. Regardless of your ultimate professional goals—be they counseling, health care, working with youths, community organization, or research—all social workers operate within the confines and consequences of policies that determine *who* may be helped and *how* help may be provided.

One of the most important concepts that underwrites both social work practice and policy is that you must understand the underlying issues before you can craft a proper intervention. If your understanding is of a different, earlier reality, then your assessment is likely to be wrong. Humans in general, and educators in particular, often try to draw comparisons between current conditions and historical events in order to create a more cohesive narrative. Although sometimes these comparisons are reasonable, too often they lead to an incomplete understanding of current reality. Too often, the reality expressed in some of the policy literature owes more to the past than it does to the future. The world and economy today are shaped by modern forces in a way that has never been experienced before. These differences matter in how you approach social policy. Understanding what the changes are and how they affect your world allows you to create policies that successfully address current challenges.

THIS BOOK IS DIFFERENT

This book is unlike other books used in the many social welfare policy courses that exist today. This book explicitly deals with the emerging information economy, the rise of globalization, and the developing environmental crisis. These are forces that real policy efforts are dealing with at the state, local, and national levels. Although other textbooks touch on these issues to some extent, this book provides a tightly integrated way to understand these forces and use them in practice.

Years ago, life was different. The United States was primarily a manufacturing nation. The economy today is far more sophisticated than the one that existed during the Great Depression or the dawn of the industrial period. Technology was primitive by today's standards. The United States felt protected by two broad oceans. Today's speedy transportation wasn't available. Although there were environmental emergencies, the scale was generally more local and the population was also smaller. Although some feel that this earlier time was more idyllic, this is more wishful thinking than reality. Many of today's rights were not available to earlier Americans, especially the poor and members of excluded groups.

In today's world, instant communication is a given, knowledge work is highly prized, information is immediately available, and things that happen across the world have immediate ramifications for life in American communities. There are also massive economic dislocations, environmental crises, and unstable governments. All of these factors make life more complex but open up new and exciting opportunities. The underlying forces that power these changes will continue to evolve and create new challenges for social workers.

PLAN OF THE BOOK

The book introduces you to basic ideas concerning the three major forces operating in the world today—globalization, the information economy, and environmental threats—and describes the terminology essential to understanding the realm of social welfare policy. Next we examine the past, present, and future of social welfare policy and discuss tools in the social work field that you can use to analyze and advocate for solutions to problems. Even in challenging times, you can affect your own fate and the fates of clients, for whom and with whom you work. The section begins by outlining the importance of values and ideology for the eventual shape of social welfare policy in any polity around the world. It then shows you how to conduct your own policy "quick analysis," and finally how to take that information and advocate for desired solutions.

The final chapters encompass six traditional arenas of policy study: child and family services, health and mental health, poverty and inequality, housing and community development, crime and violence, and aging. Each arena is approached with a common structure and set of questions to answer, examining how they function in the broader context of social forces while also identifying what concerns have remained constant and universal. In this way you can see the power of following large-scale trends and their effects on individual policy areas. The problems of people can either be diminished or exacerbated by the overarching trends discussed here, depending on how they are addressed.

The book ends with a short coda, not to summarize the material, but to ensure some closure. It will be quite a journey that you embark on in this book, and it is always nice to spend a bit of time making sure that the experience is savored when it is about to end. For the many reasons discussed in this text, the present is unlike the past and the future is being shaped and reshaped daily. You will face challenges that social workers in the past never had to meet. This book will prepare you to address these challenges.

Our Thanks

We would like to thank our publisher, David Follmer, for his persistence in seeing this project through, and Tom Meenaghan of Lyceum Books who strongly supported the book as well. The reviewers of earlier drafts—Michael Dover, Robin Ersing, Susan Grossman, Thomas McLaughlin, Victor Manolo, and Alice K. Butterfield—deserve credit for helping us think through the ideas. There are other reviewers whose names we do not know, but their critiques also inspired us to improve the manuscript in numerous ways. Naturally, we take full responsibility for the areas of the book that fall short.

Many people in our lives supported us when we needed support, and left us alone to wrestle with our thoughts when we needed that, as well. John would like to think his frequent technology collaborators including Jonathan Justice, Kate Boland, Lauri Goldkind, Steve Hick, Goutham Menon, Roger Lohmann, Michael Ahn, Irene Queiro-Tajalli, David Carter, and Lori Brainard, who helped me focus my ideas and look for exciting avenues to explore. Many of my students and colleagues have led me into intellectual areas that were both unexpected and exciting. I would also like to thank my mentors, particularly David Austin, Robert Sigler, Ken Sanchagrin, and Donald Anderson. Finally, to Marcia, I dedicate my part of the book.

Rick's gratitude extends to those people who have inspired him to think about social policy and why we have the type of policy we do. Intellectual forebears such as John Tropman and Jack Walker, and other faculty at the University of Michigan, helped kindle my interest and provide me needed skills. Colleagues at the University of Texas at Arlington, where I have worked for over twenty years, provided encouragement and support. The many students who asked questions and learned along with me deserve my thanks, too. I dedicate my portion of this book to my daughter, Sharon, a social work graduate herself, and most especially to my wife, Paula, who has seen me work far into the night on far too many days.

Chapter 1

Welcome to the Future:
Your Many Roles

As you begin this book, take a moment to consider your situation as it currently stands. Like most people, you are undoubtedly in flux, ending some aspects of your life, beginning others but mostly continuing many of the roles that are part of how you see your life moving forward. One role that you will certainly be playing is student.

Although you may be taking on the role of student for the first time in a while, you have already had years of experience with it. You were in elementary, middle, and high schools where you learned about this role in those different settings. Being a student at a college or university carries different responsibilities than those earlier forms of schooling.

But you're not just *any* type of student; you're a student in a social work class. You're likely either a BSW or an MSW student and you may have a concentration in a level of service (individual, group, organization, or community) or a field of practice (mental health, child welfare, addictions, or schools) or both. This type of role specification helps you define who you are to yourself and others. It helps you become better at what you do by having a tighter focus to your knowledge and skills.

Such specialization can also put you into self-made or organizationally defined silos where you hardly ever interact with people who are not in the same narrow specialty as you are. You can become immersed in the small world of your current classes, job, or position. You could stop learning about your profession and the world more broadly. This leaves you knowing very little about how other people (even social workers) operate and what they know. It certainly leaves you unaware of how you are affected by factors beyond your specialty area.

Your social work education tries to counteract this problem of overspecialization by requiring you to take classes that may, at first glance, not be related to what you want to do as a social worker. You're required to take courses in research methods, human behavior in the social environment, and social policy. Take a look at how these classes can be helpful to you.

1

Research courses provide tools for knowing what effective practice is. They help you confront your prejudices, expand your limited knowledge, and see connections between different factors in clients' lives and operations. Human behavior classes present different theories that explain why people do what they do, when they do. These theories operate at the individual, group, organizational, and community levels. Exploring the ramifications of human behavior theories in a serious way will force you out of your silo quickly!

This book is an introduction to the area of social policy, which is one of the most important silo-breakers in social work. At first glance, knowledge of social policy is of use only to people interested in macro social work. But all social workers operate within the confines and consequences of policies that determine *who* may be helped, *when* they may receive help, *how* often they can receive help, and in *what* ways help may be provided. Knowing what the rules are is a vital element for effective and ethical social workers.

But your knowledge of social policy "dos and don'ts" cannot end there. Professional social workers must also learn how to change policy that is detrimental to client success, built on incorrect assumptions, or possibly even counter to social work ethics. Anyone who wishes to fully take on the role of professional social worker must not only know what policy currently exists but also what actions can be taken to make existing policy more effective, more just, and more beneficial.

This book is designed and written to help you understand the context of current social work practice and policy as well as the trends that continue to affect life in the United States for everyone. You need this knowledge to be effective in your social work career no matter what social work role you play.

WHAT IS SOCIAL WELFARE POLICY?

All government entities and many other types of organizations create policies to guide and structure their activities. Policies give direction to organizational activities and allow for complex interventions aimed at problems and challenges. Policy is an essential part of organizational and societal life. Properly developed, policies can protect human rights, assure the delivery of benefits, and create opportunities. Governments design an enormous range of policies aimed at all sorts of issues and problems. Policies are created by different branches of government at different levels.

Public policy is usually considered to be all the decisions that the government makes and the laws, regulations, and other artifacts that result from these decisions. Where highways go, what types of things are allowed in food, and how student financial aid is allocated are all examples of public policy. Policies include laws, regulations, budgets, plans, and other things that guide and structure governmental action.

Social policy is composed of those decisions that affect social well-being. Health care, education, telecommunications, environmental protection, and so forth are examples of social policy. There is a vast array of social policy decision-making and all social policies are part of public policy.

Social welfare policy is composed of those aspects of social policy that involve mutual aid or people helping people (Warren, 1963). Mental health policy, child welfare, and social security policies are examples of social welfare policy. Environmental regulations help people by preventing the impacts of environmental destruction but are not social welfare policies because they do not involve mutual aid. They are, however, social policies and public policies.

Policies are often interrelated. It is important to note that economic policies (which are public policies) frequently have an impact on antipoverty and social insurance policies (which are social welfare policies). It is also worth noting that policies are frequently in conflict with one another. The nature of that interaction is becoming more and more complicated as time goes on and society changes from an industrial economy to one based on information. This doesn't mean that that is what is intended. Sometimes there is a tight connection between two policy domains. An example is unemployment compensation, which was intended to have a stimulating effect on the economy when a recession created unemployment. This is called an automatic stabilizer because the money spent for aid is also supposed to stimulate the economy and help end the recession. In other cases, the link is less direct and some policies may even work against each other. Figure 1-1 portrays the relationship between public policy, social policy, and social welfare policy.

Most of the things that social workers are concerned about are part of social welfare policy. Most of their programs (child welfare, mental health, health care, and aging) are covered by social welfare policy. On balance, the entire range of public policies can affect the welfare of people so social workers must be concerned about all of those issues. Air pollution, for example, can lead to important health consequences for the entire population. Air pollution can lead to respiratory disease. Groundwater contamination can lead to cancer. The outcomes of transportation policy can have an impact on wealth and poverty when rural communities are left behind or intercity communities lack public transportations to job sites (Wilson, 1996). Although these are not

Figure 1-1
Relationship between Public Policy, Social Policy, and Social Welfare Policy

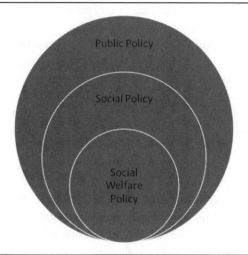

specifically what you may think of as social welfare policy, they are obviously important to people who are concerned about human well-being. Public policy is an interconnected world and all of it affects the well-being of part of the population. Many traditional treatments of social welfare policy essentially ignore some important public policy and social policy issues.

Environmental policies, for example, are critical to the health and well-being of our population (Brown, 2009; Hoff & McNutt, 1994). As evidenced in the aftermath of the 2005 Katrina/Wilma/Rita storms in the Gulf coast and Hurricane Sandy on the East coast in late 2012, the environment has significant impacts on wealth, poverty, and homelessness. If you ignore the ecological base of social welfare policy and the social problems that it tries to address, you will arrive at an incomplete understanding of the problem and an inadequate solution.

Telecommunications policy, long considered irrelevant to social welfare concerns, has emerged as a major driver of the newest form of social injustice, the digital divide. A related set of issues, the net neutrality debate, will also contribute to inequality and may hold the key to free speech in the future.

Perhaps the biggest omission in much of the social work literature is a credible discussion of the range of economic policies. Because much of what social welfare policy makers do depends on the underlying state of the economy, this is a serious omission. The current condition of state budgets has had and will have an enormous impact on what policies can be mounted at state and local levels and, because there is a good deal of cost sharing in many federal policies, will determine many choices made by the federal government.

Many policy makers find economic logic more compelling than that offered by other experts. Just because you do not like the logic of economics does not mean that you can ignore its almost overwhelming impact on the policy debates. This, in turn, means that social workers are often unprepared to function in these policy areas even when it is in their interest to be able to do so.

Policy develops in a confluence of social, cultural, economic, and political forces. All of these forces shape the policies that social workers make and the problems their clients and communities deal with. Understanding what is happening and what is possible is critical to understanding policy and ultimately social work. What you can accomplish as a social work practitioner depends on the severity of the social problems and what society has done to address them. It also depends on the resources available to address the problem. All of these factors are addressed directly or indirectly by the policy enterprise.

Professional Responsibilities Concerning Social Policy

Sometimes social work students are unclear why they should know about social policy. After all, most see themselves as working directly with clients, not studying laws, history, or techniques of lobbying. This is a natural reaction to your past experiences. Still, understanding the total package of becoming a professional social worker may help explain the necessity of understanding and being able to understand and affect policy.

Becoming a member of any profession, including social work, is a daunting task. In addition to learning about human behavior, social work practice, research methods, and a number of other things, there is the transition to becoming a professional which carries with it a new set of expectations and responsibilities. There are the responsibilities of professional ethics, the expectation of professional behavior, and responsibilities under law and regulation. There are also the ethical responsibilities of upholding the values shared by social workers. Although all professions hold social betterment as an article of commitment, social work goes further and makes it a strong ethical principle. The National Association of Social Workers (NASW) Code of Ethics makes it quite clear that all social workers—not just the ones who choose careers in macro practice—have a responsibility to work for social change. Upholding this professional expectation is impossible without a thorough grounding in what social policy is, how it affects what social workers and clients can and must do, and what affects policies and laws.

Social workers have another set of responsibilities that go beyond the professional realm. There are the responsibilities of citizenship. Certainly they include voting, staying informed about issues, participating in public meetings, completing jury duty, and paying taxes. These are important but there are more. You are a citizen of your community. Making your community better is your responsibility. You are a citizen of your nation. National issues are something that you should care about and try to address. You are also a citizen of the world. Although there are many good things in the world, there is no shortage of evils. War, slavery, desperate poverty, disease, and a host of other terrible things afflict our world. A question that every social worker must ask is "Do we do something or do we look away?"

Most social workers look at the problems that negatively affect our communities, our nation, and our world, and want to make a difference. It would be difficult to profess the values of the social work profession and not want an end to poverty, crime, and disease. The truth is that people can make a difference. It might be difficult, costly, and take a great deal of time, but it can be done.

Making a difference combines your roles as citizen and social worker. How you choose to make a difference depends on the opportunities and resources that you have.

The skills that you learn in social work education can be applied to discharging your responsibilities as a citizen. You learn how to assess people and situations, how to interview, how to work with groups, and how to organize. These are all incredibly useful skills. This book will take you further and introduce you to what may be a new role for you: Applying your knowledge and practicing your skills allow you to make a difference with your clients, the organizations you work in, and the communities you live in. Some change agents have an impact at state, national, and international levels.

This book is designed to help you become the change agent that social work students aspire to be. It has been developed to help you understand the issues you face and are likely to face in the future. It will give you the opportunity to do something productive in the service of positive social change.

WHAT MAKES THIS POLICY BOOK DIFFERENT?

Although this policy book is likely to be one of the few that you, as a student, ever read, it is really quite different in some important ways from other policy

Street scene in Seoul demonstrating urban congestion and population growth. Seoul is a quickly growing city and a powerhouse in the global information economy.

books. Your instructor likely chose this book for your class because of these differences.

This book is different in three major ways from many other policy books: (1) It uses the global information society as an important point of departure for the analysis of societal trends affecting policy. (2) It devotes considerable attention to the environment as a major social policy issue. (3) It emphasizes *doing* policy analysis and advocacy as well as *learning about* policy. It thus deals with social policy and public policy as an integrated knowledge and skill area for your life as both a professional and a citizen.

A QUICK PEEK AHEAD

The world is facing transformative social change. This is not unlike the change that early social workers encountered when they went to work in the teeming slums of major American cities in the midst of the Industrial Revolution in the 1800s. There are three major things looming in the very near future:

Toronto, a highly developed post-industrial city

- The Rise of the Information Economy: People today are in the midst of a major transformation from an industrial economy to an information economy. This will change all the social institutions and change the nature of people's lives. Although many of the impacts of the information society will occur in the future, quite a few have already happened and many are occurring now. The pace of change is often quicker than people realize and change is difficult for most people.

- The Continued Pace of Globalization: Although there has always been international trade, the pace of globalization has increased radically. Americans now compete with people throughout the world. The development of technology has made trade easier and more immediate. Globalization has both benefits and costs. The loss of many jobs and the devastation of communities are clearly costs of international trade. On balance, people's ability to benefit from trade is considerable. The fact that you can interact with people all over the world is a huge benefit and one that can enrich both your working life and your personal life. In addition, having products made in low-cost areas of the globe makes them less expensive for American consumers when they are sold in the United States. The influence of globalization challenges what is meant by "citizenship" and "statehood" by giving people a view of themselves as part of a larger system.

- The Need to Conserve and Protect the Environment: After centuries of ignoring the health of our planet and environment, the bill has come due. If people do not stop overconsuming and despoiling their resource base, they will run out of resources. It is also true that many of the things that people put into the environment will hurt the health and the life chances of future generations.

These are key issues that will define your life and your work. They are things you cannot ignore. They will create problems and difficulties. They are, however, forces that you can ultimately manage. This will take knowledge, skills, and commitment.

Social work and social welfare currently exist within the context of these three streams. You definitely should care about them because they affect your work and your professional future. But you must also care because of your role as a citizen. The message is that if you are a social worker you must care about the information society, globalization, and the environment because these forces will have a major impact on your professional and personal life.

In order to make a change you must first understand the issues. Change for change's sake is rarely beneficial and frequently disastrous. This book gives you a good overview of the major issues and how they work, although you will have to continue to learn about the issues as time passes. This book will introduce you to policy analysis and advocacy skills. These are skills that will help you understand the issues and make constructive change when the opportunity presents itself. The book also gives you questions to think about, further resources to consult, and exercises to do.

This chapter has served as an introduction to the world of social policy and how it is vital for social workers to understand it. The next chapter discusses in more depth the terms and vocabulary that you will need so that you can communicate clearly. It looks at three forces within the context of these concepts— the coming of the information age, globalization, and environmental issues. It blends in information from sociology, political science, anthropology, and economics to make these concepts understandable. These two chapters comprise an introduction to social policy in the information age.

Chapter 3 presents a history of social policy, primarily in the United States. This chapter looks at the history of social policy and places the three major issues in chronological perspective. It reviews the history of social welfare and social policy using a developmental perspective. This is not a comprehensive overview of social welfare history. It is intended to illustrate how the development of society and its institutions has affected and will continue to affect social policy and social welfare. Only by knowing the foundation of America's current system can one explore recent changes leading to social policy in the information society. Chapter 4 presents the book's central thesis, that the nature of society is changing and so too are the problems of society. This is a more in-depth treatment of the information society within the context of a global society and an environmental crisis. This chapter provides additional theory and issues to ponder. The changing nature of social problems calls for reexamining the solutions that social workers are called to create and implement.

With these four chapters of foundation firmly laid, the next three chapters explain tools for understanding and affecting social policy. Chapter 5 discusses the role of values, ideology, and political philosophy in social policy. These issues are critical to understanding the current debates on many issues central to social policy and what solutions may be found for them. This chapter examines social policy values using examples from around the world. The range of potential policy is much wider than is usually discussed in the United States, so it is important to place the United States in a global perspective. Chapter 6 gives you real world tools for analyzing and critiquing policies. This approach uses a process called quick analysis. This policy analysis chapter provides a conceptual overview but it also provides some realistic ideas on how to do a basic analysis. This chapter provides content on the political and economic content of policy analysis and also offers practical guidance for your initial stab at completing the policy analysis process. Chapter 7 provides information on how to advocate for the solutions deemed best. Because advocacy is a component of ethical social work practice, all social workers must have grounding in advocacy.

The final six chapters provide information and application of the three vital trends that are occurring as people move further into the information society. Six topical areas are covered: poverty (chapter 8), health and mental health (chapter 9), children and family policies (chapter 10), crime and violence (chapter 11), housing and community development (chapter 12), and aging (chapter 13). Each of these chapters examines a current issue in terms of the three forces and looks at both existing policy and potential policy.

The first of these chapters looks at poverty and the probable poverty and income issues that arise. It examines the problem of poverty and its measurement. It also looks at domestic and national statistics and considers theories about the problem. It then examines current issues and policies and considers how well those policies square with both current and emerging needs.

Chapter 9 focuses on health care and mental health. This is an area that you will likely see a great deal of discussion about in the next few years. This chapter looks at health and disease, how these issues are measured, and what theories are critical to following the issues. The chapter also describes how environmental problems contribute to health issues.

Children and family policies are the subject of chapter 10. Children are society's most vulnerable group and this chapter looks at the problems that they face and the policies that can help them. American society can do a better job for kids and their families.

Crime and violence are constant problems in society. How people deal with the victims and the perpetrators is important. Why are there such different perceptions of the harms caused by white collar crime, which steals billions of dollars of wealth, and street crime, which has much less financial impact? The United States has the highest incarceration rate in the world. Is this really in our best interest? Chapter 11 deals with these questions.

Chapter 12 explores the related areas of housing and community development. Community is important in the United States and could receive better treatment at the hands of public policy. The recent crisis in housing and mortgage lending has had a tremendous negative impact on the world economy. It has caused thousands of people to lose their homes, with some ending up homeless. American society can do better.

Chapter 13 looks at the role of aging in an information society. This will become an ever more important area as the United States becomes a society with a higher proportion of aged people. Although poverty among the post-sixty-five-year-old segment of the population is relatively low, it has increased in recent years. Seniors also have a number of problems that are related to their age, particularly health issues.

Social policy, in the United States and in the world today, can be much better. It can be more adequate, fairer, and better organized. More important, it can change the way people live in the world.

A lot of this discussion is about social work and your role as a social worker. You can make a difference. You can also make change as a citizen in all your various roles. All of this together is about living your life as a force for a better, more just world. At the end of the day, why are you here?

The book concludes with a short coda, bringing together the themes presented through all of the chapters.

HOPE FOR THE FUTURE

The United States and, indeed, the world, are faced with enormous challenges. The task of adapting to a new stage of societal evolution is one of them. Another charge is preserving the environment. Living together as a global village is still a third challenge. This is certainly enough work for any group of people and any generation. The labor will be hard and the risks will be great.

You are about to embark on a great quest—creating the future of your society. This society faces many challenges from both within and without. Some of those challenges are familiar, such as the growth of poverty, a shortage of health care, domestic violence, immigration, and so forth. Others are not so familiar, such as globalization, the decline of social capital and civility, and the rise of international terrorism. All of these problems that are confronting the social welfare system beg for solutions. To survive as a society, people must adapt to a new set of realities. The issues are difficult ones and it will take creativity and commitment to make the difference that is needed.

Social work is certainly about dealing with today's issues, but it also has always been about building the future. You are about to become part of that proud tradition. Social workers in direct services build a future for their clients by working with them as individuals, couples, families, and small groups. They take a future that wasn't so rosy and make it into something livable and more satisfying. Direct service workers fight for social justice every day (see Pierce, 1984).

Community organizers, administrators, and social planners create new organizations, programs, and even new communities, thus forming the structure of future environments and helping systems (Gilbert & Specht, 1974). Finally, policy practitioners create the framework of laws, regulations, and other elements of the framework that makes it all work together (Jansson, 2007). Working as a team, social workers create a positive, empowering future for all that makes clear their commitments to social and economic justice, diversity, and protecting the rights of special populations. Everybody on the social work team contributes to the final product.

Social welfare policy shapes the social work profession and influences what practitioners can do. It is a basic part of our environment. It's also likely that change in social policy will change the profession. Social work can be proactive and help make the changes that are necessary. Change is inevitable but the nature of the change can be guided, planned, and influenced. This book will give you some of the tools that you need to be part of that change.

It is helpful to note that social workers are well positioned to change policy (Hoefer, 2012a) and can use the techniques necessary to design, analyze, and advocate for appropriate policies. It is both part of social workers' values and ethics and an occupational necessity. If social workers fail to address the need for new policies, their jobs will become more frustrating and they will be unable to deal positively with human needs.

The hope is that you will finish this book with a new understanding of what is happening in social welfare and social work as well as a commitment to make the changes that are essential for the future. This will be an exciting journey for you. Creating the future is a fascinating prospect. You can choose many of the ways that your future will play out. It's important that you make the critical choices.

Once there was a time like this time. People struggled to meet the demands of a new economy, they worked to save the environment, and they dealt with a global labor force. They had names like Jane Addams, Frances Perkins, and Mary Richmond. They called themselves social workers. You can use what this book offers to make the world a better, more just, and more positive place. Social workers have been doing that for a long time. You can make change now and in the future. It's your turn now. This is the time.

Questions for Discussion

1. Why should social workers get involved with things like environmental preservation and climate change? Isn't that somebody else's problem?

2. I just want to work with individuals and families. How is social policy going to help me?

Exercises

1. Write your obituary. What did you accomplish by the end of a long and satisfying life? What would you like to say that you did? What would you like your peers to say and think about you? After you have created the obituary, think about what it means and what it says about your values. What is important to you? How can your career reflect what your values endorse?

2. Map your concerns. This exercise gives you the opportunity to see where the things that you care about are connected. Start with a large sheet of paper and several colored magic markers. List the issues that you care about in a circle around the paper. Draw a line between the ones that you think are connected. Which things seem highly connected? Which seem to be independent?

Websites

The Do Something Awards: http://www.dosomething.org/programs/awards

Future Majority: http://futuremajority.com/

Harvard Institute on Politics: http://www.iop.harvard.edu/

Idealist: http://www.idealist.org/

Netroots Nation: http://netrootsnation.org/

Serve Next: http://www.servenext.org/

Further Reading

Brown, L. R. (2006). *Plan B 2.0: Rescuing a planet under stress and a civilization in trouble*. New York, NY: Norton.

Cohen, L., & Young, D. (1989). *Careers for dreamers and doers: A guide to management careers in the nonprofit sector*. New York, NY: Foundation Center.

Idealist.org & Land, S. (2009). *The Idealist.org handbook to building a better world*. New York, NY: Perigee.

Steffen, A. (Ed.) (2006). *World changing: A user's guide to the 21st century*. New York, NY: Harry N. Abrams.

Chapter 2

Society and Social Welfare in Agrarian and Industrial Societies

Social welfare policy is a critical part of any social worker's conceptual tool kit. It provides the means by which assistance arrives and services are made available. It is society's response to the problems that people in society experience. Social work, as it is generally understood, is not possible without social welfare policy. Social work, as a profession, depends on social sanction to operate. That sanction comes from the organized frameworks that are part of the social welfare enterprise.

Like other social institutions, social welfare exists in the context of a society's culture, the economy, the social structure, and the political system. These other systems have a tremendous impact on social welfare policy making. They also are very influential in determining what kinds of problems the social welfare system encounters and what problems it can address. Some think of social institutions as constants; they are, in fact, frequently changing entities.

Social institutions are the structures that allow society to meet the critical needs of its members. Generally, the economic system, the family, the government, religion, and social welfare are considered to be social institutions (Gilbert & Specht, 1974; Warren, 1963). Each of these institutions meets a core set of needs (fulfills a social function) but may address other needs as well.

SOCIAL WORK, SOCIETAL FUNCTIONS, AND INSTITUTIONS

If you were suddenly stranded in a completely uninhabited locale, with just one other person with whom to procreate, how would you set up your new society? Assuming you had sufficient natural resources, and were lucky enough not to have any deaths due to childbirth, accidents, or illness, how would you organize your time and the time of others in your family?

As you think about it, you'd have to accomplish at least a few minimum tasks in order to survive: You'd have to have shelter, food, and water, as well as tools to make your work more efficient and effective. You'd want to establish some way to set rules and enforce them, particularly as your group became larger. Education of the young is important so that knowledge is transferred

15

BY THE MAGISTRATES & TOWN COUNCIL IN GRATITUDE FOR THE LIBERALITY AND KINDNESS OF ARCHIBALD JOHN EARL OF ROSEBERY PROVOST OF THIS BURGH TO WHOM THE INHABITANTS ARE INDEBTED FOR A BLEACHING GREEN & THIS SUPPLY OF WATER

1817

This sign in a local community south of Edinburgh, Scotland, thanks the provost, a local municipal leader, for providing the community with clean water. The provision of clean water (as we expect it today) was long in coming in even developed nations and remains a dream for people in many parts of the world today.

and possibly enlarged. You may want to develop a way to have all the people in your group feel included and to have ways to acknowledge a sense of the transcendent. You might want to foster a sense of mutual interdependence as well. These are the functions that any group of people needs to survive, though some are more primary than others. Without sufficient food and water, for example, other needs are irrelevant. One expression of this idea is from Abraham Maslow, with his "hierarchy of needs" (Maslow, 1954).

What you've done in this thought experiment is to informally lay out the primary functions of a society. The next step is to look at what the five main social functions are and what social institutions help achieve those functions, at least to some degree.

FIVE SOCIAL FUNCTIONS AND THE SOCIAL INSTITUTIONS THAT ADDRESS THEM

This section describes five social functions and the institutions that are designed to achieve them. Despite the many variations and debates about

Figure 2-1
Social Functions and Social Institutions

Principal Societal Function	Primary Institution
Production-Distribution-Consumption	Economy
Socialization	Family/Schools
Social Control	Government
.Social Participation	Religious/Civic Organizations
Mutual Aid	Social Welfare

functionalism, the main tenet is easily understandable: In any society, there are needs to be met and institutions are developed to meet these needs.

Figure 2-1 shows the principal social functions and the primary institutions developed to handle them. Each function will be discussed in turn. Two caveats should be kept in mind when looking at this figure. First, more than one institution can play a part in fulfilling any particular function, and second, these assignments can change over time.

Social Function 1: Production, Distribution, and Consumption

This function refers to the way that a society "earns a living" and is met through the institution of the economy, a system that allows for products and services to be created, distributed, and consumed by and for its members. This might mean anything from hunting and gathering to a complex global information society. Individuals within the economic system decide what is produced and how it is distributed. They set priorities for what kind of goods and services are created. They control the distribution system and determine the prices that people pay for what they need or want. Economic systems vary from those that are guided completely by market forces to those that are governed by economic planning. This is generally a matter of degree rather than all one or all the other.

Pure market economies operate with complete autonomy from another of the institutions, government. This is the type of economy that was advocated by Adam Smith and the early political economists and is echoed in some contemporary authors and politicians such as Ayn Rand and Rand Paul. They argue that a free market is the most efficient way for an economic system to operate and if the government played no role, the market would manage itself. This concept, the self-regulating market, was generally called into question after the Great Depression. There are very few nations in the world that have this completely hands-off way of dealing with the economic system. Most nations have at least some planning and some regulation.

At the other extreme are pure command economies that are operated completely by government planning. Planners determine what is made and how it is distributed. This is the ideal of socialist governments. Many socialists feel that markets ignore social justice and equality so that a command government is a better choice for the people who live there. Again, there are few, if any, pure communist nations. Even socialism, which is a variant of communism that accepts limited markets, is rarely practiced in anything like a pure form.

Both of these extreme positions have proved problematic in practice and very few thinkers advocate for either of these positions. The United States has a mixed economy that includes both planning and the market as decision-makers. The U.S. market system is regulated by a host of laws and institutions that are designed to deal with the problems of pure markets. There are organizations such as the Federal Reserve Bank that plan economic activity and intervene where there are problems. People use monetary and fiscal policies to manage the economy, and they regulate many aspects of business and finance. Monetary policy manages the amount of money in the economy in an effort to control inflation, or rising prices. Fiscal policy concerns government spending and taxing arrangements, hoping to influence unemployment levels and avoid the free market's tendency toward instability.

Sometimes the operation of the world economy frustrates a nation's ability to control the domestic economy. Because of the interdependent nature of world economies it is very difficult to resist the forces in international markets. The energy issue regularly reminds Americans that they are part of a world economy. Although it is possible to isolate a nation from the world economic system, it is rarely a successful strategy because few countries can supply all their needs for energy, food, and other necessities without engaging in trade with other countries. The world economy is governed not only by economic forces and the laws of the various nations; it is influenced by a complex array of treaties, institutions, and agreements. These constraints often affect domestic economic behavior.

Social Function 2: Socialization

Socialization is the societal function that assures that all members have the knowledge and skills needed to function in a society. This means that new members (either by birth or by migration) must learn a wide range of things. To ensure that this occurs, society creates mechanisms to make that happen. The family is a primary agent of socialization in American society, supported by the educational system. In addition, organizations socialize their members, as do social groups and communities. In most cases this is positive but sometimes people are socialized to engage in "deviant" behavior that threatens societal integrity. Cults, gangs, and other groups are examples of negative influence.

Socialization also influences how people choose to participate in public policy and how well they are involved. Family socialization can contribute to a desire for civic involvement or it can repress that need. Organizations also contribute to socialization. Putnam (2000) argues that associations are used to provide people with the training and experience needed to participate (what Verba, Schlozman, & Brady, 1995, call civic skills) in the governmental and political system.

Socialization through families and educational organizations is generally successful in meeting the major demands of society for most people. In some cases, however, it breaks down or prepares people for deviant life styles. At that point, society relies on agents of social control to control behavior.

Social Function 3: Social Control

Social control is the means to assure that society has rules and that the rules are followed. This means both formal rules, such as laws and policies, but informal rules as well. No organized activity is possible without mutual expectations and it is difficult to conceive of even a simple society without enforced ground rules in place. The most obvious formal agents of social control are law enforcement officers and the criminal justice system. Although social workers might prefer not to think of themselves as formal agents of social control, their activities in mental health, child welfare, and other areas are clearly aimed at controlling deviant behavior. Some (see Galper, 1977; Piven & Cloward, 1971) argue that almost all social welfare is a form of control. Informal agents of social control are ubiquitous. A word, a nod, or even a negative expression can serve to control behavior. The internalized sense of society's expectations is usually enough to prevent most deviant behavior.

The governmental institution is the principal agent of social control but it also discharges many other functions in modern societies. Government is involved in all of the other functions to a greater or lesser extent.

Governments vary in the extent to which the governed are included in decision-making. Pure democracies, which allow complete control of the government by majority rule, are rare, at least at the national level. Totalitarian governments, which control their citizens to a high degree, are unfortunately not so rare. This is, again, a continuum from anarchy (no control) to totalitarianism.

Governments tend to be reflections of particular sets of values that are inherent in the rules about social control and other functions. Chapter 5 discusses a wide variety of political values.

Social Function 4: Social Participation

Social participation refers to the networks and relationships that make it possible for people to undertake complex societal tasks. One aspect of this is that people are able to work with other people constructively. Religious beliefs, and the institutions that transmit them, act to bring people together around common values and beliefs, and instruct believers on how to interact with people of different beliefs. Participation in society is eased by having religious institutions bringing like-minded people together, as long as there is tolerance for other groups' views. When only one religious (or ideological) view is allowed to exist, problems, such as discrimination, persecution, and even genocide, can occur. This sort of misuse of the power of social cohesion and participation tears societies apart. When religious tensions threaten, successful societies turn to creating secular institutions and values to provide a sense of community. This approach to social participation and cohesion is referred to as nationalism. It, too, can lead to problems if the cohesion of the society depends on creating an external threat or enemy that must be vanquished.

At a more local level, non-religious civic organizations assist in enabling social participation. Civic organizations, such as sports clubs, fraternal societies, professional associations, and the like, allow individuals to organize themselves to accomplish tasks that otherwise would be beyond the abilities of individuals on their own. Such organizations help create what is called "social capital." Social capital (Putnam, 2000) is a capacity that is built through social participation in networks that can bring benefits to the individuals involved in them. Social capital is also vitally important to both the commercial and political systems because people with high levels of social capital can translate this into benefits for their families, organizations, and communities.

Political participation is one aspect of social participation. Having a democracy requires participation in order to make it work. Of course many people do not participate and are not involved (Verba, Schlozman, & Brady, 1995) and thus their views and ideas are less likely to be embedded into policy and law. Political parties, groups, and associations try to encourage people to participate in the political system (Putnam, 2000; Skocpol, 2003).

A concrete expression of social capital is the concept of civil society. This term has roots going back to early philosophical discussions about morality and the roles of people and governments. Although the term is now used widely and with considerable variation in meaning, it generally refers to a non-market-, non-government-based set of organizations that do not distribute profits and that are private, self-governed, and voluntary (Salamon, Sokolowski, & List, 2003). According to Salamon, Sokolowski and List (2003), organizations in civil society perform tasks such as "advocacy, cultural expression, commu-nity organizing, environmental protection, human rights, religion, representa-tion of interests, and political expression" and provide concrete services, such as the "provision of health, education, or welfare services" (p. 9). The National Association of Social Workers, the National Rifle Association, and your local reli-gious institution are all aspects of civil society.

Social participation is also important to other aspects of society. It supports mutual decision-making and the development of a functioning society. This par-ticipation is encouraged by the voluntary organizations, groups, and nonprofit organizations that comprise civil society (see Salamon, 1994). An important part of that collection of groups is religion and the faith community.

Social Function 5: Mutual Aid

Mutual aid is the function that provides help for those in need. More specifi-cally, mutual aid is people helping people. This can mean organized social wel-fare but it can also include acts of individual informal helping and the development of support networks. Mutual aid is different across societies and subcultures in societies. Societies differ in what mutual aid consists of, how it is delivered, and how it is regarded by others. The study of mutual aid is the study of social policy.

CHANGING SOCIETY CHANGES INSTITUTIONS

The functionalist perspective has a focus on answering the question "How do societies maintain themselves?" One answer is that the institutions in the soci-ety are effective enough to keep enough people from demanding change so that large-scale changes are unneeded. Of course, sometimes mechanisms of social control can be used to stifle dissent and lead to persecution and repres-sion in order to avert change even when large numbers of people desire it.

Another answer, and one that is more positive, is that social institutions can be agile enough so that desire for change is foreseen or at least accommo-dated without creating society-destroying alterations. One can see differences in the level of adaptability between different societies (such as the peaceful shift from one leader to the next in the American political system compared to countries gaining new leaders only as a result of military force or extreme political uprisings).

The functionalist approach posits that all of the social institutions work together and have overlapping boundaries. When one institution changes others must adapt. For example, when levels of social participation increase and additional categories of people become active, new types of government policy may emerge with social control mechanisms changing as well. The civil rights movement in the United States during the 1950s and 1960s shows how a group of people who were denied the right to participate fully in society were able to use the institutions of society to promote an equal status. In this case, social control mechanisms were first used to thwart civil rights for African Americans, but advocates' social participation through largely nonviolent means eventually caused institutions to change. Now, institutions are set up to promote equality. Laws prohibit discrimination in the workplace, schools promote inclusion of all children, and people of color receive benefits from social welfare institutions. (Current social institutions do not actually achieve the promise of equality, but principles are now in place that replaced the raw racism of earlier laws.)

CHANGING FROM AGRARIAN TO INDUSTRIAL SOCIETIES

Over the course of human history, society has changed many times. Lenski and Lenski (1982) identify several types of societies, one leading to the next: hunting and gathering, horticultural, agrarian, and industrial. Each of these types has a different core technology, a different way of handling society's needs, and a different means of organizing how society discharges its other functions. This chapter focuses on the social institutions in agrarian and industrial societies and their differences (see Figure 2-2). The purpose is to point out how institutions change even if they fulfill some of the same functions as earlier incarnations of the institutions. This chapter also lays the groundwork for a more in-depth discussion of the history of social policy as a reflection of the changes in institutions.

Agrarian Societies

Agricultural or agrarian societies came after horticultural societies (Lenski and Lenski, 1982). Most of human history has occurred within agrarian society. This section describes agricultural society and provides a short history of how agrar-

Statue in Birmingham, England, of three of the most important figures in the industrial revolution. Boulton, Watt, and Murdoch were key contributors to the development of steam power.

ian societies grew and changed in the Western European and American contexts, using the five social institutions covered earlier as organizing principles.

The Economy

The economy of an agrarian society is built on farming: the cultivation of fields, rather than smaller, more garden-like patches of land as occurred during the horticultural period that preceded it. The key difference between horticultural

Figure 2-2

Changes in Social Institutions as a Consequence of the Shift from Agrarian to Industrial Society

Institution	Agrarian Form	Industrial Form
Economy	Land, Animal, & Human Power (Subsistence economy)	Complex, Factory System (Wage economy)
Family	Extended	Nuclear
Government	Small, Personalistic Justice, Government Divided into Many Small Units	Advanced, Bureaucratic Government, Justice Nation-States
Religion/ Civic Organizations	International Church/Guilds	National Churches/ Labor Unions
Social Welfare	Small, Church Centered	Secular, Government Run

and agricultural types of society is the use of plows which allowed farmers to plant larger areas and grow just one type of crop, such as wheat, barley, or corn. Greater production of food allowed society to enlarge the size of communities and to support a larger population. People also created larger surpluses that supported enterprises like social welfare (Dolgoff & Feldstein, 1980, 2007). This leads to more capacity to support separate social institutions and for society to become more complex, leading to diversification and specialization (Polanyi, 1942). Urban areas became larger and trade became more complex and far reaching. This development led to corresponding changes in political and military institutions.

The economy in an agrarian society is tied to the land. The source of wealth is land and what can be grown or raised on it. Production and movement is powered by water, wind, animals, and humans. Products are made on a small scale, based on local resources, in decentralized cottage industries, and generally traded or sold in a limited area.

The Family and Schools

Because the key element of agrarian farming was human and animal power to plow, grind grain, and produce foodstuffs, large families were an economic necessity. Extended families, with multiple generations living together, produced what was needed for their survival and more. Because technology did not change often, elders could provide useful information to younger generations to help everyone in the family. Even in the larger communities that developed, the norm was to have three generations living together. Learning a practical trade, such as the making of shoes, barrels, or bread, passed from parent to child, as did other livelihoods that were important to the population. Everyone, whether in the city or on the farm, had a role to play to ensure the prosperity of the group.

Education tended to be limited to a small group of the population, and often was limited to learning how to do practical tasks. Before printed books were available, and before literacy was commonplace, there was really little need for most people to receive much of an education beyond how to do the work required of them. Education was given to people destined for the clergy in order to be able to read the Bible, but this was a small part of the population. Private tutors were employed by upper class families. The establishment of universities in Western Europe began as an outgrowth of the need for clergy and administrators for the church. Over many hundreds of years, these became more secular in nature as government took on the task of providing and paying for universities.

Government

In an agrarian society, government tended to be small and limited in scope. Government was divided into small territories, with local chieftains or leaders taking charge. The chief reasons for any government at all were to defend the population or expand the territory of the country, provide rules regarding trade, and mete out justice. Often, at least in Europe, government was ultimately in the hands of kings who were thought to rule from divine right.

The administration of justice tended to be more personalistic than objective. Both the determination of guilt and the assignment of punishment related to who you were and what role you had in society. Persons of royal and noble blood had rights, but ordinary people frequently had none. Absolute rulers could, and did, bend the law to fit their own desires.

Religion/Civic Organizations

For most of Western Europe's history, religion *was* the Christian Catholic Church. It transcended national borders and the Pope had as much authority as leaders of countries. As the state religion for much of the continent, it had a significant impact on the culture of the population. Catholic theology held that work was punishment for sin and that the charging of interest for money loaned (usury) was a sin. Catholicism also preached that wealth was a sign of ungodliness and that wealthy people were more likely to be punished for their lives than rewarded. Despite this theology, some in its hierarchy abused their power and the Catholic Church accumulated vast amounts of wealth. This created the desire for change on the part of some of the clergy for a more "pure" church and also some secular rulers wanted the church's wealth for their own purposes.

Change came through the Protestant Reformation (Weber, 1956) which attacked Catholicism's ideology and created the first of the national churches. It began as a reaction to corruption in the Catholic Church. In 1517, Martin Luther nailed to a church door his ninety-five theses, which spelled out many objections to the way that the Catholic Church conducted matters. Open conflict and wars between Catholics and Protestants continued for centuries. Most of the major Protestant denominations can trace their origins to this time.

Catholicism functioned as a theocracy prior to the Reformation. The emergence of new faiths led to an erosion of Catholicism's monopoly on Christianity in Western Europe (the Eastern Orthodox church based in Constantinople had split from the Roman Catholic Church in the Great Schism in 1204). This not only broke the control of Catholicism over government and civil society, it allowed a change in ideology which was more supportive of income accumulation and wealth.

The civic organizations that existed apart from the church in the Middle Ages were few but included various craft guilds which controlled manufacturing and trade in Middle Ages Europe. A guild was a group of people who were in the same business (such as bakers, blacksmiths, and cloth makers) who banded together to protect their livelihood from others entering their market. They became involved in community affairs through being on city councils, providing charity, policing the streets, and doing other civic and charitable activities. They also provided basic education for their members (Betcher, n.d.).

In more recent agrarian societies, civic organizations grew to encompass a greater proportion of people. With the invention of the printing press and greater levels of literacy, people were able to exchange ideas more easily and across greater distances. In the American colonies and, later, states, clubs dedicated to civic improvements were formed that took on projects to improve everyday life. De Tocqueville wrote of the spirit of volunteerism that animated American life in *Democracy in America* (1835), indicating that Americans freely banded together to perform civic tasks that in other countries would be done, if at all, by government.

Social Welfare

In agrarian societies, social welfare is small scale, local, and centered on the church. The social welfare function before the Middle Ages was primarily controlled by the church, its clerics, and its related organizations such as orders of monks and nuns. These religious individuals took vows to live in poverty and frequently provided social services such as health care, education, and assistance to the poor and those with disabilities. Most people lived very similar lives, and when drought or natural disaster struck, everyone in the vicinity was likely in a position of need. Only the church had connections with other areas that might be able to send help. For individual cases of need, the relatively well-off would provide alms or other funds to the church for the relief of the poor. People in need were often known personally to the people giving funds or assistance.

In Europe after the fall of the Roman Empire, a feudal system evolved that provided for farming by serfs who were tied to the land. Serfs were not slaves but they nonetheless had few rights and lived hard lives. They were provided protection by feudal lords who owned the land the serfs worked. Social welfare was a function of local lords and the church. This arrangement remained constant until the Black Death or the Plague decimated the population of Europe in the 1340s. This was a pandemic that spread quickly through Europe and Asia. Entire communities were struck by this illness and a large portion of the European population died.

The deaths of so many people reduced the pool of available laborers. This, of course, raised the cost of labor and created competition for workers and further reduced the viability of the feudal system. New laws were passed in response to this crisis. For example, in Great Britain, the Settlement Acts were passed to prevent workers from migrating to areas with higher wages. These new policies led to changes in medieval society, including many that were central to the future of social welfare policy.

Much of what this book discusses regarding early social welfare and developments such as the Elizabethan Poor Laws is a product of the agrarian period in Great Britain and the United States. (This topic is covered in detail in the next chapter.)

Industrial Society

What people think of as industrial society began in the mid-to-late 1700s when the first Industrial Revolution started in Britain. The impact of the Industrial

Revolution is assessed by the Nobel Prize winning economist Robert Lucas Jr., in this way: "For the first time in history, the living standards of the masses of ordinary people have begun to undergo sustained growth" (2002, pp. 109-110).

There are two Industrial Revolutions. During the first, great improvements in productivity were created by mechanizing production of textiles and iron, and the use of steam power was made practical by improvements in the design of steam engines. Steam engines were able to power rotary mechanisms needed in production and were also designed to be powerful and portable, making them useful for transportation. Other aspects of the first Industrial Revolution involved improvements in manufacturing chemicals such as sulfuric acid and sodium carbonate, which are needed in other industrial processes. A process for making Portland cement was created, allowing for expansions in building tunnels and other structures. Precision-made machine tools were created from metal as another aspect of the Industrial Revolution. Standardized metal screws, for example, needed to hold together machines, were able to be manufactured for the first time. Glass and paper-making processes were also mechanized and improved. As you can see, things often taken for granted as being inexpensive consumer goods have been available for a relatively short amount of time.

Building upon the first wave of changes, the second Industrial Revolution is marked most prominently by the replacement of iron with steel. Steel is a much more easily shaped metal and is less brittle than iron. Improved techniques for making steel (thus decreasing its cost) and incorporating it into other products galvanized improvements in industry and consumer goods. Other aspects of the time included further changes in chemical production, the discovery of useful purposes for petroleum along with reliable and economical methods for refining and distributing it, the entire electrical industry (from creation of this source of power to the enormous number of products that could use it), and the development of practical automobiles.

If you consider the changes in the 200 years from 1800 to 2000, you must be awestruck. The shift from an agrarian society to an industrial one allows nearly everyone in Western Europe and the United States to have access to products and processes that enhance their physical existence at every turn. Of course, the Industrial Revolution has had many negative consequences as well, but the degree of squalor and poverty that was common in agrarian societies has been greatly reduced.

Figure 2-2 shows how the Industrial Revolution affected the institutions of society. The following discussion ranges across time, as factors impinging one social institution often are happening many decades before factors affecting other institutions. In the middle of the eighteenth century, many different strands of history met, allowing a powerful and productive capitalistic economic system to emerge. Political and religious philosophy affected thoughts about the economy and governmental institutions, and technology made amazing strides. If one of these strands had not existed, the Industrial Revolution would have been much delayed.

Economy

Industrialization is characterized by complex interactions in producing, distributing, and trading products. What is made in one place in vast quantities must be sent to other places in order to be purchased. The infrastructure thus needed includes reliable and inexpensive means of transportation, methods to create and enforce contracts across jurisdictions and countries, and a supply of labor willing and able to move to cities and work in factories. The infrastructure also must include a societal and legal ethos to drive innovation (such as valuing the making of profits and wealth and the granting of patents to inventors). The needs of the industrial economy have thus led to many changes in other institutions.

Family/Schools

Changes in the economy have altered the way most people live. Instead of living in extended families of multiple generations, most people in industrialized societies live in nuclear families or even on their own. Two aspects of the Industrial Revolution, working together, caused this change. First, machines were invented that greatly reduced the need for agricultural workers. As the need for laborers decreased, their wages and their working conditions worsened, if they could find jobs at all. Second, the factory system began in cities where transportation of manufactured goods to far-off places was easier. There was a need for additional workers in factories. Thus, individuals were being both pushed from the land and pulled to cities so that they could find work.

Organized schools funded by the public became common in the United States. By the 1870s, all states had free elementary schools. Schools educated and socialized youth and immigrants in ways that were beneficial to people looking for work in an industrial society where literacy and basic knowledge was needed.

The growth of urban areas was not without its problems. Cities became despicable places that promoted poverty, disease, and despair. People who migrated to these places were often unprepared for what they found. Housing was often difficult to find or inadequate or both. Industrial jobs were frequently dangerous and public health programs were often nonexistent. Workers (which often included children) worked many hours in very poor conditions for little money. They had few, if any, rights in the workplace. Many of the factory owners subscribed to social Darwinist views about the nature of society, accepting that people with great wealth were better adapted to the social need for the survival of the fittest.

Government

Government in an industrial era is larger and takes on more issues. It is also bureaucratic, attempting to interpret the law in the same way for all, regardless of the relationship to the judge. In industrialized countries, government is an instrument of the nation-state, often encompassing large areas of land and highly developed societies.

The rise of nation-states was an important development that created a unified political system in an area. This facilitated commerce and began systems of commercial law and money that also made trade easier. This also broke much of the power of the Catholic Church, at least in part of Europe. In England, for example, the reign of Henry VIII included the creation of the Church of England (1536) and the seizing of all of the land previously held by the Catholic Church. This included all of the monasteries and churches that had previously provided services for the poor. Because land is the major driver of wealth in an agrarian society, Henry benefitted considerably from his efforts. This, of course, left the crown responsible for the social welfare activities that were previously carried out by the church. The English government responded with laws such as the Elizabethan Poor Laws that devolved responsibility for the poor to local government efforts. These sorts of laws and patterns of belief came with the English settlers to the American colonies and later were put into effect by American states and the national government.

As industry and factories became more important to the economy in the eighteenth and nineteenth centuries, government did little to limit problems or enforce safety of workers. Under the presumptions of contract law, workers were supposedly free to take or leave factory employment, and it was assumed they did so as consenting participants. Even small children who worked were not protected by regulations as it was presumed that their parents consented on their behalf.

Forms of government did change over time, though, as legal theory accepted equality before the law for all. The American and French Revolutions enshrined aspects of equality into government, and even European countries with monarchies had to share power with elected legislatures. Government became less personalized in its application of law in criminal trials. As national government projects became larger in scope, regularizing rules and standards became important. Military equipment such as firearms and uniforms were made to be identical and this could only be done when the government could describe precisely what was to be manufactured. Supporting the enforcement of equality and regulations, bureaucracy (in the form of a professional cadre of civilian workers, rules applicable to all people, opportunities for advancement based on merit, and so on) became the organizing principle of government.

Religion/Civic Organizations

As noted earlier, in order for the Industrial Revolution to take place, society had to esteem the building of wealth. The professed ideology of the Catholic Church was not conducive to capitalism, but most Protestant denominations were. Religion in Europe was also not immune to change. The Catholic Church was split asunder by the Reformation which promulgated a very different relationship between God and His followers. Although the Reformation was not caused by industrialization (indeed, it happened at least 200 years before), the new churches had laid the groundwork for a society in which great wealth was a sign of divine favor, not a sign of future condemnation. Instead, poverty became a sign of moral problems.

Non-church-related organizations came into being during the industrial age. Although guilds existed as far back as the Middle Ages to protect worker livelihoods, labor unions were created to demand safer workplaces, shorter work days and weeks, and an age limit on child labor. Unions were almost always strongly and often violently opposed by factory owners. Political movements and parties came into being to support the rights of working people as well. Communism and socialism were two such civic movements. Immigrants to the United States founded organizations to provide support to each other and a way to maintain common cultural traditions. Women also formed societies to tackle important issues in their communities and country.

Social Welfare

The institution of social welfare confronted many changed circumstances moving from an agrarian society to an industrial one. In industrialized societies, social welfare tends to be impersonal, secular, and government-run. The providers of assistance follow rules for the distribution of help and do not otherwise know the people receiving aid. Government is the main source of social welfare funds and so recipients are often called upon to behave in approved ways (such as looking for work, making sure children attend school, and so on) in order to be eligible to receive government funds or services.

Ideas about social welfare at the start of the Industrial Revolution were consistent with a laissez-faire approach to government. These principles included ideas that people were responsible for their own welfare, and, failing sufficient resources from their own efforts, could look to government at the local level or church-related organizations for relief. The Principle of Less Eligibility stipulated that the amount of aid given was to be lower than what could be earned because otherwise it was too easy to spoil human initiative.

THE CHANGES CONSIDERED

Industrialization was a wrenching experience in Western Europe and eventually in the United States. Since then, the process has been repeated in much of the less developed world under the banner of globalization, economic development, or modernization theory. This transition created major shifts in the nature of social institutions.

The Industrial Revolution was accompanied by major dislocations and the people affected sometimes fought back. The Enclosure Movement allowed for the taking of publicly used land (such as for grazing) and turning it into privately held land, enclosed by fences or hedges. In Great Britain, Parliament passed two Enclosure Acts, one in 1801 and another in 1845. Nobles gained exclusive access to the land for their own use and began larger-scale farming and livestock raising. Peasants and crofters lost a valuable resource.

At about that same time, technology was affecting livelihoods as well. In 1812, in most parts of England, for example, skilled laborers and crafts makers whose jobs were eliminated joined together in the Luddite movement. They destroyed threshing machines, power looms, and other elements of the onrushing industrial age in protest. Riots took place and on more than one occasion, protesting workers were arrested, convicted, and then imprisoned, deported, or executed.

Industrialization also spurred changes in the status of women. One example comes from the textile mills of Lowell, Massachusetts. Young, single women from throughout northern New England were recruited to work in the mills there. They were paid between $3.00 and $3.50 per week, much more than they could receive in rural areas. Living in boarding houses at a distance from their family members, they had a measure of independence they would not have had under their parents' roof. Research shows that only about one-third of these workers returned to the countryside to take up the expected role of "farmer's wife" (Dublin, n.d.).

Female mill workers protested against high boarding house charges and long working hours by leading "turn-outs" (what would be called strikes today). These occurred in 1836 when 2,500 women struck for two months before achieving their goal of lower costs for their food and board, and in 1846 when strikes went on for two years in an effort to reduce the working day to ten hours from the standard twelve hours (Dublin, n.d.). Such actions led to later involvement by mill-working women in other social movements, such as labor unionization, immigration reform, and the abolition of slavery.

When society changes, everything in it tends to change. Sometimes these changes are predictable and at other times they are not. The environment, economy, and political systems are closely linked. Other systems (religion, the family, social welfare, and civil society) respond to those changes. If there is a lag between changes, people are not as well served by their institutions.

The next chapter describes some of the social welfare policies that are rooted in both agrarian and industrial society problems. It shows how social welfare policy has adapted to the times.

Questions for Discussion

1. What social changes are likely to affect your area of practice most seriously?

2. What do you think the consequences will be if the profession ignores the changes in society?

3. Apply knowledge from other courses you have taken (perhaps in the fields of sociology, political science, or economics) to what is in this chapter. Do those other disciplines have similar or contradictory perspectives?

4. What will social work and social policy be like for you in ten years? How about at the end of your career?

Exercise

1. Write a job description for a social worker in 2025. What will they be doing? How is this different from what social workers are doing today? How will the skills needed in 2025 differ from what social workers need today?

Websites

Bill and Melinda Gates Foundation: http://www.gatesfoundation.org/

National Association of Social Workers: https://www.socialworkers.org/

World Future Society: http://www.wfs.org/home.php

Visual Media

John Green, "The Nerd's Guide to Learning Everything Online": http://www.ted.com/talks/john_green_the_nerd_s_guide_to_learning_everything_online

Further Reading

Bell, W. (2004). *Foundations of futures studies: Human science for a new era*, vol. 2, *Values, objectivity, and the good society*. Transaction Publishers.

Ife, J. (2012). *Human rights and social work: Towards rights-based practice* (3rd ed.). New York, NY: Cambridge University Press.

Mason, M., & Gammonley, D. (2012). Public policy and the future of social work in long-term home health care. *Home Health Care Management & Practice, 24*(3), 125–131.

Reisch, M. (2013). What is the future of social work? *Critical and Radical Social Work, 1*(1), 67–85.

Chapter 3

Social Welfare History in Developmental Context

Social welfare exists in a context of a larger society that dictates many of the issues that the system must address. Social welfare history cannot be properly understood without looking at the larger society and what forces were affecting the other social institutions. Social welfare is affected by values and culture, economics, politics, and the level of societal development. It is also affected by other historical developments. Trying to understand social welfare without understanding its social, economic, and political context is a fool's errand. Most factors that drive the social welfare system are external forces that radiate from other institutions.

One issue that is rarely discussed on social welfare policy is the impact of the physical environment (Hoff & McNutt, 1994, 2008; Mary, 2008). If you examine the history of social welfare, there are quite a few times that ecological forces have driven effects in both the economic system and the social welfare system. Several of those instances (such as the impact of the three hurricanes that hit the U.S. Gulf Coast in 2005, Hurricane Sandy in 2013, and the 2010 oil spill in the Gulf) have been remarkably easily linked to environmental change by nearly everyone although others have been less easy to connect. If you understand that there is an intimate connection between the economy and the environment and that the economy is an important driver of social welfare and social welfare policy, it stands to reason that the environment will constrain social welfare (Hoff & McNutt, 1994; Sachs, 2008). It is critical to make that connection in any discussion of social welfare policy. The rest of this chapter expands on these views.

OVERVIEW OF SOCIAL WELFARE HISTORY

This is not a comprehensive review of social welfare history. The purpose in this chapter is to place this book's central argument in historical perspective. The growth of social welfare within a societal development perspective is critical to understand this argument and, in point of fact, the current state of social welfare. The next pages provide an overview of some of the most important laws that illustrate the shift in the social welfare institution from an agrarian to an industrial society.

The Poor Laws

The poor laws were a set of laws created in Great Britain over time, as first one policy was tried and then another. These laws reflect the shifting of charity from the church to the state due to the King of England starting a state-church and seizing the Catholic Church's property. At the time the Poor Laws were initially created, England was still an agrarian society. As it moved into industrialization, in the late 1700s and through the 1800s, the Poor Laws were amended to deal with higher rates of unemployment with a punitive shift in ideology and view of the poor.

In 1531 the Principle of Government Provisions was enacted by the English government (Dolgoff & Feldstein, 1980, p. 49). This law attempted to differentiate between people who were poor due to circumstances beyond their control (the worthy poor) and those who were seen as just unmotivated or lazy (the unworthy poor). This distinction became important as legislation developed. Those who were worthy were given certification for begging and those who were not considered worthy were punished. A centralized secular administration replaced the religious administration offered by the church as welfare became a civil responsibility. The final codification of the English Poor Laws was passed in 1601.

The Settlement Act of 1662 added the idea of residence requirements to the poor laws. This meant that local governments were empowered to remove the poor that had been found in areas other than their home area. Charity was thus tied to where one was settled, not to where one relocated to find work. This saved money for the jurisdictions that saw net in-migration of people who were, or became, poor.

Other laws were passed related to employment and the poor that tried to regulate and classify the poor. A significant aspect of this was the use of almshouses, workhouses, or poor houses. This is also called indoor relief. The 1723 Workhouse Test Act required anyone seeking assistance to enter a workhouse. These were squalid places and they created the opportunity for many types of social problems. Mentally ill patients, the sick, and even common criminals were thrown in together. Because workhouses were intentionally very unpleasant places, a great deal of desperation was required before accepting this option.

Another law, Gilbert's Act of 1782, prevented the able-bodied poor (the unworthy poor) from entering workhouses. Local government was still obliged to provide for this group of the indigent, but could only do so by providing work or "outdoor relief." Indoor relief was reserved for the elderly, ill, and/or disabled adults, as well as dependent children (Bloy, 2002c).

The Industrial Revolution was picking up steam when the Speenhamland system was created at a meeting of the justices of the peace in Speenhamland in 1795. This approach to assisting the poor was a sort of "guaranteed minimum income" scheme. It tied the amount of government assistance to the price of bread (the bread scale). Workers were to receive as much income as possible per week from their own labor but if they did not earn enough to meet the level of income called for by the bread scale, the difference would be made up from government coffers. The Speenhamland system was a departure from the punitive tone of the poor laws but had unintended consequences and problems. One problem was that employers offered only low wages, knowing that the workers could get additional income from the "welfare system." Lower wages to employees meant higher profits for employers but strained local government budgets (Bloy, 2002c).

In 1832 a royal commission was created to study the Poor Laws. In 1834 this commission's recommendations led to a spate of new laws abolishing the system of aid to the poor that was created in 1601 with the Poor Laws (Bloy, 2002a). Under this new approach, outdoor relief was prohibited for able-bodied men and women and their families. The poor and their families would be enrolled into workhouses, the purpose of which was to be so unpleasant that no one who had any other real option would take refuge in them (Bloy, 2002a). Families were put into different areas where men, women, and children were housed separately, with little possibility of contact with each other (Bloy, 2002a).

Exceptions to the outright ban on outdoor relief were created within a few years. By 1844 some categories of people could receive assistance without going into a workhouse. These were the following populations: those who themselves were ill or had sick family members; those who had suffered an accident or had a family member who had had an accident; new widows (within six months); widows with dependent, legitimate children; widows of soldiers; and children of soldiers (Bloy, 2002a).

Over the years, this system struggled with the balance of providing indoor and outdoor aid. The numbers of poor people during economic downturns made it impractical to contain them all in workhouses as the law demanded. Outdoor relief was much cheaper than workhouses, and rate (tax) payers wanted their rates as low as possible. Protests and even riots erupted when laws became too punitive, forcing legislators to rescind overly harsh policies. Some local organizations and officials did their best to obstruct the law's implementation (Bloy, 2002a).

The idea of less eligibility was an important part of the new law's ideology. Originally a correctional concept, it means that the poorest person not on welfare should be better off than the richest person on welfare (Bloy, 2002b). This approach to social welfare remained until Great Britain brought its social insurance system into play in the early twentieth century. (The concept still is a significant aspect of welfare policy in the United States.)

The Poor Laws in America

In their earliest times, American colonists were living very close to the survival margin. Cases of extreme need were handled informally, up to the capacity of the local group to do so. As society became larger and more stable the colonies began to emulate their home nations. The English colonies moved to implement the poor laws that existed during that time. In general, the poor law administration in the American colonies and then the independent United States paralleled that of the system in England (Trattner, 1998). The United States was an agrarian society until the middle of the nineteenth century and the agrarian-based poor laws from the English heritage seemed appropriate in the new country. Nonetheless, the American experience with the poor and other populations demanded new approaches as well.

The Institutional Period in the United States

As a new nation, the United States had no well-developed social institutions when it began. There were traditions rooted in the English system, and some Americans wanted to emulate the French, but much of society, and its responses to social issues, had to be developed from the ground up. During the early decades of the 1800s, states and localities retained control over social welfare policies, although they frequently emulated what was happening in other states. As a whole, the United States turned to residential institutions to deal with many of the social issues that it encountered such as crime, mental illness, and the condition of children. Prisons, mental hospitals, and orphanages were some of the tools that were developed to deal with these social problems.

Prisons

The United States pioneered the use of institutions for correcting criminal behavior. Other nations used their jails to hold people for corporal or capital punishment. They banished or exiled people to other parts of the world. The Walnut Street Jail and Eastern Penitentiary, both in Philadelphia, began the movement toward true correctional institutions. Eastern Penitentiary was built to segregate inmates from each other. The programming included spiritual reflection, exercise, and other elements designed to encourage positive behavior. Prisons in other states, most notably New York, introduced reformatory programs into their correctional systems. Another American innovation, probation, was pioneered by Boston tradesman John Augustus.

Mental hospitals

Mental illness was not well understood in earlier times. Some people thought it was a moral problem, a character defect, or infestation by evil spirits. Victims of mental illness were often thrown into jails, workhouses, or worse. The emerging mental hygiene movement fought these ideas and these practices but making change was hard.

Dorothea Dix, a remarkable social reformer, conducted a grassroots campaign to build mental hospitals throughout the Eastern states. She campaigned with the public, with state legislatures, and others to build these state hospitals, and was successful at establishing one in almost every Eastern state. She finally took the case to the federal government. Congress passed the Indigent Insane Act in 1856. This law would have given federal land to support the creation of mental health facilities at the state level. It was vetoed by President Franklin Pierce who argued that the care of the mentally ill was not a federal responsibility (Dolgoff & Feldstein, 1980).

Orphanages

In the early 1800s, children, particularly children of immigrants, were seen as an "at-risk" population that needed to be assisted. Thousands of orphanages were set up at that time and for the next century, in hopes of creating "good Americans" out of the children of the poor. What is not widely known is that orphanages were created not just to house children whose parents were dead, but many other types of children as well. Only about 10 to 20 percent of children were "real" orphans, with both parents deceased. Poverty was the main reason that children were taken from their families or that parents relinquished responsibility for their children. The poorhouses that were in use at that time were the source of most children put in orphanages, and tens of thousands of children were taken from one institution (the poorhouse) and put into another (the orphanage) (Crenson, 1998).

According to Crenson (1998), orphanages in the 1800s were both highly regimented and dangerous. Meals were dull or not very nutritious, and older boys were able to bully younger ones with impunity. Many orphanages' goal was to "save children" from poverty and "immoral" parents. Thus youth were sent to "good" foster homes in their city (who sometimes sent the children back). Others were put on "orphan trains" to the Midwest so they could live in the "purity" of rural American life but the children often become little more than indentured servants. Native American children were forced from their families to become "Americanized" in mission boarding schools. The treatment of the children was frequently inhumane and the policy worked to destroy Native American cultures.

All of these problems necessitating institutions were made worse in the transition from an agricultural society to an industrial one. The Northeastern and Midwestern areas of the United States were well along the path to industrialization at the time the Civil War began in 1861. Southern states were largely agricultural societies and relied on enslaved laborers, particularly on cotton plantations.

The Civil War and Reconstruction

The Civil War was obviously a perilous time for the United States and many of the issues that were fostered by the war are still felt today. Reconstruction was also difficult. The war and its aftermath added to the social welfare problems experienced by American communities. The war left many Americans dead or disabled and much of the limited industrial base of the South was destroyed.

As it was before the war, social welfare was deemed to be a responsibility of local charity and state and local governments. There were three exceptions: the Freedmen's Bureau, the Bureau of Indian Affairs (BIA), and the Civil War Veteran's Pension Program (Dolgoff & Feldstein, 1980).

The Freedmen's Bureau was created to address some of the problems experienced by people who had been enslaved and then freed. The agency created freedmen's schools to educate former enslaved people and created organizations to help them succeed in small businesses. Early in Reconstruction, freed people who had been enslaved made progress in claiming the rights long denied them. Sadly, this was not to last. The creation of "Jim Crow" laws in the former slave states restricted their freedom and prevented many from exercising their rights.

The Bureau of Indian Affairs (BIA) was created to deal with the needs of Native Americans. This is a different set of relationships than what existed with other groups. The agreements between the tribes and the United States are treaties. The BIA provided social welfare and educational services to the reservations. In point of fact, the relationship between the BIA and the Native American peoples has often been contentious. Native Americans often did not receive full rations and other goods they had been promised in the treaties. In short, the government of the United States broke the treaties with Native tribes and often left their people hungry, without adequate shelter or food, and without the rights that were guaranteed them in the treaties.

Much of the prevailing mood among elites was influenced by emerging cultural values such as social Darwinism and paternalism. The idea of social Darwinism revolved around evolution and the concept of "survival of the fittest" (a concept actually formulated by Herbert Spencer rather than Charles Darwin). This idea, when applied to human society, suggests that the progress of humanity depends on weeding out the less successful parts of the human race. This would mean that any display of altruism would actually damage the ultimate progress of all. If you were poor, it was because you were less able and inferior. Paternalism also assumes that some people are less capable than others but argues for taking care of those who cannot compete in the market. Current ideas about empowerment were not part of the mix.

Private Charity and Industrialization

Private charity has always been a part of the social welfare mix. In fact, because the church is often considered part of the nonprofit sector, it dominated social welfare before the coming of the poor laws. The development of private charities that aided the poor was a feature of both English and American social welfare approaches.

Charity Organization Societies (COS) and the settlement house movement are two institutions that are generally credited as having significant roles in the creation of social work and major parts of the U.S. social welfare system. Both have roots in England and both have strong ties to the industrial middle and upper classes. On balance, these two organizations represent substantial poles in the nonprofit approaches to social policy. — Different Approaches

Charity Organization Societies (COS) began in England and were copied in the United States, starting in Buffalo in 1877. The primary issue addressed was the coordination of charity and the prevention of over-giving to the indigent. One of the major ideas behind the COS was that over-giving to the poor was morally dangerous. The COS tried to prevent the poor from receiving more from different charities than was actually needed. This central coordinating body hired paid investigators to determine each family's need. Agencies and charities would coordinate to prevent anyone from receiving more than was needed. The COS also created councils of social agencies which allowed communities to plan for their welfare needs. Another aspect of the COS system was the implementation of "friendly visitors," volunteers who visited poor families. These volunteers were charged with helping the poor develop the attitudes that were desired by the upper classes. Many of the friendly visitors were the wives or daughters of business leaders.

Settlement houses were organized quite differently. They were located in impoverished areas and the settlement house staff lived and worked in the surrounding community. Settlement houses provided socialization and adult education. They also engaged in social action. The last task was the one that settlement houses are most identified with. Settlement house workers, including Jane Addams, Grace and Edith Abbott, Frances Perkins, and others, were involved in creating child labor laws, the juvenile court system, fair wage and hour legislation, and a host of other progressive causes.

Although there were many other nonprofit charities, organizations following these two approaches represented much of the nonprofit social welfare activity as the United States entered the Industrial Revolution. The COS eventually gave rise to the United Way movement (Brilliant, 1990) and formed much of the organized nonprofit human services sector. The settlement house workers continued to exist in poor neighborhoods but their social action activities continued to develop and expand. Settlement house workers were involved in much of the progressive legislation that was created in the time following the coming of industrialization.

Social Work Emerges

This is the point that organized social work began to become recognized as a professional occupation. As Lubove (1965) points out, an initial task for the new profession was separating social workers from volunteers. A specialized knowledge base was needed and eventually developed. Professional schools were created, beginning with the New York School of Philanthropy. Eventually, professional organizations were created and standards for practice were developed. Although there were certainly some ideas about ways to deal with the issues of the day, early social workers were forced to create a lot of their practice principles from their experience in the field. Mary Richmond's *Social Diagnosis* is an example of a set of principles derived from practice. Eventually more formal ideas were incorporated but these early attempts are important because the social workers who dealt with industrialization were breaking new ground.

Progressive Era

The Progressive Era began in the 1890s and lasted until 1920. Its start can be linked to public reaction to scandals and the horrific after-effects of the Industrial Revolution. Reformers addressed many of these problems and created a series of protections for workers, the poor, and vulnerable groups like children. The White House Conference on Children was held in 1909. It led to the formation of the Children's Bureau. Little by little, a social safety net for children and their families was beginning to form. Child labor laws, the juvenile court, public health policies, and a host of additional progressive legislation came on the scene during this time (Leiby, 1978; Trattner, 1998). Agitation for rights for women, in both the economic and political spheres, strengthened during the Progressive Era. Jane Addams was one of the leaders in the progressive movement.

There were also the beginnings of concern for the physical environment, particularly under the leadership of President Theodore Roosevelt. The national parks were established and wild areas were protected. This was at odds with the belief, prominent at the time, that nature was an inexhaustible resource.

The Coming of the Welfare State

The latter part of the nineteenth century saw a shift in thinking about social welfare. Perhaps the most significant shift was the beginning of the social insurance movement. Bismarck created the first social insurance system in Germany in 1889. Many of the industrialized nations followed suit, creating a system of social protections for their citizens. In Great Britain, the Beveridge Commission, chaired by Lord William Beveridge, in 1942 created the design of the welfare state that eventually replaced the poor laws. The new system gave rise to comprehensive pension, health, and social safety net policies that were a major transition from the restrictive policies of the poor laws. In short order, most of the advanced nations of the world developed a welfare state. Only the United States and Sweden were hold outs among the Western Democracies.

The Associative State and the Red Scare

The early part of the twentieth century brought the rise of the associative state (Skocpol & Ikenberry, 1983) in which business and government worked together closely. This was a conservative force that often ran counter to many of the ideas that were advanced by the progressive movement. Most Americans endorsed the idea of a free enterprise system with minimal government intervention. This viewpoint was shared by many policy makers. There was some government intervention in the economy but it was limited.

One of the social welfare innovations that grew out of this period was workers' compensation. Until the early days of the past century, companies were shielded from liability by the fellow servant rule. This rule held that if a worker was injured as the result of another worker's actions they could not sue their employer. This theory protected employers from lawsuits from their employees. Given the terrible working conditions that existed, this was significant protection. When this protection was removed by the Supreme Court, the business community looked for an alternative. Workers' compensation was the solution. This was insurance for workers' injuries and illnesses. Every state in the nation had a program by 1919.

At the same time, many of the industrialized nations, including the United States, began to fear the possibility of socialist revolution after the Bolshevik Revolution in Russia. In the United States, the Red Scare created a chilling environment for social change activism.

This was a conservative time for America. The belief that business could deliver a good life for most people was rarely questioned. Guided by a flawed orthodox economic belief that the economy is self-regulating (a cornerstone of classical economic theory), the U.S. government failed to take action when action would have helped. In the late part of the 1920s, things began to fall apart.

The Great Depression

The Great Depression, for many people in the United States, began on October 29, 1929, when the stock market crashed. It began as the world economy in general, and the American economy in particular, began to wind down. The stock market crash was preceded by a meltdown in the agricultural sector. Some of this was caused by economic policy, particularly the inability of traditional markets to address the agricultural sector (this is frequently referred to as the farm problem). It was certainly influenced by environmental destruction. One particularly serious situation in the Midwest is frequently referred to as the "dust bowl." This refers to the destruction of topsoil in much of the farming heartland of the nation as a result of poor farming practices and a massive drought. The situation in many farming areas bordered on revolution.

The Great Depression was nothing short of a catastrophe for most Americans. In the absence of economic security protections available in many other nations and economic regulating activities not yet developed, Americans were on their own. High unemployment, bank insolvency, and other perils plagued the American family. Many lost their homes, their jobs, and their life savings.

The Depression was a surprise to policy makers who believed that if government just stayed out of the economy, the market would correct any problems. This was a major article of faith for adherents of classical economics. The argument was that if the market was allowed to function freely, the system would reach equilibrium and all problems would be solved. Supply would create its own demand. Although there was economic regulation prior to the 1930s (such as antitrust regulations), such policies were few and far between. Most serious economists today, including many very conservative economists, accept a role for government in managing the economy.

The stock market and the financial sector were largely unregulated in the 1920s. This lack of regulation led some decision-makers to take serious risks which resulted in instability in the financial services organizations they managed. As a consequence, bank failures were quite common in the early 1930s. Even well managed institutions had to deal with "runs" on banks and the resulting failures. Many of the protections people count on today (such as the FDIC which insures bank deposits) were created in reaction to this horrific situation.

President Herbert Hoover finally intervened after it was clear that market forces alone wouldn't end the nation's suffering. He asked the Red Cross to distribute government resources to the needy (Eherenreich 1985). This proved to be beyond the ability of the Red Cross or any other nonprofit organization.

Most professional social workers were identified with the nonprofit sector. There was a certain amount of tension between the nonprofit social service agencies and the emerging federal system of income support for the unemployed, poor, and ill. Leaders of the nonprofit sector believed they could more properly guide the poor and indigent than government programs could and resisted government "takeover" of their programs (Eherenreich, 1985).

[margin note: Radical Solutions]

On the other hand, a group of social workers favored more radical solutions than proposed by Charity Organization Societies. Known as the rank and file movement, they advocated for fundamental changes in the economic system. Bertha Capen Reynolds and Mary Van Kleek were among the leaders of this group.

[margin note: inadequate]

The American social welfare system that did exist was small and relatively sparse. There were public agencies, private charities, and nonprofit organizations. There were also churches and social organizations. Given the massive social problems that existed at the time, these groups were clearly inadequate to deal with the issues.

[margin note: Critical time]

This was a critical time for the United States and the world. Civil society was under great stress and social stability was in question. Problems with the economy drove political unrest and led to the election of fascist dictators in Germany (Adolf Hitler) and Italy (Benito Mussolini). In the United States civil unrest was part of the landscape in many communities. Populists such as Huey Long pushed for a redistribution of wealth as millions of Americans had little work while a few had millions of dollars.

[margin note: Comparisons]

The Great Depression was a severe crisis. Although it left an indelible stain on the nation's consciousness, it is hardly relevant to today's crisis. Although some are quick to compare any current economic crisis with the Great Depression, this is often not helpful. The United States economy was quite a bit smaller, less diverse, and less regulated then than it is today. This is also true of the world economy. The global economic system is more integrated than it was eighty years ago. Unfortunately, because of the simplistic way those economic issues are often treated in the media and elsewhere, many Americans fail to comprehend what is different about a modern economy or how the system actually works. The tools that people have developed for managing the economy were not available at the time of the Great Depression, and many nations, including the United States, did not feel that managing the economy was a proper role for government. The economy of the 1920s and 1930s is not the economy that exists in the second decade of the twenty-first century. The society is also very different today from what it was back then.

The New Deal

In the 1932 election Americans elected New York governor Franklin D. Roosevelt as the new president. Roosevelt had been Secretary of the Navy and suffered from polio through much of his adult life. In his inaugural speech he promised that "we have nothing to fear but fear itself." That was probably far from the truth. Unemployment was running at historically high levels and many banks had closed. Civil unrest was common in some areas (particularly the farming areas of the Midwest). Clearly, the situation called for decisive action.

In his first hundred days in office, Roosevelt met the problem head on. He made major changes in the economic regulatory system. These included cre- *Action* ating a system to manage and secure the banks as well as regulations for the stock market and other areas of the economy. He also put forth legislation to create the National Recovery Administration (NRA). The NRA was a major effort to blunt the effects of the Depression. Programs included the Works Progress Administration (renamed the Work Projects Administration in 1939) and the Civilian Conservation Corps which put the unemployed youth to work on pub- lic service programs. Many state parks and other public works still show the results of WPA and CCC efforts.

Harry Hopkins, a social worker from Iowa, headed the Federal Emergency Relief Administration. This was one of Roosevelt's initial efforts and Hopkins had led a similar effort in New York. Hopkins was a driving force within the Roosevelt administration and was heavily involved in the creation of the New Deal and the Social Security Act.

In the past, government policy makers believed that the economy was self- regulating and that government intervention should be minimal at most. Pre- vailing economic theory advocated for this course. Given the shambles that the economy was in, it was not surprising that policy makers felt like they needed a different model. They looked for a theory that described how government could intervene in the economic system in a helpful way.

Lord John Maynard Keynes, a British economist, provided that approach. Keynes dismissed the idea that the economy could not be planned and that government intervention was inherently bad. This was the birth of fiscal policy and government action to regulate the economy. Keynes argued that by rais- *Economy* ing the level of aggregate demand in the economy people could reduce unem- ployment and by lowering that demand they could lower inflation. Government spending, because the government is such a significant consumer, could reg- ulate the economy by adjusting its spending. A recent example of this type of approach is the American Recovery and Reinvestment Act of 2009 (ARRA) (P.L. 111-5) which was created early in the Obama administration. Often called a stimulus package, this type of policy pushes money into the economy to reduce unemployment and spur economic growth. This was an acknowledgement that the economy was not self-regulating.

Keynesian economic theory led to policy development that met people's needs at the same time they were stimulating the economy. Unemployment compensation is a case in point. When unemployment rose, the unemployment compensation program added money to the economy by paying people who had lost their jobs and could not find another one. By maintaining buying power, the level of aggregate demand is also maintained. When buying power shrinks, so does the need for consumer goods. With no demand for products, additional factories are closed and those workers become unemployed as well. Thus, keeping money in people's hands so they can spend it keeps others from losing their jobs as a negative spiral develops. These payments also address the immediate income problems of unemployed workers. Programs that operate in this manner are called automatic stabilizers. This makes the development of social welfare programs related to other activities involved in managing the macroeconomic environment vital.

The Social Security Act of 1935

The Social Security Act of 1935 is probably the most significant piece of legislation in American social welfare policy history. It made two critical differences in American social welfare. First, it defined the nature of the system for decades to come. An important part of this definition was the leadership role given to the federal government. Second, it moved the United States into the ranks of nations with a social insurance system. Neither of these contributions should be taken lightly.

Most Americans are familiar with the Social Security Act's old age pension. This is an important provision of the act but represents only a small part of what the act includes. Box 3-1 lists the major programs included in the original legislation. It's clear from looking at this list how central the Social Security Act is to America's welfare system. Over the last eight decades, Congress has added a number of programs to social security. Disability and survivors insurance was added. Later, Supplemental Security Income (SSI), Temporary Assistance for Needy Families (TANF), Medicare, Medicaid, State Children's Health Insurance (SCHIP), as well as many others were added to the framework. One component that did not become part of the original legislation was national health insurance. Opposition from various interest groups forced Roosevelt to forgo this important program. This was partially fulfilled with the creation of Medicare and Medicaid in 1965. In 2009 Congress passed the Patient Protection and Affordable Care Act, which created a historic extension of coverage for health care.

The Social Security Act was the product of many forces. Certainly, there was Roosevelt's underlying concern for policy that would promote human well-being. The Townsend movement was also an important force. The Townsend plan would have established a national retirement pension plan for every person over the age of sixty, with a monthly benefit of $200 that had to be spent within thirty days. In 1935, 56 percent of Americans supported the plan, despite widespread opposition from economists and establishment leaders (Dewitt, 2001). Enormous political pressure existed to satisfy the desire for some national pension system.

The United States was almost alone among the developed market economies in not having a social insurance system. One of the most influential American economists of the first half of the twentieth century, John Commons, shaped ideas that were first adopted in Wisconsin and later as elements of the successful Social Security Act of 1935. Also vital was the leadership of Harry Hopkins and Frances Perkins. Perkins, Roosevelt's Secretary of Labor, earned a master's degree in sociology at Columbia and was part of Roosevelt's administration in New York.

The Social Security Act of 1935 should be seen against its historical period. This is particularly true of the old age pension provisions. The breakdown of the extended family created the issue of who would care for older workers after they retired. Poverty among the retired was a critical problem. The United States was largely a manufacturing nation when the Social Security Act was originally passed. People often spent their working lives employed by a single employer.

Box 3-1

Major Parts of the Social Security Act of 1935

Benefits for Individuals
Old Age Pension: Provides coverage for workers who have reached retirement age.
Unemployment Compensation: Provides coverage for many unemployed workers for a specific period of time while they locate new employment.

Grants to the States for:
Old Age Assistance
Aid to the Blind
Aid to Dependent Children
Maternal and Child Health
Crippled Children
Child Welfare
Public Health

This was a life that started young and ended relatively young. Higher education was available to few and many did not finish high school. A long and healthy life meant something quite different than it does today. According to the Social Security Administration (n.d.), "*Life expectancy* at birth in 1930 was indeed only 58 for men and 62 for women." Industrial work was hard, often hazardous, and not everyone survived to retire.

Many occupational groups were not covered under the original Social Security program. Section 210 of the original legislation excluded many workers from coverage, as this quote shows:

> Federal Old Age Benefits (Title II) Coverage (see 210b):
>
> Old age benefits are to be paid to all employees based upon wages received in employment in any service performed within the United States, Alaska, and Hawaii except:
>
> 1. Agricultural labor;
> 2. Domestic service in a private home;
> 3. Casual labor not in the course of employer's trade or business;
> 4. Officers or members of the crew of a vessel documented under the laws of the United States or of any foreign country;
> 5. Employees of the United States Government;
> 6. Employees of a State or political subdivision;
> 7. Employees of nonprofit institutions operated exclusively for religious, charitable, scientific, literary, or educational purposes, or for the prevention of cruelty to children or animals;
> 8. Employees of a carrier as defined in Railroad Retirement Act of 1935.
>
> (Public Law No. 399, 74th Cong. [H.R. 8651]).

Little by little, excluded groups became part of the coverage pool.

The constitutionality of the Social Security System was tested in the court system and eventually upheld by the Supreme Court. Additional legislation brought refinement and additional coverage to the Social Security program.

Shortly after the passage of the Social Security Act, war clouds began to gather in Asia and Europe. The Depression was a worldwide phenomenon and that helped to fuel existing tensions and rivalries. War broke out in the 1930s in both Europe and Asia and eventually spread to other areas. Many in the United

States hoped to stay out of the growing war but that proved impossible after the Japanese attacked the American naval base in Pearl Harbor on December 7, 1941. This act led the United States to declare war on Japan and its allies, Germany and Italy. The Second World War changed many of the dimensions that Roosevelt was forced to deal with and added others. The war became his principal concern until his death in 1945, shortly before the war's end.

Finally, the war ended and the United States found itself in a different position with regard to the rest of the world. As the only major nation to emerge with its entire economic base intact, the United States moved into a dominant position. Still, the war brought with it a social welfare burden that was painful for the nation. Families and dislocated people needed help. Many people returned from war with physical and mental issues that required years of care.

The Veterans Administration (VA) grew substantially after the war. Many veterans returned with problems that were addressed in its hospitals and clinics. Passage of the GI Bill of Rights in 1944 (actually called the Servicemen's Readjustment Act) led to educational possibilities for many Americans and college enrollments blossomed. Colleges, once only for people of means, were flooded with veterans. This legislation led to a rise in social mobility and new opportunity for many Americans, including women and members of minority groups who had served in the U.S. armed forces in record numbers.

Much of the rest of the world ended the war in shambles. Most of the industrial base of Europe was destroyed. The United States created the Marshall Plan, which began in April of 1948, to rebuild Europe. This was, in many ways, one of the most massive social development efforts ever conducted. Although foreign aid is not generally considered to be social welfare, an argument can be made that it constitutes mutual aid if it is for humanitarian assistance. Much of America's foreign aid and the foreign aid of a number of other nations is primarily for military assistance.

The group of nations that defeated the Axis powers of Germany, Italy, and Japan included the Soviet Union. This alliance unraveled after the war ended. Concern over the menace of communism grew throughout the United States and Great Britain. Confrontations in Berlin and a war in Korea created a real fear of another world war, this one with nuclear weapons. The United States, Great Britain, and France led the development of a treaty, called the North Atlantic Treaty Organization (NATO), among Western European countries with democratic governments. This group of nations confronted the Soviet Union and its allies, a group known as the Warsaw Pact countries. The ongoing struggle between these two groups became known as the cold war. There was also a growing concern about the issue of internal subversion. This became a period like the Red Scare of the 1920s.

The Fifties

The fifties introduced a sense of conservatism that rivaled that of the associated state period. The cold war, the McCarthy period (named after Senator Joseph McCarthy, a Republican from Wisconsin, one of the primary actors), and the Red Scare made it very difficult to propose progressive legislation. Many progressive thinkers found themselves the focus of attacks. People who were communists or even suspected communists were blacklisted and harassed. Two congressional committees spearheaded many of the investigations but federal law enforcement agencies were involved. Combined with a conservative president (the former Army general who commanded all troops in Europe fighting against Germany and Italy, Dwight D. Eisenhower) and a national mood of fear and distrust, progressives found it hard to pursue their agenda and there were hard battles to maintain some of the gains made during the New Deal.

There was a certain amount of policy making for social welfare. The Social Security Act was amended several times. Aid to Families with Dependent Children replaced Aid to Dependent Children and the Supplemental Security Income program or SSI was developed in lieu of Aid to the Permanently and Totally Disabled (APTD).

The profession of social work saw the creation of the National Association of Social Workers and the Council on Social Work Education. Both of these organizations were composed of many smaller organizations. In the 1950s, it was generally thought that bigger organizations were better. Social work also suffered through a schism between the diagnostic school and the functional school.

The South saw the beginning of what was to become the civil rights movement. The Montgomery bus boycott in 1955 was certainly one of the early actions in a struggle for equal rights. The year before, the U.S. Supreme Court ruled on *Brown v. Board of Education of Topeka, 347 U.S. 483* (1954) and decided that the separate but equal principle used in the public schools in some states was unconstitutional. This did not end school segregation but began the process of moving toward fairer schools. The struggle for equality had reached a significant milestone.

The nature of American communities also began to change. The growth of the national highway system, which prioritized individual drivers of automobiles over public transportation, along with other forces, began the long process of suburbanization. This had both social and economic consequence and ultimately led to environmental consequences. The American sense of community was in decline. Putnam (2000) argues that the decline of social capital occurred as people reduced their civic engagement to follow more individual pursuits.

The post-war period of the late 1940s to the late 1950s was a conservative time in American history. Many Americans were happy with the improvement in lifestyle, fearful of world communism, and ignorant of poverty and discrimination that existed in their midst. Others were unhappy and dreamed of better times. Things were about to change.

The War on Poverty and the 1960s

The sixties appeared to be heading toward a repeat of the fifties to many early observers. The narrow victory of Senator John F. Kennedy over Vice President Richard Nixon was a harbinger of another possible future. Kennedy was young, enthusiastic, and inspirational. Although he was president for only a short time, Kennedy set the tenor for the times. The press spoke of Camelot and the New Frontier.

During Kennedy's campaign for the presidency, his brother and confidant, Robert Kennedy, visited poor areas of West Virginia and saw the extent of deprivation in the Appalachian region. Other events, such as the publication of Michael Harrington's *The Other America*, brought the problem of poverty to the national stage. Many Americans, who had been content to believe that poverty happened in other places, found this was untrue.

Kennedy's major contribution to social welfare was the Community Mental Health Centers Act of 1963. This law, built on the idea of preventative psychiatry, was aimed at reducing the population of mental hospitals. It was a bold step and, coupled with a number of important court decisions and the development of psychotropic drugs, opened the door to the deinstitutionalization that took place during the 1970s.

Kennedy also created the Peace Corps (Rice, 1985). During his campaign for the presidency, Kennedy asked a crowd of students at the University of Michigan if they were willing to volunteer to work in an underdeveloped nation for two years. After his election, Kennedy worked to fulfill his promise to institute such a program (with some apparent nudging from Vice President Johnson). In 1961, he created the Peace Corps by executive order. The passage of the Peace Corps Act solidified the effort. This program asked Americans to volunteer two years of their lives to help people in the third world. It was a bold and long-lasting program that changed the lives of many Americans (the Peace Corps celebrated its fiftieth anniversary in 2011) and led the way for the development of many national service programs in subsequent decades.

On November 22, 1963, President Kennedy was assassinated in Dallas, Texas. A shocked nation recoiled from the loss of an inspirational leader. Kennedy's death put Vice President Lyndon Johnson in the White House. Johnson, who had been a Civilian Conservation Corps director during the Depression, had strong progressive leanings. After being the longtime leader of the Democrats in the Senate, Johnson was chosen by Kennedy as his vice presidential running mate, a move to help ensure support of Southern voters. Johnson was able to have legislation passed by Congress to support a broad effort he called the Great Society.

In his 1964 State of the Union address, President Johnson declared War on Poverty. Part of this effort was the creation of the Office of Economic Opportunity (OEO), which included a variety of programs aimed at helping the nation's poor. Although the OEO was created by executive order, the Economic Opportunity Act of 1964 (P.L. 88-452, 78 Stat. 508) created a more permanent entity. Box 3-2 outlines some of the major programs that came out of this legislation.

The OEO often developed parallel institutions that created new pathways of opportunities for the poor. Cloward and Ohlin's (1960) opportunity theory provided many of the ideas that underpinned the War on Poverty effort. These efforts, which often came into direct conflict with local power structures, made considerable use of community organization techniques and promoted inclusion and community empowerment.

Box 3-2

Major Programs of the War on Poverty

Community Action Agencies/Community Action Program: CAAs coordinated community action efforts in a geographic area. The activity included community organization and advocacy.

Head Start: Provided developmental education for children from underprivileged families.

Job Corps: Job training for young people.

Legal Services: Provided lawyers to represent the poor.

VISTA: Volunteers in Service to America: National Service Volunteer Program for Americans to work with a poverty community.

The OEO experience was marked by continual struggle and political controversy. Local power structures frequently objected to the Community Action Agencies/Community Action Program methods. Eventually, this friction reached Congress, which restricted OEO's activities. The Green Amendment, passed in 1967, reduced the political impact of OEO. Eventually OEO was dismantled by the Nixon administration.

Johnson's Great Society ushered in other programs as well. Model Cities brought social and physical planning to America's cities. Urban renewal efforts changed the nature of many cities. Private efforts, like the Ford Foundation's Gray Areas Project, also addressed the problems of America's cities.

Medicare and Medicaid became part of the Social Security Act in 1965. This represented a substantial improvement in the social safety net. Medicare provided health care coverage for those over sixty-five or falling into several other categories of risk while Medicaid covered those with low incomes.

Social movements made an indelible mark on the 1960s. The civil rights movement, the antiwar movement, the women's movement, the Native American movement, the environmental movement, and efforts for gay rights made huge changes in the American national character and social structure. Many of those movements continue today. These social movements led to policies that protected voting and employment rights, rights to political participation, and a host of other freedoms that people often take for granted today. The movements also provided the motivation to protect the environment and insure future resource adequacy. The people who came through these movements changed professions like social work in profound ways.

The civil rights movement began in the 1950s and grew steadily in the early 1960s. After post-Civil War Reconstruction, many of the rights that enslaved people had won were taken from them by campaigns of fear and laws that restricted their rights. Voting rights were restricted by the Jim Crow laws. Terror campaigns conducted by various white supremacy organizations resulted in lynchings and beatings throughout the South. Civil rights leaders such as Reverend Martin Luther King adopted a strategy based on the peaceful resistance ideas used in India by Mahatma Gandhi. The Southern Christian Leadership Conference conducted marches in many cities in the South to push for equal rights. Their efforts were often met with violence. Protesters faced violence and death to promote their civil rights and the civil rights of others. The passage of federal laws protecting civil rights and voting rights was a response to the movement.

The Vietnam war dragged on, negatively affecting the Johnson administration, and Johnson decided not to run for his second term. Support for the war was low and his efforts to resolve those issues were unsuccessful. There was also a good deal of civil unrest that proved difficult to resolve. The antiwar movement involved many college campuses and many major cities. Marches and demonstrations communicated the anger of many Americans toward what they saw as an unjust war. The 1968 Democratic National Convention in Chicago was the scene of a major confrontation. The student movement and the antiwar movement occupied similar ground but the former had broader aims. Organizations like Students for a Democratic Society (SDS) organized on many campuses on a multiplicity of issues. Ultimately some of the people involved in all of these movements moved toward becoming committed international radicals.

Richard Nixon was elected president in 1968. He promptly dismantled many of the programs that Johnson had created. He also created a system he called "The New Federalism" which returned control of many federal programs to the states through revenue sharing. Revenue sharing took money collected from federal taxes and gave it to states and localities to decide how to spend. Many social programs were moved toward the private sector. Although there was some scaling back of the programs of the 1960s, there was also much progress, particularly in the area of health care.

Environmental awareness was a growing force among the American public. Earth Day in 1970 focused attention on air and water pollution as well as resource shortages. There was legislative progress on the environmental front. The Clean Air Act (42 USC §7401 et seq.) was passed in the 1970s, followed by the Clean Water Act (33 USC §1251 et seq.) in 1972.

Nixon's second term was marked by the Watergate scandal and he resigned in 1973. He was succeeded by Gerald Ford, who had become vice president when former Vice President Spiro Agnew resigned. The war in Vietnam finally ended in 1975 when the North Vietnamese occupied the city of Saigon.

In 1973 and again in 1979 the people of the United States were subjected to a surprising and painful reality—an energy crisis that made oil and gasoline hard to get. Gas shortages and increased prices shocked people who counted on cheap and abundant energy. This created major problems for the economy and for every part of American society. Although these two episodes were partially political in character, they showed Americans what the future might look like if energy issues were not addressed.

Georgia governor Jimmy Carter became president in 1976 after defeating Gerald Ford. Carter encouraged a number of policy innovations in mental health and child welfare but challenges in the international and economic realms diverted his attention from social welfare. Knowledge and service work began

Nuclear power plant in Salem County, New Jersey. Nuclear power is cleaner than coal but promises long term issues storing nuclear wastes and potential accidents. This facility is near Philadelphia and Wilmington.

to replace manufacturing work, leading to mass layoffs and a souring economic situation for many Americans. There were several policy developments in the child welfare area. The Child Abuse Treatment and Prevention Act of 1974 was passed. This law created a framework for child protection that went far beyond what was in place up to that point. The foster child permanency movement, perhaps best represented by the Oregon and Alameda Projects, became part of the federal policy with the passage of the Child Care and Adoption Act (P.L. 96-272) in 1980. There were also policies for special education and battered families.

Carter was defeated for reelection in 1980 and Ronald Reagan, former actor and California governor, became president. Reagan shifted much government spending toward the military and took an aggressive posture toward the Soviet Union and its allies. His efforts resulted in huge deficits and increases in the national debt and a reenvision approach to social welfare.

Reagan vigorously attacked the idea of an activist government. He believed that, in many situations, government was the problem and not the solution. His charismatic style and communications ability made him successful in pushing his agenda forward.

Reagan worked to dismantle the welfare state that was created over the previous four decades. Although the system suffered consistent attacks from the Reagan administration, most of the major elements remained in place. The movement toward privatization continued. One huge change was passage of the Omnibus Budget Reconciliation Act of 1981 (P.L. 97-35) which converted a range of categorical programs (specific programs for narrowly targeted beneficiaries) to a series of block grants (a smaller amount of money than the sum of the categorical programs' funding, given to states and localities to be spent on a wider variety of programs).

During the Reagan years, there was a movement toward deregulation of the financial industry and scaling back of environmental regulations. Energy conservation was downplayed. Toward the end of Reagan's second term the nation encountered the savings and loan crisis. A number of savings and loans failed during this emergency. Deregulation was one of the culprits in this crisis. Although this was a relatively minor predicament at the time, the nation would be visited again by bank failures in the future.

Reagan's presidency also saw the hard edge of economic restructuring as the manufacturing sector of the economy lost jobs to overseas competition (Bluestone & Harrison, 1982). Large areas of the Midwest suffered massive unemployment. Entire communities were decimated as the industrial plants that they depended upon closed and jobs moved to factories in distant countries. This process has continued for decades as the information sector continues to push out the manufacturing sector in the United States and globalization continues to advance.

Devolution, the movement moving responsibilities for social programs toward lower levels of government, was part of a world wide trend. This, combined with privatization and outsourcing by social agencies, created a situation that encouraged smaller organizations. This policy creates greater variability in who receives funds for specific situations because these decisions are made at the local and state levels, not the national level. One jurisdiction may find ways to reduce spending on programs that support African Americans while promoting programs that enhance the lives of whites.

Reagan's vice president, George H. W. Bush, succeeded him into the presidency in 1988. A much more moderate Republican, Bush lacked Reagan's charisma. He also inherited a huge budget deficit from the Reagan years. In the first Gulf War, Bush led the nation in ejecting Iraq from Kuwait. The substantial popularity he gained as part of this successful effort was reduced by the serious recession that occurred shortly after. It was also during his presidency that the Soviet Union disintegrated. Social welfare contributions of the Bush years included the Americans with Disabilities Act of 1990 (42 USC § 12101) and a number of child welfare policies. Bush also put emphasis on national service and private charity.

William Jefferson Clinton was elected president in 1992 and pursued a number of social welfare policy proposals including national health insurance.

After losing control of Congress in 1994, Clinton had difficulty putting forth progressive policies. His welfare reform efforts were criticized by many. Scandals plagued the Clinton Administration but progress was made on many fronts.

First Lady Hillary Clinton led the move toward national health care. This had been a goal of welfare-state policy making since the original Social Security legislation in the 1930s. The commission that she chaired proposed a national health plan called managed competition. This would have involved competing health plans in each geographic area. Resistance from the health care industry as well as political inexperience and a lack of political support were factors that helped defeat the plan.

Some health care legislation was adopted during the Clinton years. These policies included the State Child Health Insurance Program (SCHIP) (Title 21 of the Social Security Act) and the Health Insurance Portability and Accountability Act (HIPAA) (P.L. 104-191). These laws, both championed by the late Senator Edward Kennedy, greatly expanded the right to health care. They also addressed privacy concerns and insurance portability.

The National and Community Service Trust Act of 1993 (P.L. 103-82) created the Corporation for National and Community Service (CNCS) and brought together national service opportunities. AmeriCorps was part of this legislation. VISTA became a part of this and a number of new efforts were added.

Welfare reform was a Clinton campaign promise. He pledged to "end welfare as we know it." Clinton brought together a group of social welfare scholars to create a vision of welfare postulated on communitarian values. His original vision for welfare reform was deflected by Georgia representative and Speaker of the House Newt Gingrich's successful Contract with America and by the political necessity of dealing with a Republican Congress. The final bill that emerged (the Personal Responsibility and Work Opportunity Reconciliation Act) changed Aid to Families with Dependent Children (AFDC) into a program called Transitional Assistance for Needy Families (TANF) (Hoefer, 2012c). TANF was a block grant and participants did not enjoy the entitlement status of AFDC. States could make choices about program design within the block grant. The administration had previously allowed states to make changes in the AFDC regulations, but this act provided even more flexibility.

Clinton advocated working with the faith community to deliver services. He created a number of opportunities to involve faith-based programs and policies in the social services mix.

The nature of politics and the political system intensified during the Clinton years and continued during the following administrations. This is often referred to as the culture war and it speaks to a lack of commonality and civility between political actors. Social issues such as abortion, gay marriage, and stem cell research have become tremendously divisive as the culture war continues.

The economy expanded greatly during the Clinton years. The technology sector led considerable growth and created substantial wealth. Trade agreements with other nations (most notably the North American Free Trade Agreement or NAFTA) facilitated trade by removing barriers. These trade agreements also accelerated the displacement of American industrial workers. Vice President Gore's interest in the environment put a strong voice for protection at the highest level of government.

The Clinton administration was able to eliminate the federal deficit and actually accumulate a surplus. His time in office saw an economic expansion and an absence of protracted conflict overseas. In spite of a series of scandals, Clinton was very popular with Americans as he left office and since that time.

George W. Bush was elected in 2000, after a contested battle with Clinton's vice president, Albert Gore. Gore won the popular vote but a Supreme Court decision stopped a recount in Florida that would have decided the election. This unusual action left the nation in a divided state and the new president without much of a mandate to govern. The Republicans did have many members in Congress and there was a growing conservative faction in the Supreme Court.

Early Bush policy proposals cut the tax rates for wealthy Americans by substantial amounts. This, along with downturns in the economy and costly military actions, eliminated the surplus and created an ever-deeper deficit. Bush's conservative policies created a negative message for social welfare. Although Bush billed himself as a "compassionate conservative," his administration did little to advance the cause of social-welfare policy making. Perhaps the most important contribution was the introduction of a prescription drug benefit as a part of Medicare.

On September 11, 2001, terrorists crashed airliners into the World Trade Center and the Pentagon. Thousands of people died in the resulting destruction and the United States entered a period of renewed concern about national security. This heightened security concern created a tremendous disincentive for progressive organizing. The Uniting and Strengthening America by Providing Appropriate Tools to Intercept and Obstruct Terrorism Act of 2001 (the USA PATRIOT Act) (P.L. 107-56), passed after the attack, created a significant number of new law enforcement and surveillance powers.

The United States invaded both Afghanistan and Iraq. Although there were initial successes, both wars dragged on and support waned as American casualties increased. The Iraq war became more and more unpopular with the American people.

Bush continued Clinton's support of faith-based organizations (FBOs) in social welfare. Wineburg (2007) observed that the emphasis was on smaller FBOs as opposed to the more traditional religious nonprofits. Wineburg suggested that this had more to do with incorporating evangelical Christians into Bush's political base than supporting the faith-based social service community.

An early corporate scandal involved Enron, a Houston based energy company that failed in the fall of 2001. This huge financial mess led to the passage of the Sarbanes-Oxley Act (P.L. 107-204) which put some controls on corporations. The scandal also fueled a national debate over corporate responsibility.

In the fall of 2005 a series of three hurricanes (Katrina/Wilma/Rita) devastated the Gulf Coast of the United States, laying waste to parts of Texas, Louisiana, Mississippi, Alabama, Kentucky, Ohio, and Florida, as well as the major cities of New Orleans, Biloxi, and Mobile. Nearly 2,000 people were killed in the Katrina storm alone. The economic cost was also substantial and the impact on the economy was enormous. Two important implications were a national outrage over the lack of an effective federal response and a national debate regarding the role of global warming in the creation of the disaster. *The Economist's* cover for the week of the storm (September 10-16) featured a distraught woman with the caption "The Shaming of America."

The 2006 election saw the Republicans losing control over both houses of Congress. Congresswoman Nancy Pelosi became the first woman Speaker of the House of Representatives.

Much higher energy prices during 2007 and 2008 raised the issue of energy supply and alternative sources of energy into the national psyche. Climate change and energy independence have become serious issues in the current policy environment (see Brown, 2006; Walt, 2008). This was the final blow for much of the automobile industry, which saw declining sales revenue. In 2009, both General Motors and Chrysler filed for bankruptcy protection.

The end of Bush's second term was characterized by an ever deeper recession and a loss of public confidence. High energy costs and the explosion of the housing bubble added strain to an economy already stressed by huge federal deficits (a consequence of tax cuts and the wars in Iraq and Afghanistan) and balance of payment issues. Questionable mortgage practices by some of the nation's largest financial institutions threatened to bring many of those institutions into insolvency. Although there are certainly a complex set of issues that contributed to the housing and economic crisis known as the Great Recession, deregulation of the banking and financial service industries loomed large.

In the end of 2008, the United States government moved to bail out a number of major financial institutions that were at risk as a result of the mortgage crisis. Congress passed the Emergency Economic Stabilization Act of 2008 (P.L. 110-343) which created the Troubled Assets Rehabilitation Program or TARP. This was a response to one of the most serious financial crises since the Great Depression (see Galbraith, 2008).

On November 4, 2008, voters elected Barack Obama as the forty-fourth president of the United States. He defeated Republican John McCain. Obama is the first African American president. Among the themes he stressed were health care, community, service, environment, and cohesion. He inherited an economy that was in a shambles and a problematic relationship with much of the rest of the world.

President Obama moved quickly to shore up the U.S. economy by supporting a $787 billion stimulus package, the American Recovery and Reinvestment Act of 2009 (P.L. 111-5). This bill was designed to be spent quickly to reinvigorate the nation's slumping economy. Although this bill was strongly criticized in some quarters, it is difficult to envision an alternative course of action other than a stimulus package.

Obama set out an ambitious plan for promoting service, reforming health care, building education, and creating a green economy. Much of his agenda was not enacted while the Democrats had majorities in both the Senate and the House, as elected officials were reticent to spend the funds needed. The federal deficit and national debt had grown substantially and prudent spending was the order of the day. The passage of a greatly reduced health care plan early in 2010 was one major victory in pursuing the issues that he had campaigned on. This law, entitled the Patient Protection and Affordable Care Act (P.L. 111-148), but frequently called "Obamacare," provides historic levels of protection for the health care of all Americans.

In 2010, the Obama administration suffered a loss as the Republicans took back control of the House of Representatives. Groups like the Tea Party movement (a small government, low tax movement often supported by conservative foundations and ideological interest groups) had an impact on the election and subsequent policy making.

The presidential election of 2012 saw the Republican candidacy of Mitt Romney unable to overcome Barack Obama's popularity with women and people of color, despite a sputtering economy that usually presages the defeat of an incumbent. Obama himself had to recover from a botched televised debate with the challenger. In the end, however, he won handily, with 332 electoral college votes, compared to Romney's 206 votes (270 are needed to have a majority). The Senate remained in Democratic hands and the House of Representatives' majority stayed Republican.

The divided Congress elected in 2012 was one of the most partisan in recent years. Senate and House Republicans, particularly those associated with the Tea Party movement, were intensely against the president's agenda, particularly the Affordable Care Act (Obamacare). House Republicans, for example, held nearly 7,400 votes against this law, along with a filibuster effort in the Senate, even though President Obama would certainly have vetoed any bill that passed to kill the health care reform (Posner, 2013). In the end, the 113th Congress is considered by the public as one of the least effective in modern history. Two-thirds of American respondents polled in December of 2013 indicated that this Congress was the worst of their lifetime and 73 percent indicated that Congress had done nothing to address the country's problems (CNN, 2013).

The non-presidential Congressional elections of 2014 handed Republicans a majority in both the Senate and the House of Representatives. Republicans continued to vow to repeal Obamacare. Such a repeal would cause millions of Americans to lose the health insurance they had just recently gained. The Supreme Court, in a series of decisions, affirmed the constitutionality of the Affordable Care Act. Partisanship looms large over the run-up to the next presidential election.

WHERE IS AMERICA NOW?

The previous chapters, along with the current one, have covered a great deal of material. Figure 3-1 provides a quick overview of some of the most important information discussed. Societal elements are shown, along with how these are seen in the industrial society and current reality. The main conclusion from Figure 3-1 is that the industrial society model and current reality have a large discrepancy between them. The next few paragraphs will briefly go through the figure line by line.

In the area of the economy, the industrial model has been discussed in chapter 2 at great length. The next chapter will discuss at length how the industrial economy our society is built on has already begun to change and will continue to develop as an information economy. Partially because of the Internet and social media, which are results of the information age, government is shifting

Figure 3-1

Gaps Between the Industrial Model and Current Reality

Element of Society	Industrial Model	Current Reality
Economy	Industrial economy	Mixed information and industrial economy
Political System	Centralized	Decentralized devolution
Focus	Nation-state	Global network
Work	Job-based model	Theater-based model, contingent work arrangements
Social Problems	Effects of industrialization	Effects of environmental destruction and dislocations of economic change as well as industrialization in some parts of the world
Environment	Assumed to be unlimited	Clearly limited/resource constraints
Social Welfare	Address side effects of modernization—residual model	Address side effects of economic dislocation—institutional model
Social Work	Residual—aimed at solving problems at the interpersonal level	Institutional—aimed at solving societal problems

from centralized in nature to more decentralized. People expect more trans-parency and the ability to influence policy decisions through electronic means and at the local level.

Although nation-states are clearly vitally important, many efforts are inter-national in scope. Even the United States, with the mightiest military on earth, works closely with other nations in its efforts to stem terrorism, improve health conditions around the world, jumpstart ailing economies, and improve the deteriorating environment. Certainly, other countries are sometimes more con-cerned with these and other issues than the United States is, but it is clear that many problems can now only be addressed using a global, rather than only a national, stage. Issues of economic and political dislocation of millions of peo-ple create problems that cannot be solved by building walls but only through multinational agreements and efforts.

The nature of work has changed for many people already. The days of choosing one company to work for all one's life have been left behind for one where changing one's employer every few years will become the norm. Job skills will need to be maintained and improved as technology alters the work environment frequently. What are considered important social problems that need to be addressed will no longer be limited to the effects of industrialization. Although unemployment and the lack of income it causes, for example, will be considered a social problem in the future, environmental destruction and the more-or-less permanent problems associated with the rise of an information society will also be seen as problems. The industrial era view of the natural environment is that the earth's riches are unlimited and that humankind's impact on it through the use of fossil fuels and harvesting of its resources is negligible. This view is no longer sustainable.

Because people will recognize the long-term impact of a changing economy, they will need to change the social welfare system. Instead of looking only at income support for temporary and short-term periods from a residual welfare system perspective, they will need to understand that everyone needs assistance at times as a matter of course. This will move our country towards an institutional approach to our social welfare system. This shift in perspective will have an impact on the profession of social work, which also will need to understand that most problems that individuals experience stem from their environment. The emphasis on individual solutions to homelessness, lack of skills, recovery from natural disasters, and so on will need to make way for understanding the systems that should be put into place to alter the impact of large-scale changes in the economy, government policy, and environmental shifts. This too represents a change from a residual view to an institutional view of social work.

WHERE FROM HERE?

What is the future likely to be like? That will depend on the decisions that people make and the efforts that they put forth. The transition to an information economy is well under way. There is also an environmental crisis. The economy, like many of today's difficulties, is global in nature. It is unlikely that what you will experience in the future will be like the three most significant periods for social welfare in the United States: the progressive period, the Great Depression, and the sixties. Those periods contributed substantially to social welfare but today's world is almost completely different. This applies to the economic, political, and sociocultural aspects of American life. You can look to these periods for inspiration but many of the lessons that they would teach you are no longer relevant. The next chapter explains what has been happening as America and the world have entered the information age.

Questions for Discussion

1. How are the changes that social workers face today different from those faced by social workers at the turn of the Industrial Revolution?
2. Do all societies evolve in the same way? What are the implications for social welfare?
3. You know that the environmental crisis is serious today, but how has the environment affected older societies and social welfare systems?

Exercise

1. Imagine that you are having a conversation with a social worker working for the Settlement House Movement in the 1800s. How would their job compare to yours? What progress have we made?

Websites

Social Welfare History Project: http://www.socialwelfarehistory.org

Social Welfare History Archives: http://special.lib.umn.edu/swha/

Social Welfare History Group: http://depts.washington.edu/sswweb/swhg/index.html

Social Work History Links Centennial Archives: http://www.socialworkers.org/profession/centennial/sw_history.htm

Visual Media

Awakenings (1990). Directed by Penny Marshall. This movie portrays Dr. Oliver Sacks's work with victims of the encephalitis epidemic.

Water (2005). Directed by Deepa Mehta. This movie examines the fate of widows in poverty in India and the coming of social change.

Further Reading

Herrick, J., & Stuart, P. (Eds.) (2005). *Encyclopedia of social welfare history in North America*. Thousand Oaks, CA: Sage.

Reisch, M., & Andrews, J. (2014). T*he road not taken: A history of radical social work in the United States*. London, England: Routledge.

Chapter 4

Current Conditions and the Coming of the Information Society

People get used to their assumptions about how the world has evolved. Change is so subtle sometimes that it is difficult to notice. It is easy to consider today's reality in terms of yesterday's experience. Even in a period of very substantial change it is easy to assume that fundamentally, nothing has changed. These assumptions are reflected in the way that social welfare policy is described and analyzed in the social welfare policy and services literature in social work. Many very thoughtful people completely ignore the coming of the information society or treat it like it was just another phase of industrialization.

Many current social welfare policies are based on ideas and assumptions that are no longer completely true. They are based on the assumption that the American economy is primarily a manufacturing one and that society reflects that situation. Because much of the expansion of social welfare took place during the 1930s and 1960s, times when the United States was an industrial nation, this is understandable. Newer policies will have to be based on an understanding of the changes in the economy that this chapter will describe.

Chapter 2 discusses what the functions and institutions of society are as well as how the shift from agrarian to industrial society changed societal institutions. The next great societal transition is the movement from late industrialization to an information society. This process is already well under way in the United States, much of Europe, and parts of Asia. This is a worldwide development and one that will change how current and future generations live, just as the previous change affected how people lived their lives.

In short, an information society is one where the information sector of the economy has become dominant (see Dillman, 1991). The dominance of the information sector not only comes at the expense of the other sectors, it changes their nature in important ways (Bell, 1973; Beniger, 1986, 1988; Dillman, 1991). Information technology is changing both agricultural and manufacturing processes (Dillman, 1985).

67

THE INFORMATION SOCIETY

In the mid to early 1970s the United States and a number of other economically influential nations began to shift toward an information society (Porat, 1977). An information society is one in which the information sector of the economy is prominent. The information sector includes a range of both service and manufacturing components. In an information society, knowledge is the greatest store of wealth (Cleveland, 1985; Huey, 1994). In earlier times it was material goods and land. Although these are still valuable, the real wealth in an information society is knowledge. This leads to huge changes in the way that economies work and how wealth is allocated. Think of Bill Gates, for example. His billions of dollars of wealth came from creating software that people used to process information. He did not amass wealth from owning real estate, manufacturing steel, or running railroads. The fortunes made by the developers of Facebook, YouTube, and Google are other examples of how creating tools for information processing has resulted in tremendous financial gains.

Much of the traditional labor in the agricultural and industrial sectors is either affected by information technology or completely automated (Beniger, 1986, 1988). Cars are now made by robotic assembly lines and contain several computers as part of their various systems. This system has replaced, to a great extent, long lines of human workers. In addition, computer-aided design (CAD) tools have greatly affected how almost all products are designed, reducing the need for some types of labor as well.

Knowledge work, work that requires highly specialized training to perform and yields products with considerable knowledge components, replaced the skilled labor of the industrial age as the work that is most highly compensated. This change, from industrial to knowledge work, accounts for much of the rash of job losses that characterized economic restructuring in the 1980s and 1990s. The outsourcing of jobs and the flight of capital characterized this transition period. This caused considerable pain in many communities and destroyed the lives of individuals. It also constituted a huge emergency for social welfare programs at a time when a conservative political climate was pushing for scaling back social programs.

If you look at the history of social welfare you can see a series of transitions that have changed the landscape of society (Garvin & Cox, 1987; McNutt, 2005). These transitions have four characteristics in common. First, they represent substantial transitions that affect almost everyone in a society. These transitions were difficult periods in the existence of most societies. Second, they alter the nature of social institutions. This means not only do they change existing institutions but they separate new institutions from others. Karl Polanyi (1942) pointed out that in earlier societies there were only a few social institutions and the functions of other institutions were embedded in the existing institutions. The family was the only institution in hunting and gathering societies. Other functions were discharged through the family until this was no longer practical. Eventually, other institutions emerged. The implication of this for an information society is that there may be additional social institutions to come.

Third, these transitions occur at different times in different societies. Although earlier development thought held that all societies go through social transitions in a similar way (a formulation called modernization theory), many social scientists have pulled away from that assumption (see Rostow, 1960; Todero, 1985). Development can be steered by a society's values and by situations that occur during a society's existence.

Finally, the change does not take place immediately. The change happens over time and may seem almost glacially slow to some. Diffusion of innovation scholars (see, for example, Rogers, 2003) write about social change efforts reaching critical mass and critics like Malcolm Gladwell (2002) talk about reaching the "tipping point." What this means is that many small changes finally result in huge changes. It also means that social change can be a slow and deliberate process taking many years to show results.

You can see the effects of the coming economy in some of the issues that confront American society. Hoping for a return to the past where things seemed more controllable is not really an option. If you look at past societies, the population was smaller, life expectancy and general health status were lower, and there were huge numbers of problems that do not exist today. Although the jury is still out on whether progress is inevitable, it is clear that the decisions that people make can have a major impact on the type of society that they have. Most views of progress have both utopian and dystopian views. One view says that society will be wonderful after people make changes while the other predicts that a worse world is coming. For example, having a cell phone means that you can communicate wherever you please but it also means that you have less privacy (people can call you anywhere) and that others can track your movements via the GPS chip in many cell phones. This list of pros and cons goes on and on. You can choose the more desirable course or have others choose the course life takes for you.

A sign for Coca-Cola on a building in the city of Gori in the Republic of Georgia. The reach of multinational corporations is immense and their impact is significant.

Information and communications technology is important in an information society. It supports the creation, storage, and dissemination of knowledge. It also supports collaborative work and data analysis. The networks created with technology have changed the nature of society in important ways. Technology has also changed the way that industrial and agricultural work is performed.

Technology and the growth of the information society have accelerated relationships with people in other parts of the globe. Although globalization is a separate social process, technology and the growth of information economics add to the impact of globalization.

GLOBAL TRADE AND THE INTERNATIONAL ECONOMY

Information economies are global economies (Castells, 2009). The globalization phenomenon that occurred over the past thirty or so years is clearly supportive of this global search for talent and capacity. Industrial societies are also global societies. Much of what is made in the United States and other nations is intended for export.

Economic theory suggests that outsourcing occurs because firms can get a higher return on their capital by locating production somewhere else (Todero, 1985). If people can manufacture a car or a piece of electronics somewhere else, and the cost of transportation doesn't rule out making it there, then most firms would decide to outsource, even if it eliminates jobs in their home country. This is called comparative advantage in international economic parlance. People can grow tropical fruit in Maine in the winter but it would be far costlier than growing it in the tropics and shipping it to Maine. If the United States has comparative advantage in research and development and the People's Republic of China has comparative advantage in manufacturing, then, theoretically, both sides would win in a trade situation. Very few people would argue with this logic. Unfortunately it is an exchange that is rarely as clean as people might like.

There is only an advantage if both sides benefit. If all of America's manufacturing work goes to another nation and America cannot use its advantage in knowledge work, then the exchange becomes one-sided. This means that Americans lose jobs and the American economy is reduced in size. What happens often depends on how international trade is managed.

Most economists argue that international trade benefits everyone if the terms of trade are fair. Unfortunately, this is frequently a problem. The postwar terms of trade are set forth in a document called the General Accord on Trade and Tariffs (GATT). The original 1947 document is often called the Bretton Woods agreement. In 1994 the final round of GATT was created and the World Trade Organization (WTO) superseded it in many ways. The WTO is an organization and a deliberative body that can sanction member nations that violate trade rules. There are also more limited agreements such as NAFTA (the North American Free Trade Agreement) and the European Union, which deal with regional trade.

This does not mean that everyone in a society benefits. A serious issue is which sectors/people/communities get hurt by outsourcing and which sectors benefit. Many industrial workers in the United States feel that international trade has sent their jobs overseas. That is an accurate perception. Those manufacturing jobs are now being done by people who live in other nations.

Trade has devastated entire communities by removing the industrial concern that was their economic base. Nations can deal with this by imposing protective tariffs to prevent competition or by retraining their workers to meet new challenges. Sadly, retraining workers has not always been a priority in many societies. The United States has lost a substantial number of manufacturing jobs over the past five decades. Figure 4-1 presents these data.

Figure 4-1

The Decline in United States Monthly Manufacturing Employment 1986–2014

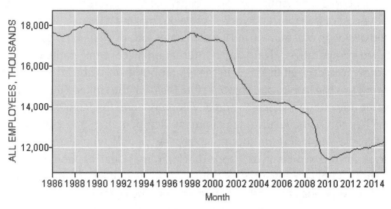

http://data.bls.gov/pdq/SurveyOutputServlet

In many economic transactions between nations there are winners and losers within societies. In the 1990s the technology and financial sectors were the winners in the United States. The manufacturing sector was a clear loser, especially in terms of automobiles and textiles. This was especially bad news for the Midwest and the South. In many ways, these changes echoed earlier transitions in these areas. The textile industry, at one point, flourished in New England. The mills eventually moved to the South for cheaper labor and lower taxes. They subsequently moved to other areas of the world for the same reasons.

Assume that the government could force these firms to stay in the United States, either by putting a heavy tariff on goods produced overseas or making it illegal for firms to move their production overseas. What would happen? In the first place, the costs of these goods would rise. This would generally lead to a lower standard of living for all citizens. Other nations might retaliate by putting tariffs on American goods. These retaliatory tariffs would hurt American industry and American workers. It also would mean that America would not make the transition to more productive pursuits.

Trade also doesn't mean that all nations are treated fairly. Economists have long documented how the nature of trade is an advantage for some nations and a serious disadvantage for many nations (particularly poorer nations). Dependency theory and world systems theory (Todero, 1985; Wallerstein, 1974) discuss this issue at great length. Contemplation of terms of trade is both a complex and controversial matter that goes beyond the scope of this book. It is, however, an important topic, particularly where the fate of communities is concerned.

None of these issues is new. International trade has been a growing occurrence for centuries and although relative terms of trade are fairly recent, they are certainly not new. The United States' Revolutionary War was fought, in part, over trade issues. One really doesn't need an information economy to have these forces occur, although it does change the way such forces often play out in nations and communities.

The changing nature of the global information economy will create incentives and disincentives for certain types of social programs. One example is national health insurance. American car manufacturers must pay for their employees' health insurance and for retirees, something that is unnecessary in nations such as Canada that provide health care coverage. This raises the cost of American-made cars and puts American manufacturing plants at a distinct disadvantage when selling their products.

The next issue in globalization is the rise of international organizations and international networks. Multinational corporations can be huge entities that are often larger in terms of net wealth than some smaller nations. As a group they have incredible amounts of influence. There are also international governance organizations such as the United Nations, International Monetary Fund, the International Criminal Court, and the World Bank. International NGOs like the International Red Cross, World Wildlife Fund, and Amnesty International have varying degrees of influence.

International networks, some of them completely informal, are also gaining in power. The Internet can bring people together to challenge older national powers in important ways as was seen in the Arab Spring movement that toppled autocratic rule in several North African countries in 2011. Insurgents were able to use social media channels to communicate, plan demonstrations, and react to government efforts to stop the uprisings. On a more gruesome note, the Islamic State organization has used social media effectively to spread video of beheadings and mass executions, and to recruit fighters to its cause.

Massive international social justice issues exist. World poverty is a serious and dismal issue that will take significant international cooperation and an enormous amount of resources to address. The international health care crisis is in a similar situation. There are many human rights and social justice issues throughout the world. Basic freedoms and rights are frequently ignored by tyrannical governments. Terrorism, war, and mass violence are problems that touch every continent.

ENVIRONMENTAL DESTRUCTION

All societies face the constraints of their resource base. It determines what can be done now and what can be done in the future. Years of neglect of conservation and environmental protection have brought people to a point where this base is in question. Even such gigantic natural resources as trees in the Amazon rain forest, or fish in the ocean, can be over-used to the point of exhaustion.

The sum total of unsustainable resource use and environmental destruction has begun to catch up with American society (Brown, 2011; Daly & Cobb, 1989). Climate change, a looming energy crisis, food shortages, droughts, and other resource shortages suggest that people are reaching the carrying capacity of the planet. It is not only true that the pace of resource use has increased but the growth of population aggravates the rate of resource depletion. A simple example of the complexities of this type of situation is the growth in demand for quinoa, a grain grown in the Andes for hundreds of years. As it has become more popular in the United States, farmers are planting more to meet demand which then nets them higher income and a higher standard of living. Unfortunately, planting more quinoa destroys natural habitats, upsetting the balance of nature in these areas. More income leads to larger families because children survive their infant years. More people can grow more quinoa and put more stress on the limited resources of the Andes.

The health of the environment has major impact on the economy. The spike in oil and gasoline prices after the Katrina/Rita/Wilma disasters in the American Gulf Coast placed considerable stress on the U.S. economy. As available resources decline, the prices for these resources will increase. This will have an impact throughout the economy. This will, of course, have a direct impact on the social welfare system.

To put it more simply, having fewer natural resources will stress the economic system and, subsequently, reduce the resources available to the social welfare system. Environmental destruction also stresses individuals and communities and makes it far less likely that many social problems can be avoided. This increases the cost of health care and related services and makes the likelihood of a successful outcome less possible. If people live in a polluted world that affects their health, it will be much harder to deal with the costs of health care.

Hurricane damage in Pensacola, Florida, in 2005. Climate change promises more destruction from weather, especially in coastal areas. This community was damaged prior to Katrina.

Many, if not most, treatments of social policy treat the natural environment as a given. That's really no longer tenable as a position. Climate change continues, threatening coastal communities and spawning more violent atmospheric disturbances such as tornados and hurricanes. Implications of changes in the environment will make many things no longer possible and other things more likely. Building along coasts may be inhibited or banned due to frequent damaging storms, for example. Droughts in agricultural areas such as California pit fruit and vegetable growers against city dwellers for use of remaining water. Political fights for water rights will create losers and winners, changing where people live, the jobs they work, and the style of life they enjoy.

GREEN SOCIETY

Not every information society needs to be green or sustainable (Brown, 1981) but, given the state of the planet, it is difficult to see a future where preservation of our environment won't be a policy priority. In addition to the growth of the information sector of the economy, there is an ecological crisis created by growing population, resource depletion, and environmental destruction (Hoff & McNutt, 1994, 2008). This will further constrain many of the traditional aspects of the economy. All of this happened before in the prelude to the Great Depression. The dust bowl phenomenon of the 1930s, caused by drought and poor farming practices, led to a large internal migration from Oklahoma, Texas, and several other states to California and other agricultural areas. Healthy economies are rarely built on unhealthy ecological systems (Brown, 1981, 2009; Speth, 2004).

A number of serious challenges, including resource destruction and depletion, climate change, and energy shortages, exist. Over-consumption and over-population are serious threats to the resource base. The gradual warming of the earth due to human activity is another serious threat to all of humanity. Climate change would be a considerable problem even if the burdens were randomly distributed; however, they are not. The poor suffer disproportionately from environmental destruction. Environmental justice is a major issue throughout the world.

What is happening today is not unlike the Industrial Revolution in the 1800s. There is a transformation of the way that society makes its living. The change is different but the process is familiar. The issues of globalization and the physical environment have become more profound. This change will be evident in the social institutions and the people, organizations, and communities that depend on them.

SOCIAL INSTITUTIONS IN FLUX

Much of what will be changed as society transforms is the nature of social institutions. Recall that these are the structures in society that meet human needs. Many of the changes discussed here have already happened or will happen in the next few years. Some of the changes will take longer and involve much effort and more time. Using the same approach as in chapter 2 will help pinpoint the nature of these institutions in the industrial and information societies. Table 4-1 summarizes some of those potential changes. Although this chapter examines each of the institutions separately, there are certainly areas that overlap. This discussion parallels what was said in chapter 2 about the transition from agrarian society to industrial society.

Table 4-1
Changes in Social Institutions

Institution	Industrial Form	Information Society
Economy	Complex, Factory System	Decentralized System Virtual Organizations Supply Chain Management
Family/Schools	Nuclear/Local Public Schools with Little State or National Rules	Nuclear or Extended/Considerable State or National Rules
Government	Advanced, Bureaucratic Government, Justice Nation States	Network-based Government, E-government and E-democracy
Religion/Civic Organizations	National Churches/ Labor Unions	Multiple Churches/Self-formed Networks
Social Welfare	Secular, Government Run	Network-based Mixed Economy of Care/Social Enterprise

Economy

The element of society that will probably be most affected by the initial shift will be the economy. The economy is the part of society that creates the goods and services that people need and finds a way to distribute those goods and services. The information revolution will change the primary engine of economic growth, the nature of work, the type of organizations, and a number of other factors. This makes the production, distribution, and consumption of knowledge the activities that the economy finds most important. Although other forms of work will continue in society, knowledge work stands out as a critical activity. Knowledge work is the type of effort that creates and uses knowledge. It requires education and special skills. It requires a body of knowledge. Knowledge work requires judgment and independence. Engineers and scientists are knowledge workers but so are psychologists and social workers.

Knowledge work is different from industrial work in other ways. Knowledge work can be done in far flung places, while industrial work must be concentrated to take advantage of the factory system. Because of virtual teams and information technology, telework and telecommuting are possible. This means that you can live where you choose and work where you want. This will not be true for all work or even all knowledge work (some of which requires physical proximity) but for a growing part of the population this could reverse the major force that has been tearing communities apart for almost two centuries. It would break the tie between capital and community. That could create a new and positive relationship between community and economy.

Capital mobility has been a destructive force in American communities for some time (Bluestone & Rose, 1997). Some communities have engaged in relatively difficult back and forth relationships between owners of capital, industrial organizations, and their workers. Factories can threaten to leave a community unless concessions are given such as lower (or no) taxes, subsidies for operating costs, and infrastructure improvements. Smokestack chasing (local leaders trying to lure manufacturing plants to locate within their borders) often costs communities years of needed tax revenues in an attempt to keep their people working. On balance, a virtual workplace can ignore location and get the people that it needs from throughout the world. The close relationship between jobs and industry, begun at the birth of the factory system, can now be discarded in many industries. Because capital mobility can be a likely side effect of globalization, this is becoming more and more important.

This could also have profound implications for immigration. Although there are certainly a number of reasons to move to another nation (such as climate or political persecution), a major reason is the search for work. People sometimes come to one of the industrialized nations, work, and send money back to their family in the poorer nations that they come from. This is a tremendous dislocation. A virtual workplace could make many immigration trips unnecessary. People can do knowledge work where they live now. This, of course, is already happening. Call centers have been outsourced from the United States to other nations. Friedman (2005) observes that tax preparation is frequently done overseas with returns passed back and forth over computer networks. In some places, instructors are outsourcing their grading. The legal profession is now seeing work performed by lawyers in other nations and shipped to U.S. law firms ("Offshoring Your Lawyer," 2010). Professional practice is always knowledge work and social workers can look forward to changes in the way that they practice.

Where Will People Work?

Bridges (1994) argues that even the concept of jobs is obsolete. People will have work but will be hired when their skills and a particular task match. They will then go on to another employment situation. People will evolve from a period of steady employment to a theater model of employment. Like actors or crew in a theatrical production, people will work on a project until they are no longer needed. They will then move on to another project where their skills are needed. This is called a theater model of employment. Most people who work in the theater industry expect employment to be short term. Projects (plays, movies, T.V. shows) have a beginning, middle, and an end and then employees go on to other projects. This adds a great deal to how agile an organization can be and is a feature of virtual organizations. There is a considerable amount of built-in insecurity in this arrangement. This is expected in the film/T.V./theater industry but is unexpected for most of the labor force. America's social welfare programs are not designed to support this type of situation, at least not completely. As it gets more common, significant problems will occur.

A familiar example of this type of arrangement is much of the academic job market. Although many faculty members are on some type of tenure line, many others are not. Numerous higher education courses are taught by adjunct faculty who are no longer employed after the course ends. They may work for multiple institutions but their services and their pay are only available for the term of contract.

Social workers who are hired by agencies with grants sometimes find themselves in the same situation. They are hired to work on the program and with the clients funded by the grant but if the grant is not renewed, and the agency does not find other revenue, the social workers need to find work elsewhere.

All of this means that there can be a great deal of flexibility in future work arrangements. In a lot of ways, this could be a wonderful option for those who find life in traditional organizations confining. Others will feel stress over the lack of security.

There may be changes in organizational structures as a result of the information society. Technology can increase span of control (the number of people that a person can supervise) and that can lead to flatter organizations (Burris, 1998). Flatter organizations can often be smaller and in some cases more egalitarian. It is also possible to create virtual organizations. In a virtual organization there is a central core of workers but most other functions are outsourced; that is, people are contracted to complete a specific task that needs to be done. Outsourcing is clearly connected to the theater model of employment discussed earlier. Although non-virtual organizations often find it hard to respond to new challenges and opportunities (because their staff and equipment are fixed), virtual organizations can adapt quickly by changing outsourcing partners. This capacity makes this form of organization highly prized in a very competitive environment. Technology makes the virtual form of organization easier to develop and manage.

E-commerce is, of course, the most likely marriage of technology and the economic system. This means transacting business online. E-commerce has created a major series of problems for "brick and mortar" retailers who find it difficult to compete on the basis of price or selection with online stores. This has been especially difficult for travel agents and certain types of financial professionals but the eventual range of those affected is unknown. Some predict that every worker will compete with every other worker in the world economy because of the reach of technology.

Who Will Be Left Behind?

Not everyone can participate in the information economy. Those who lack skills or access to information technology and networks like the Internet will be excluded (Ebo, 1998; McNutt, 1996a, 1998; Norris, 2001). This issue is often called the digital divide and may be one of the severe civil rights issues of the next decades. Access to technology is a relatively easy and inexpensive issue to address (Wilhelm, 2004).

There is a growing amount of information on the digital divide. Internationally, a measure called the Digital Opportunity Index (DOI) (http://www.itu .int/ITU-D/ict/doi/index.html) has been developed by the International Telecommunications Union to assess differences between nations in terms of the technology opportunities available to their citizens. There are eleven indicators over three clusters. In late 2007 (the latest year the index is available), the Republic of Korea ranked first on the DOI while the United States ranked twentieth.

One of the lessons of the information age economy is the importance of higher education both as source of an educated labor force and as a driver of innovation. People who didn't finish high school and many with a high school diploma are likely to find that their job prospects are less bright than they were in previous years. The manufacturing jobs that once could have been gotten with these credentials no longer exist in the United States. This is also a warning to states and communities that do not prioritize education. One of the key elements in a decision to relocate companies is that there must be a well-trained labor force. If an area is weak in this regard, it will be passed over.

As technology, information, and jobs change, the labor force will need a continuous stream of retraining as new knowledge becomes available and workers move from one part of the economy to others. New careers will constantly emerge and workers will need additional training to take advantage of these new possibilities. These needs may be filled by on-line coursework or nimble private institutions willing to teach any class that can pay for itself.

The educational system has already changed in important ways. Traditionally, higher education meant campus-based systems mostly run by non-profit and state-supported institutions. Off campus programs were small and secondary. Things have certainly changed. The largest private university in the United States now is the University of Phoenix, a for-profit, campus-free institution. On-line instruction has blossomed. The cost of traditional higher education has skyrocketed. A recent innovation in online education is the MOOC (Massive Open Online Course) which is a class offered free to anyone who desires to enroll. Although only a very small percentage of people who sign up for the course complete it, the model of easy access to coursework and information is now on the playing field. Modifications to this approach, such as having students pay a fee to have access to "learning guides" may prove necessary to make the approach function well. All of these forces promise to change the future trajectory of higher education.

Globalization (or actually just international trade) can lead to a movement of manufacturing jobs to other nations (Friedman, 2005; Todero, 1985). Competition is no longer between firms in the same town, state, or country but between firms throughout the world. Many nations can produce items much more cheaply than the United States. As a consequence, the manufacturing jobs go to those areas. This means that U.S. workers lose their jobs if they work in the affected industries, but can be retrained to work in more competitive sectors. It should be noted that most models of international trade consider this a beneficial impact of competition. It means that consumers receive the cheapest goods and those workers with relative advantage receive the jobs. It could also mean that American workers could be retrained for better jobs in other industries.

Changes in the economic system have been under way for some time. In comparison with the economic system during the sub-eras of the industrial society, such as the Progressive period, the Great Depression, or even the 1960s, the present economy is vastly different. This is also true of America's other institutions.

Family and Schools

The Industrial Revolution led to a major change in families. The extended form of family was replaced with a nuclear variety to support industrializations needed for a mobile labor force. This had real consequences for child rearing and the care of the elderly and the physically challenged. The information revolution and the different demands of knowledge work, coupled with concerns about the care of the aged and young, may push the model back to a more extended model. Families also exist within communities that not only share their socialization function but also support their ability to exist.

The family shares its socialization role with the education system, the media, and peer groups. All of these influences are affected by new technologies and changes in society. Texting, social networking sites, and video sharing sites have extended the nature of peer groups that children and adolescents must deal with. Technology has had a tremendous impact on the developmental experiences of children, teenagers, and young adults. There is even research to suggest that today's interactive, networked technology physically changes or rewires users' brains (Prensky, 2001a, 2001b).

The role of education is likely to be different as time progresses. Children today live in an information-rich environment. Education will need to take advantage of that environment and of the technology that supports it. There is an increase in the number of children who are home-schooled, growing to about 1.77 million in 2013, up from 1.5 million in 2007 (Smith, 2013). Technology makes this much more practical than ever before.

At the same time as larger numbers of children are being taken out of public schools, states and the national government are expecting more from teachers and students. Alarmed by what they see as falling levels of knowledge, officials have implemented tests to assess what children know and to judge teachers' and administrators' performance. Although this approach is not yielding the results that were hoped for, it recognizes the importance of knowledge in an information society. It does show that policy makers are beginning to grasp the critical importance of a highly educated workforce.

Government

It is useful to divide the political institution into the political decision-making system (politics) and the implementation role of government in providing services to citizens and others (government administration). Government has a more complex role to play than in the past. Globalization and the rise of complex relationships between sectors have made the mandate less clear and lines of authority less pronounced. Government leaders have become negotiators and organizers as well as leaders and administrators.

Some have argued that the scope of today's government is far less extensive than the government in the past. They call it the hollow state (Peters, 1994) and question if this is the best way to be governed. Political rhetoric charges that government is broken. Government is changing from the way it once was. This chapter will look at some of the changes that have occurred as a result of our transition to an information society.

Electronic democracy and electronic campaigning have the potential to change how political decisions are conducted. Electronic government can change how services, including social services, are delivered (Holzer, Manoharan, Shick, & Stowers, 2009). This could be a very positive eventuality or a negative outcome (Lathrop & Ruma, 2010). It could also reinforce the existing way of politics and further enshrine those who are powerful in the current system. The use of data on voting patterns down to the individual block level has allowed the creation of gerrymandered districts that keep elected officials in office.

The development of legislative information systems, "wired" legislatures, and electronic town meetings has been a huge movement forward in rewiring government for an information society future. New developments are announced almost every day. The U.S. government now has a chief technology officer, as do many states.

Political campaigns use technology at an impressive rate. In the 2012 campaign for president, all of the national campaigns made considerable use of technology to inform and engage voters and to channel the efforts of supporters. In many ways the rise of Web 2.0 techniques, such as blogs, wikis, and so forth, can spell the end of traditional campaigns where substantial effort is expended on controlling the message. On the other hand, it may mean that Web 2.0 approaches will be used more to get the campaign's message out through additional channels and to define the debate in every way possible.

Advocacy campaigns are also using technology to make change (Hick & McNutt, 2002; McNutt & Menon, 2008) and organize communities. These organizations often develop large networks of supporters because of their use of technology. One example is MoveOn, which started as an effort to prevent the impeachment of President Clinton. It is now arguably the largest advocacy group in the world.

One of the unique things that electronic communications can bring to government is enhanced transparency (Baxandall & Wohlschlegel, 2010). Transparency means providing access to government. Many of the negative things that happen in official circles cannot continue if they are well documented and visible. Systems are being developed to increase transparency in deliberation and influence. Wikileaks garnered international attention by using the Internet to release sensitive documents that revealed many embarrassing facts about governmental activity. Edward Snowden, a source for leaks about the United States' intelligence agencies keeping track of nearly all telephone calls in the country, used Wikileaks to distribute information about government practices that have been called illegal by the courts.

Electronic government has major potential to improve and enhance the way that government interacts with its constituents (West, 2005). West (2001) observes that "e-government refers to the delivery of information and services on-line through the Internet and other digital means" (p. 3). In practice it can mean many things from the government end of e-commerce to a rather substantial reinventing of government. Some contend that e-government is more about making government more effective. Layne and Lee (2001) argue that e-government can be thought of as an evolutionary development starting with the presentation of information and moving through organizational transformation. Their stages of development include information cataloging, transaction (such as renewing a driver's license online), vertical integration (internal change within a system), and finally horizontal integration (bringing a system of agencies together). The last stage addresses one of the more serious issues facing the social services system—multiple agencies addressing the same population in multiple ways. This is often referred to as fragmentation.

It is not all positive however. The information revolution also has the potential to turn the political institution into a surveillance state where everyone's movements are monitored (Britain has made a huge investment in closed-circuit television (CCTV) systems to observe people on the street). Face recognition software can be used to detect and monitor a person's whereabouts from the images on these CCTV systems. People can live in a society that offers little freedom and controls its population in ways that despots of old never dreamed possible. Electronic records have been intercepted by both government agencies looking for terrorists and by criminal hackers looking for information to access credit accounts. Privacy will become an ever more serious issue as technology develops new ways to provide surveillance.

The Internet also has the potential to allow hate groups to organize more easily. Terrorists have made widespread use of the Internet as well. Government agencies use the Internet to track access to sites that may be related to terrorism as well as spy on their own citizens. The cat-and-mouse aspects of the situation are striking, as each participant tries to outmaneuver the other.

Politics is ultimately about values. What those values are and how they are expressed is critically important in determining the type of system that people will have. Technology may allow for competing values to be expressed and engaged.

Religion/Civic Organizations

Religion is an important institution in most societies throughout the world. Religion is one of the keepers of culture. It can be the emergent culture or the culture of past societies. It also provides the opportunity to develop community solidarity and participation. Churches and other types of community associations can make it possible to build the type of social capital that creates strong communities. Given the possibility that capital and community can be more harmonized in an information society, the religious institution can help create the glue that holds these communities together.

The rise of the "mega-church," generally regarded as a church with an average weekly attendance of 2,000 or more (Hartford Institute for Religious Research, 2012), has been fueled by strategic use of mass media (such as television and radio broadcasts on specialized religious-oriented stations) to gain followers and savvy use of social media to connect with potential or current members of congregations. On the opposite end of the spectrum, the information society provides ways for very small groups of like-minded people to organize and share their religious viewpoints and beliefs.

This same ability applies to civic groups who have what can be called "long-tail" or "niche" interests. Anyone interested in finding other people with "highly superior autobiographical memories" (National Public Radio, 2013) can start a Facebook group or use other Internet-enabled methods to find the small numbers of people with a similar interest. Other people may be interested in sharing genealogical, epidemiological, or specialized information. This type of sharing can be for social benefit or to undermine social institutions, but the information age makes it all possible.

Some people worry that civic life is in decline due to the easy access to computer networks that have people working in isolated rooms at home rather than getting out to encounter each other in person. Robert Putnam (2000) coined the term "bowling alone" as an image to underscore the idea of increased individualism. Bowling leagues were dying out, he noted, while the number of people bowling had actually risen. Attendance at club meetings had dropped by 58 percent over a twenty-five year period, for example. Not content to merely point out the decline, Putnam advocates for the building of social capital through face-to-face interactions. (A list of 100 things you can do to overcome the isolating aspects of contemporary life can be found at http://www.bettertogether.org/thereport.htm). Other authors, however, dispute the severity of the issue. Raskoff (2009) for example, notes that the percent of Americans volunteering time to address social problems has increased in recent years. Also, forms of civic participation and organization have changed, facilitated by the Internet. Putnam's analysis is based on older models of civic participation that have less relevance to people in the information age.

Labor unions, a product of the industrial age's need to protect workers and improve their quality of life, have suffered as membership has declined for decades. Although still important in some manufacturing industries, unions are not only battling private sector companies that outsource their production to other countries (globalization), but also politicians who see public employee unions and their demands for pay and pensions as extravagant burdens on taxpayers.

Generations seem to have unique cultures, reflecting the challenges that they faced. The World War II generation was hardened by economic depression and war. Their sense of civic responsibility is the standard by which other generations are regarded. Baby boomers were affected by a relatively strong economy, the civil rights movement, the Vietnam war, and the feminist movement. The millennial generation appears to be stronger in civic commitment, diversity, cooperation, and interest in global issues (see Tapscott, 1998; Zukin, Keeter, Andolina, Jenkins, & Delli Carpini, 2006).

International values are changing in terms of supporting post-modern attitudes on human rights, the environment, and diversity. This transformation is still in process but major orientations are changing.

SOCIAL WELFARE

Most of the social welfare policy that the United States currently has in place is based on the assumptions created from dealing with the problems of industrialization. It was assumed that most people would be employed in the same steady job until retirement. Although short-term layoffs were possible, the majority of people would work consistently and for the same company until retirement. People would need help in certain situations, but these would be rare. The American social welfare system was a good, although not perfect, fit for this situation. Society has changed, however, and what was good enough before is now not adequate.

Job security is the key social welfare issue for today's social welfare policy with regards to income maintenance. In the past, it was a lack of pensions and family support for those who retired after a lifetime of work. That problem is addressed by our Social Security pension program. Unfortunately, Social Security can address fewer and fewer of the issues that individuals and families face today.

Social welfare can change significantly as the other institutions begin to change (McNutt, 2005). Many social welfare services in the industrial economy are provided by employers as part of the benefit systems. This is usually called occupational social welfare (Titmuss, 1974) and includes things such as pensions, health insurance, and disability. Training and staff development are also provided by many employers. If the traditional employer-employee relationship is dissolved, then it is unlikely that these benefits will be provided. If that is the case, either employees will need to provide these things themselves or the social welfare system will have to provide them. This logic argues for national health insurance and an adequate national pensions program. It also argues for enhanced educational benefits. Without these safeguards, the risks of working in an information society might be too great to be tolerable.

Lubove (1965) observed that social services were often operated in the same style as a factory. This was a reflection of the industrial period (see also Wilensky & Lebeaux, 1958). In the future, you can expect a model that is based on a network. Contracting and the hollow state (Peters, 1994) have moved social agencies closer to that network model, but the actual workplace has changed very little. Current efforts to create "continua of care" are one way that networks are being integrated into social service systems at the local level. In the ideal situation, a person in need of services is presented with a variety of agencies, each delivering a type or level of service. This results in less competition for clients by agencies but a full coverage of different levels of need for the community. Agencies in the continuum function as nodes in a network, referring individual clients to the agency with the most appropriate level of intervention services. Of course, in many communities, the necessary variety and span of service is much less than a full continuum requires and service gaps exist.

Combining these themes, agencies could be replaced with something like an exchange. Clients would come to the exchange and link up with a social worker. The exchange could handle billing insurance and additional referrals could also come through the exchange. This would have the effect of making all workers private practitioners. Arrangements like this already exist and it may just be a matter of time before they are commonplace. The development of virtual human services organizations is clearly in the cards. In a lot of ways that is what managed care has become. If you are a social worker on a provider panel the relationship is more between the worker and the funder as opposed to the agency and the funder.

This evolution of professional practice could have some interesting implications for the social work profession. Some of this is happening already and other components are in the planning stage. Social workers who do on-line therapy (Finn, 1999; Postel, de Haan, & De Jong, 2007) will be able to treat people in other nations or in underserved areas of the United States. This could bring in many new wrinkles in individual practice, including licensing of social workers in multiple states.

More and more, fundraising and development are done online. Changes in attitudes toward e-commerce and generational changes are fueling this new reality. Better software tools are now available, increasing confidence in the security of the transactions. Mobile technology for donations is improving rapidly to meet the needs of the vastly increased number of smartphone and tablet users. Other approaches to funding nonprofits using the Internet now exist and some pioneering agencies find them very useful (Hoefer, 2012b).

This transition provides the opportunity to build a better system than the current one. It can be fairer, more comprehensive, and make better use of the human talent that powers social services. Whether such a better system gets built, or whether people build upon the imperfect current foundation, remains to be seen. Improvements will not be made without a careful analysis of the past and a thoughtful embrace of the emerging approaches.

Technology makes many things possible, but it can also exclude people and groups from economic activity. The digital divide (McNutt, 1996b, 1998; Norris, 2001) means access to the skills, technology, and network enjoyed by most of the population and essential to participation in the new economy. The digital divide stacks up as one of the major civil rights problems of the new millennium as people are excluded from society based on their access to technology and their skills at using it. Organizations in the social welfare system that understand and use technology will prosper more than will others in terms of fundraising and sustainability.

THE INFORMATION SOCIETY CONSIDERED

The transition to the information society is under way in the United States, most of Europe, and parts of the rest of the world. When the process is complete, it will transform everyone's life. It will change society and the social institutions that people go to for help and support. This stage of social transformation will bring vast new vistas and potential wonders. It will also bring with it terrifying possibilities. Although some of those things are outside our control, others will depend on our choices. No one can understand our future, or even our present, without understanding the information society and how it could develop. Understanding this process also requires an appreciation of the global economy and the current state of the environment.

This is a huge challenge for all social workers. The challenge is not unlike that faced by early social workers in the settlement houses and Charities Organization Society. They saw firsthand the issues created by an earlier transformation and they built a system to address those challenges. Today's task is to look at the future and build the system that can best anticipate and address those needs.

Questions for Discussion

1. How is the current transition from an industrial to an information society like the transition from an agrarian to an industrial society? How is it different?
2. How does the environment influence social welfare policy?
3. What new needs are created by an information society? How can social welfare policy address those needs?
4. What are the major issues created by globalization and international trade?
5. What will happen if people do nothing to preserve the environment?

Exercise

1. Where was your stuff made? Look at the things that are in your room. Where were they made? How much of your stuff came from the United States? What are the implications for society?

Websites

TED: http://www.ted.com/. Wonderful presentations by exciting people in many fields.

The Student's Guide to Globalization: http://www.globalization101.org/. Maintained by the Levine Institute as part of the State University of New York.

The Globalization Website (Emory): http://www.sociology.emory.edu/globalization/about.html

Visual Media

An Inconvenient Truth (2006). Directed by Davis Guggenheim. Al Gore's award-winning film about global warming.

1984 (1984). Directed by Michael Radford. Film version of George Orwell's novel.

Further Reading

Brown, L. R. (2009). *Plan B 4.0: Mobilizing to save civilization*. New York, NY: Norton.

Gore, A. (2006). *An inconvenient truth: The planetary emergency of global warming and what we can do about it*. Emmaus, PA: Rodale.

Howe, N., & Strauss, W. (2000). *Millennials rising: The next Great Generation*. New York, NY: Vintage.

Lawless, J. L., & Fox, R. L. (2015). *Running from office: Why young Americans are turned off to politics*. New York, NY: Oxford University Press.

Chapter 5

Values, Ideology, and Political Philosophy in Social Welfare Policy

The adage "Policy affects practice and practice affects policy" helps remind social workers of the dual role they play—practitioners, working with individuals, groups, organizations, and communities to improve current situations, and advocates, working through political means to alter or remove the causes of current and future problems. Working both in the present and for the future places social workers in a unique position.

One way to understand what may solve problems is to look at them through the lenses of values, ideology, and political philosophy. Key actors in governmental policy making are generally members of political parties and they approach their duties from a particular point of view. This point of view is based on how they understand the world and the range of solutions that they find ideal.

This chapter presents a range of political philosophies and shows how their adherents operationalize their view of the "ideal" social policy. It includes policy statements that come from political parties around the world, thus exposing you to ideas you may not be familiar with. Becoming acquainted with such ideas can only be helpful in understanding social welfare policy differences around the globe.

In essence, social welfare policy is the outcome of a process involving the ideologies or philosophies of the people who determine what is finally chosen and advocacy efforts to influence the decision-makers. By understanding the range of desired social policies, depending on the philosophy used for justification, you will see more clearly the need to choose elected officials whose views are in accord with your own and the social work profession's.

POLITICS AS IDEOLOGIES: ACROSS THE SPECTRUM OF RIGHT AND LEFT

The question "What are your politics?" is clearly understood as a question regarding your views about policy, or what your political philosophy is. It is in

Protesters from the National March for Sanity in front of a building on the national mall. The march was organized by Comedians Jon Stewart and Stephen Colbert to call attention to the dysfunction in the current political situation.

this sense that political philosophy and social policy are closely intertwined— the political views controlling a decision-making body help determine the social policies that emerge. Political views can be described as falling on a continuum from right (conservative) to left (socialist) and are more or less systematically set forth by political parties. These views and their implications for social policy are the heart of this chapter.

In order to show the impact of political philosophy or ideology on social policy, this chapter examines a number of political philosophies and their associated political parties. Each is described and then the implications of this viewpoint for social policy are discussed.

The usual way of describing ideology is to move from right to left, a byproduct of French prerevolutionary governance, where supporters of the king sat on his right and those desiring change sat on his left. Several other elements besides the desire for change are embedded in the political continuum, however. Baradat (2011) notes that the desire for change helps you differentiate ideologies but that you must also examine the depth of the change desired, the speed of change desired, and the methods to be used to create the change desired to fully describe what makes one ideology different from another. In addition, it is vital to know the values and motivations behind the desire for change in order to fully describe a political view (Baradat, 2011).

The spectrum of views acceptable in a state or country varies tremendously. Some countries have the full or nearly full spectrum represented in their political system, while other countries have an extremely truncated spectrum. What is considered far left in one country may be considered middle-of-the-road or even on the right in another country. Some countries may allow only one official political viewpoint. Even within such a one-party system, however, different factions develop along the lines of how much (if any) change is wanted, how quickly to make changes, and so forth.

Critics of the American political system argue that there is little true difference between Democrats and Republicans, particularly in an international context. Hard-core American Republicans and Democrats, however, see very large differences between (and even within) their parties. The political spectrum delimited here is purposely wider than what one finds in mainstream American politics and may also be broader than found in many other countries. It is important for students of social policy to have a broader view of possibilities than what currently exists in the United States because the experiences and ideas from other countries may better reflect solutions to the emergent needs of people caused by the shifts in context, such as the coming of the information society, globalization, and environmental destruction.

Libertarians (Neo-Conservatism)

Description

The key principles for Libertarians in the United States include greater personal and economic liberty, "a world in which all individuals are sovereign over their own lives and no one is forced to sacrifice his or her values for the benefit of others" (Libertarian Party, 2014, Platform). Libertarians thus desire considerable change from the status quo, seeking to rein in what are seen as governmental excesses (such as high taxes and social programs) but also to keep government from interfering in personal matters such as obtaining an abortion or marrying someone of the same sex. Libertarians are willing to work through the electoral system and are willing to endure a slow pace of change, but nonetheless call for dramatic shifts in current practices. The scope of desired change can be shown with selections from the Libertarian Party's political platform, adopted in June, 2014. Key aspects of the platform include:

- We hold that all individuals have the right to exercise sole dominion over their own lives, and have the right to live in whatever manner they choose, so long as they do not forcibly interfere with the equal right of others to live in whatever manner they choose (Libertarian Party, 2014, Statement of Principles).

- The only proper role of government in the economic realm is to protect property rights, adjudicate disputes, and provide a legal framework in which voluntary trade is protected. All efforts by government to redistribute wealth, or to control or manage trade, are improper in a free society (Libertarian Party, 2014, Economic Liberty).

- All persons are entitled to keep the fruits of their labor. We call for the repeal of the income tax, the abolishment of the Internal Revenue Service and all federal programs and services not required under the U.S. Constitution (Libertarian Party, 2014, Government Finance and Spending).

- The proper and most effective source of help for the poor is the voluntary efforts of private groups and individuals. We believe members of society will become more charitable and civil society will be strengthened as government reduces its activity in this realm (Libertarian Party, 2014, Retirement and Income Security).

Policy Implications

The policy implications of the Libertarian views are stark. With no income tax to generate funds, and the admonition to eliminate all federal programs and services not specifically listed in the Constitution, social policy would be purely in the hands of families, businesses, voluntary organizations, and state/local government. Libertarians believe that the American welfare system has been a failure, that welfare cannot be reformed, and that it should be ended. The role of the individual would change drastically if this policy prescription were enacted. People who cannot support themselves or their families in the labor market would be required to seek assistance primarily from family members, churches, nonprofits, or other non-governmental sources. States and local government may provide limited aid as well, but the federal government should not. This position dovetails logically with the Libertarian position that social problems are created or exacerbated by government subsidization and protection (Kristol, 2004; Murray, 1997).

Libertarians argue that the welfare system, for example, creates problems by allowing people who make poor life choices to remain relatively unaffected by their bad decisions and thus shift costs from the individual to society (other people). This can only be paid for by taxes taken from people who make better choices, and punishes those living "by the rules." Entitlements for benefits would be eliminated: "The general rule has to be: if it is your own behavior that could land you on welfare, then you don't get it, or you get very little of it" (Kristol, 2004, p. 148).

According to Libertarians, because an unregulated market allows the most freedom of choice, the principle at work in social welfare policy should be: "Let people shop for what they want and pay for what they get" (Murray, 1997, p. 93). Organizations that offer education or health care would compete on both price and service, much as organizations that offer computers or other products do now.

In addition, according to the Libertarian viewpoint, social problems can be reduced by decriminalizing activities such as alcohol and drug use, pornography, prostitution, and so on. People would still be required to act responsibly, and if they did not, their irresponsible crimes (but not the use of alcohol or other drugs, the viewing of pornography, or the selling of sex, in and of themselves) would be punished.

Conservatism

Description

Major conservative parties exist in many countries and often have the word conservative in their party name (such as in Australia, Canada, and the United Kingdom). In the United States, the term "conservative" is used by both the American Conservative Party (http://americanconservativeparty.com) and the Conservative Party USA (www.conservativepartyusa.com). These two parties are quite small, however, and do not have an important place in the political system at this time. The Republican Party is the major party generally thought to advance conservative positions. As the term implies, conservatives wish to "conserve" what they see as the best policies from the nation's traditions and to rely on a laissez-faire economy. Conservatives advocate for a limited government role in the economy (thus championing the primacy of the market in deciding the

The *Washington Post* screams "Shutdown" during the 2013 debt ceiling showdown between Congress and President Obama.

distribution of goods and income), low taxes, and little government interference in individual behavior (though some strands of conservative thought desire government action regarding issues of morality). Additional important elements of conservative thought are the importance of property rights, an emphasis on low tax rates, and decreased regulation of business. Ronald Reagan, a favorite of American conservatives, famously intoned that "government is not the solution: government is the problem" when running for president in 1980.

Conservatives, as opposed to Libertarians, accept the need for individuals to have access to social welfare services. Believing that the best government is the government that governs least, however, conservatives push for assistance to the poor to come primarily from family members and nongovernmental organizations, particularly nonprofits with a faith basis (Olasky, 2000). The Conservative Party of the United Kingdom has this policy position relating to welfare:

- Real fairness means that where people really cannot work, they must be supported—but where they are able to work, they should (Conservative Party of the United Kingdom, 2015, Manifesto, p. 25).
- We will lower the maximum amount that a single household can claim in benefits each year from £26,000 to £23,000, so we reward work (Conservative Party of the United Kingdom, 2015, p. 28).

Another conservative party, the Canadian Conservative Party, espouses these beliefs:

Our Conservative Government continues to support job creation and economic growth by:

- keeping taxes low
- helping connect Canadians with available jobs
- investing in roads, bridges, transit and other important infrastructure in our communities
- staying on track to balanced budgets in 2015 (Conservative Party of Canada, 2015, Jobs).

Conservative parties work through parliamentary or democratic methods. Some argue that people of conservative ideology hold the reins of power through their wealth, social connections, and control of the military-industrial complex (see, for example, Mills, 1956). This power may control what emerges on the governmental decision-making agenda (Bachrach & Baratz, 1962). Conservative forces frequently used violence and threats of violence in the past to thwart unionizing and other left-wing causes and this use of force continues in some places around the world.

Although there is some discussion about whether the Republican Party nominates candidates who are "true conservatives" or not, in the United States, the Republican Party is seen by most observers, both insiders and outsiders, as being conservative. The Republican Party's 2012 platform makes this clear:

- This platform affirms that America has always been a place of grand dreams and even grander realities; and so it will be again, if we return government to its proper role, making it smaller and smarter. If we restructure government's most important domestic programs to avoid their fiscal collapse. If we keep taxation, litigation, and regulation to a minimum. If we celebrate success, entrepreneurship, and innovation. (Republican Party, 2012, Platform, p. i).

- The tax system must be simplified. Government spending and regulation must be reined in (Republican Party, 2012, Platform, p. 1).

- ... we believe that marriage, the union of one man and one woman, must be upheld as the national standard, a goal to stand for, encourage, and promote through laws governing marriage (Republican Party, 2012, Platform, p. 31).

- For the sake of low-income families as well as the taxpayers, the federal government's entire system of public assistance should be reformed to ensure that it promotes work (Republican Party, 2012, Platform, p. 31).

- The Republican Party is the party of fresh and innovative ideas in education. We support options for learning, including home schooling and local innovations like single-sex classes, full-day school hours, and year-round schools (Republican Party, 2012, Platform, p. 36).

In addition, the Republican Party platform pledged to abolish the Affordable Care Act (Obamacare), seeing it as an unconstitutional usurpation of power by the federal government.

Policy Implications

As can be seen from the quotations from British, Canadian, and American political parties, there is a great deal of overlap in positions of conservatives and Republicans. Two social welfare policy authors sum up conservative/Republican policy beliefs as saying that:

> ... the traditional values of hard work, ambition, and self-reliance will lead to individual and family well-being. ... Their goal is equity. That is, if everyone is provided with an equal opportunity to compete, conservatives want to minimize policies that are designed to shape the final result (Dolgoff & Feldstein, 2007, p. 113).

This is not to say that conservatives are all of one mind in terms of their social agenda. Some who are conservative on the economic front by wanting to limit government involvement in regulating the economy are also "traditional" conservatives regarding interference with individual liberty. In other words, they do not advocate for government intervention on behalf of any religious or philosophical view to tell individuals what they can and cannot do. This type of conservative is close to being a Libertarian. Others, sometimes called cultural conservatives, who consider themselves strictly conservative in their economic views, are eager to use government power to uphold their viewpoints regarding abortion, marriage, sexual activities, and other issues of morality.

Some of the specific policies advocated by conservative parties include tax cuts for the wealthy, thus reducing government funds for human services; decreased government support for human service programs; and a stronger emphasis and reliance on private organizations (nonprofit and for-profit) to actually provide services to clients. Some conservatives argue for ending any right to an abortion and for maintaining or strengthening discrimination against sexual minorities. Social conservatives argue in favor of marriage being only between one man and one woman, against abortion, and in favor of abstinence-only programs to combat teen pregnancy.

Religiously affiliated nonprofits have become more important elements of social service provision in recent years, as President George W. Bush's administration specifically allocated money to assist faith-based organizations to receive government funding for the provision of services. Early in the Obama administration, the White House announced the creation of its Office of Faith-based and Neighborhood Partnerships (the White House, 2009) which revamped the previous administration's efforts but did not dismantle them entirely.

Centrism

Description

Centrists are generally not too upset by the status quo nor are they unwilling to see opportunities for positive change. By definition, they adopt positions that are between the more extreme views on the right (libertarian and conservative) and the left (liberal and socialist). They work within the system and tend to be pragmatic (rather than strictly ideological) in terms of proposing possible changes. The centrist approach includes making incremental adjustments to policies to improve outcomes. Center parties have established themselves in Nordic countries (Sweden, Finland, and Norway all have a "Center Party"). In Sweden, for example,

The Swedish Center Party has its roots in rural Sweden but today describes its politics as "green liberalism" and also attracts urban voters. Core issues for the party are entrepreneurialism, jobs, care for the environment and the climate. The party is pro-immigration and stands for openness and diversity (Sweden.se, 2010).

A flavor of the Swedish Center Party's approach to welfare is found on their website:

- Sometimes your life changes direction. You have children, you lose your job or you can't manage to take care of yourself for some reason. In these situations, we want that there is an ongoing social welfare system to help you and to take your life further to the next stage. The Center Party wants to make it easier to move from support to a new job.
- Economic support is an important form of protection. But it should only be temporary—the goal should always be that all people will support themselves.

An American example of centrism emerged in the early part of the twenty-first century. Noting the arrival of the information age, Halstead and Lind (2001) advocate a new movement, dubbed "radical centrism." It is based on four principles:

- Increasing the amount of choice available to individual citizens
- Holding citizens to a higher personal standard of self-sufficiency
- Providing a true safety net model of economic security for citizens
- Allowing federal jurisdiction to take over from state and local government when the outcome is expanding individual freedoms and choices (pp. 19-23).

Defined by the amount of change desired and speed at which they would like to see the change occur, Halstead and Lind do fit the idea of radical. But because they espouse ideas that tend to be between the far right and left, they are also centrists.

Centrist parties do not emerge or last long in all countries. Two-party systems develop in countries where winner-take-all elections are used, such as in the United States, and there is little room for multiple parties that siphon off the vote from one of the two major parties. For example, Independent Ross Perot is said to have helped elect Bill Clinton in 1992 by drawing voters away from incumbent President George H. W. Bush. Green Party candidate Ralph Nader was blamed by supporters of Al Gore in 2000 for the vice president's razor-thin electoral college vote loss to George W. Bush. This may explain why there is not a major Center Party in the United States, despite calls for one such as by Halstead and Lind (2001) and Avlon (2005).

Policy Implications

Centrist social policy is essentially a point between trusting the government to do the right thing, to improve social conditions (liberalism) and trusting the market's integrity and ability to improve conditions (conservatism). Policy positions frequently are a combination of ideas from a wide range of ideologies, as long as the ideas seem workable. Centrists generally believe that people want to be responsible but may need encouragement and role-modeling to know how to be self-sufficient in a market economy. Services should be available to those who are not able to work, but everyone else should be in the labor force, both for their own good and for the good of society. Specific policies put forth by Sweden's Center Party in its 2014 platform statement are:

> We believe in proximity. Sweden needs "närodlad politik" (locally grown politics) with decisions that are made as close to people as possible. We believe that jobs must be created throughout Sweden. The path to achieving this is to make it easier for people to start and run companies. Wherever they live in Sweden. And it must be made easier to get your first job (Centerpartiet, 2014).

Halstead and Lind (2001) argue that their four principles are more in line with the realities of the twenty-first century information age than are other ideologies and associated political parties. They advocate the following policies:

- Mandatory private health care system for all Americans that would ensure that the poorest and least healthy are fully covered
- Progressive privatization of Social Security, based on mandatory retirement savings for all workers
- A broadening of the ownership of financial capital so that all Americans can benefit directly from a growing economy

The implications of a centrist party are perhaps strongest in promoting a civility of discussion and a focus on what works, rather than what is in line with an ideological stance. In some ways, when government in the United States is divided between Republicans and Democrats, the only policies that are created come from the common center—neither party can force its positions into law. In these situations, if legislation is to move forward, policy positions and votes must move away from extremes and towards the center of the political spectrum.

Liberalism

Description

Within American political discourse, the word "liberal" has become, at least for some, a synonym for welfare-supporting, tax-and-spend, socialized-medicine-loving, and abortion-friendly politicians. Liberals view their ideas differently: A quote by John Kennedy when he accepted the nomination for president of the United States by the Liberal Party of New York defines "liberal" from the liberal's perspective:

> What do our opponents mean when they apply to us the label "Liberal?" If by "Liberal" they mean, as they want people to believe, someone who is soft in his policies abroad, who is against local government, and who is unconcerned with the taxpayer's dollar, then the record of this party and its members demonstrate that we are not that kind of "Liberal." But if by a "Liberal" they mean someone who looks ahead and not behind, someone who welcomes new ideas without rigid reactions, someone who cares about the welfare of the people—their health, their housing, their schools, their jobs, their civil rights, and their civil liberties—someone who believes we can break through the stalemate and suspicions that grip us in our policies abroad, if that is what they mean by a "Liberal," then I'm proud to say I'm a "Liberal" (Liberal Party of New York State, 2011).

Baradat (2011) indicates that one of the hallmarks of liberalism is optimism and Kennedy's statement expresses an optimistic viewpoint well.

A positive view of the world and people relates to the enshrinement of human intellect that emerged during the Enlightenment. Because people are so capable, the reasoning goes, they should be able to assess problems, figure out solutions, and implement their ideas. New ideas have merit and are useful in improving the world. Liberals tend to believe in the importance of achieving equality of opportunity, as well as making strides with government policy to mitigate the excesses of the market, problems such as high levels of inequality, discrimination, and injury to dispossessed populations.

Political parties with the name "Liberal" in them currently exist in Australia, Canada, the United Kingdom, and other countries. Classical liberals focused primarily on the importance of individual rights, particularly opposing the rights of kings to govern without input from the ruled. Thus, many liberal ideas were enshrined in the American constitution. Modern liberalism is based on dissatisfaction with the state of the world, a belief in the perfectibility of society, optimism, and a willingness to work through governmental institutions in order to achieve social goals. Liberals wish change to be thorough and relatively rapid, but always through a democratic process.

The views of the Liberal Party of Australia are typical. According to their federal platform,

> In summary, Australian Liberalism holds that individual people matter most, that the family is the most fundamental institution for development of the individual, that strong civil society is the most effective way to advance shared community interests and values, and that government exists to serve people and not the reverse (2014, p. 9).

The Liberal Party of Australia lays out many specific policy statements. A few of these most relevant to social policy include believing:

- In a just and humane society, where those who cannot provide for themselves can live in dignity
- In the family as the primary institution for fostering the values on which a cohesive society is built
- In the creation of wealth and in competitive enterprise, consumer choice and reward for effort as the proven means of providing prosperity for all Australians
- In the principle of mutual obligation, whereby those in receipt of government benefits make some form of contribution to the community in return, where this is appropriate
- In the importance of voluntary effort and voluntary organizations (Liberal Party of Australia, 2014)

The Liberal Party of Canada stresses its primary policy positions on various pages of its website (www.liberal.ca/issues):

- Every Canadian must have access to timely, publicly funded, high-quality, universal health care, regardless of background, physical needs, geographical location, or income (Health Care).
- Liberals believe that access to affordable, high-quality child care improves life outcomes for children, and increases the supply of workers and worker productivity (Child Care).
- Liberals believe the federal government should invest in the development of more affordable housing units to help Canadian families ease their cost of living. When people are secure in their home, they can grow, thrive and create the stability that leads to a strong economy (Affordable Housing).

In the American system, the Democratic Party is considered the more liberal of the two major parties. Although the Republican Party is sometimes seen as too conservative in nature (just as the Democratic Party is sometimes considered not conservative enough), it is the major political party that comes closest to the current meaning of the term liberal. Democrats stress the importance of equal rights for all, of opportunity for "ordinary people" rather than the wealthy, health care security for all, tax cuts for middle class families, and other provisions that expand work opportunities through government programs and improve the health and safety of the public through government regulation of business. As is stated on their website, www.democrats.org, "There are several core beliefs that tie our party together: Democrats believe that we're greater together than we are on our own—that this country succeeds when everyone gets a fair shot, everyone does their fair share, and everyone plays by the same rules" (Democratic National Committee, 2015a). These positions show a large difference from conservative ideas that stress the role of an unfettered private enterprise system to improve people's lives.

Other policy statements by Democrats are:

- . . . in our fight to stand up for civil rights for all Americans, we are committed to protecting voting rights, enacting the Employment Non-Discrimination Act, ensuring marriage equality, and equal federal rights for LGBT couples, and achieving equal pay for equal work (Democratic National Party, 2015b).

- Today, we finally are able to make real the principle that every American should have access to quality health care, and no one should go bankrupt just because they get sick (Democratic National Committee, 2015c).

- Democrats believe that a dignified retirement is central to the American Dream, and its foundation is built on two long-standing institutions charged with realizing that dream: Medicare and Social Security. These two institutions represent an unbreakable commitment to American workers, and for decades Democrats have fought to defend them (Democratic National Committee, 2015d).

Policy Implications

Liberal policy positions are in favor of government intervention in the market to improve society and protect human rights (as opposed to property rights), egalitarianism (as opposed to elitism), and personal liberty (as opposed to government intervention into private behavior) (Baradat, 2011).

A few examples of specific social policies supported by liberals are greater equality between racial and ethnic groups, as well as between men and women; livable minimum wage levels; provision of adequate levels of medical care, housing, and nutritious food to all; and sufficient regulation of business to ensure safety in food, medicine, and other products.

These positions will seem familiar to anyone who has read the National Association of Social Workers' positions on these issues. There is a clear difference in the approach of liberals and conservatives in the nature of the policies that are espoused. Liberals believe government can be a force for good; conservatives believe government is generally a force for oppression. Liberals understand that the free market needs regulation and control in order to prevent damage to individuals unable to work or to protect themselves from unscrupulous practices; conservatives understand that a free and competitive market should be left to operate on its own in order to bring about the best distribution of material goods. Liberals want to collect taxes from all in order to benefit the common good; conservatives want to decrease taxes in order for individuals to make their own choices about how to use their money. These are clear differences that are seen between liberals and conservatives throughout the world and have clear consequences for the social welfare policies that are enacted.

Social Democracy and Labor Parties

Description

Social democracy is another view espoused by political parties around the globe (for example, Australia's, New Zealand's, and the United Kingdom's Labour Parties, and Germany's, Norway's, and Sweden's Social Democratic Parties), although no major party in the United States fits into this category. Although social democracy originally was a strongly socialist philosophy, now the mainstream of many social democratic parties has moved toward the center. Such political parties now take on the mantle of the "third way," a system between pure capitalism and pure socialism, although it is still more socialist than capitalist or conservative. A common thread for all social democratic parties is repugnance concerning the excesses of capitalism, particularly inequality, poverty, oppression of various groups, and distaste for the strong individualism that negates the importance of solidarity among people and groups. According to Socialist International (SI), "Social democracy is a common denominator for those who seek progress, equality, solidarity and the affirmation of the rights of the individual and the community alike" (Socialist International, 1996).

Many social democratic political parties are connected to the labor movement in their country. It is natural that some parties belonging to the social democratic movement are called labor parties and have similar stances as social democratic parties. For example, the Labour Party of the United Kingdom says its key values are "fairness, equality and social justice" (Labour Party of the United Kingdom, 2015).

The values labor stands for today are those that have guided it throughout its existence:

- Social justice
- Strong community and strong values
- Reward for hard work
- Decency
- Rights matched by responsibilities (Labour Party of the United Kingdom, 2015: http://www.labour.org.uk/pages/what-is-the-labour-party)

The Australian Labor Party promises that it will work diligently to overcome the conservative policies in place.

- Australia deserves a government that protects the most vulnerable in our community, and Labor is committed to tackling homelessness in Australia rather than cutting services and support (Labor Party of Australia, 2015a).
- For our country to prosper, we must improve fairness, opportunity and safety for women in the workplace and in the community (Labor Party of Australia, 2015a).
- Labor is also providing flexibility to help workers balance their work and family lives (Labor Party of Australia, 2015b).
- We will fight for good and affordable education, fight for a cleaner environment and for investments in the clean technologies of the future, and fight for investments that allow all Australians to participate in the 21st century economy. And above all else, we will be guided by the important principles of fairness and opportunity (Labor Party of Australia, 2015c, http://www.alp.org.au/growthandopportunity).

Policy Implications

Social policy under social democrats follows what has been called an "institutional model" where receipt of social services is considered a normal part of life so government provides them. Although financial realities may prevent governments from providing all services that are desired, the number and scope of services are considerable and reach from "cradle to grave."

Modern social democracy takes on a variety of positions but most social democrats support:

- An extensive government sector responsible for providing mitigation of the excesses of a capitalistic system through social pensions, social insurance efforts, and means of maintaining income for people who are aged, disabled, or unemployable
- Government provision for universal access to education, health care, and child care
- Maintaining the importance of a free market to distribute goods
- Allowing the market to distribute goods while regulating companies in order to protect workers and the general public from unsafe and unhealthy business practices and monopolistic excesses
- Progressive taxes (Socialist International, 2009)

Socialism

Description

Despite the many variations in philosophy and practice that can be found among socialists, socialism has three basic features: public ownership of production; an extensive welfare state; and the desire to create a society where material want is eliminated (the socialist intent) (Baradat, 2011).

Public ownership of production is needed, according to socialists, because private ownership within a mixed or capitalist system assures exploitation of workers and thus must be eliminated. In order to make a profit, a capitalist must pay a worker less than the income that worker generates—it is the excess of income created by the worker's contribution over the costs of production (including the worker's wage) that is profit. Private owners thus always have an incentive to pay a worker as little as possible in order to maximize their own income. Nationalizing production or turning production over to cooperatives solves the problem of exploitation as no one individual benefits from exploiting workers.

An extensive welfare state is used by government to ensure access to the necessities of life. Universal education, health care, pensions, income maintenance, and other programs are instituted. This is in accord with the "socialist intent," the desire to reduce and then eliminate social problems. In this way, socialism is far superior to capitalism (at least in theory) because hunger, discrimination, homelessness, lack of affordable health care for all, and the other ills seen around the world in capitalist economies can be eliminated.

All socialists desire radical change in society. Different strands of socialism have varying ideas relating to the use of violence to achieve radical change. Democratic socialists eschew violence, believing in the power of democracy to bring about such a large change. Other branches of socialism, however, believe that the only true power for change comes from "the barrel of a gun."

No socialist party has been widely popular in the United States but parties with the word socialist in their title do exist. The Socialist Party USA has a platform which includes the following declaration:

> The Socialist Party strives to establish a radical democracy that places people's lives under their own control—a non-racist, classless, feminist socialist society . . . where working people own and control the means of production and distribution through democratically-controlled public agencies, cooperatives, or other collective groups; where full employment

is realized for everyone who wants to work; where workers have the right to form unions freely, and to strike and engage in other forms of job actions; and where the production of society is used for the benefit of all humanity, not for the private profit of a few (Socialist Party USA, n.d., http://socialistparty-usa.net/principles.html).

Policy Implications

Socialist social policy results in the most far-spreading institutional system of all the philosophies described. But it is important to understand that the key element of socialism is that society is radically transformed by eliminating capitalism. The economic system is radically different than in any system where capitalism is allowed to continue, even in social democratic countries, which also have extensive social welfare programs.

Socialists have to struggle with the fact that wherever their ideas have been tried, success has been limited. Although the former Soviet bloc countries may not be a true test of socialist ideas, they are an object lesson in ways that the socialist theory can be applied with ensuing negative effects. Other experiments in socialist governance, such as the People's Republic of China, or Cuba, have both success and failures, but may not adhere closely to socialist principles at this time. Still, on a few indicators of national health, they have outperformed the United States (World Health Organization, 2007). Critics of socialist ideology focus on the loss of individual freedom that is demanded in return for a promised freedom from material want.

Green Party

Description

As a result of ecological and sustainability problems experienced throughout the world in the 1970s and early 1980s and as an outgrowth of the ecology movement, green parties began to develop around the globe. The first Green Party was formed in Germany. In 1982, after a split between more conservative and more left-wing elements of the original organization, the Green Party of Germany emerged as a pacifist, anti-nuclear-power political party. In 1983 they achieved representation in the lower house of the German parliament. Green Parties exist in many other countries, as well. In 2001, delegates from Green Parties in seventy-two different countries met in Australia and signed a document describing their common beliefs. Building on previous statements agreed to by Greens from around the world, the 2001 document specifies the principles of ecological wisdom, social justice, participatory democracy, nonviolence, sustainability, and respect for diversity (Global Greens, 2001).

These six principles are strikingly post-industrialist in nature, referring to ecological wisdom, rather than scientific knowledge; social justice and environmental justice, rather than whether the market is better unfettered or slightly fettered; decision-making open to all; nonviolence, peace, and cooperation in the face of conflict; sustainability rather than consumption; and respect for diversity rather than enforced acculturation of those who are different. These positions are true across the globe and indicate a level of cooperation that is matched only by socialist parties.

The Green Party of the United States has ten (rather than six) core principles: grassroots democracy, social justice and equal opportunity, ecological wisdom, nonviolence, decentralization, community-based economics and economic justice, feminism and gender equity, respect for diversity, personal and global responsibility, and future focus and sustainability (Green Party of the United States, 2012a). The party has taken specific positions on topics related to American social welfare policy.

- We have a special responsibility to the health and well-being of the young. Yet we see the federal safety net being removed and replaced with limited and potentially harsh state welfare programs.
- We believe our community priorities must first protect the young and helpless.
- We believe local decision-making is important, but we realize, as we learned during the civil rights era, that strict federal standards must guide state actions in providing basic protections (Green Party of the United States, 2012b).
- It is time for a radical shift in our attitude toward support for families, children, the poor, and the disabled. Such support must not be given grudgingly; it is the right of those presently in need and an investment in our future. We must take an uncompromising position that the care and nurture of children, elders, and the disabled are essential to a healthy, peaceful, and sustainable society (Green Party of the United States, 2012b).

Policy Implications

Following through on the principles agreed to by the Green Party of the United States leads to social welfare policies being very different from what they are now in America. No other party is, for example, calling for more generous and widespread welfare payments. The Greens also declare their antagonism towards privatizing Social Security; their belief that "all people have a right to food, housing, medical care, jobs that pay a living wage, education, and support in times of hardship"; and a significant reduction in the budget for the military (Green Party of the United States, 2012b). Such positions seem to put even socialist parties to their right on the political spectrum. Although Green Parties have been included in government coalitions in many countries, they tend to have a rift between the more ideological and the more pragmatic wings of their memberships.

In the United States, the Green Party named Ralph Nader as its nominee for president in the election of 2000, despite predictions that Mr. Nader would siphon off enough votes from the Democratic candidate, Vice President Al Gore, to allow Republican George W. Bush to win. The Green Party's position was that there wasn't that much difference between the two candidates, anyway, so the Green Party would nominate a person who more fully advocated for the Green Party's position. In the end, Al Gore lost the fight for president in the electoral college over disputed votes in Florida, despite having more popular votes than George W. Bush. Although one can admire the purity of the Green Party's position, it probably led to a president who was much more antagonistic to environmental and social justice issues than if Vice President Gore had become president.

CONCLUSION

This survey of "politics as ideology" and the resultant social policies espoused by each political view leads to the conclusion that political parties have the ability to create or destroy policies and programs designed to improve people's lives—in other words, those in power, using their values and ideology, shape social policy to match their interests. In most democratic countries, however, individual people and groups are able to voice their opinions to have their own values enacted. It is to be hoped that you now better understand the range of ideas that exist to be selected from.

As the information age moves forward, it is easy to see that the speed with which information can be created, spread, and affect governmental policy making has increased dramatically. Political ideologies and parties must adapt to the explosion in information or be left behind. The speed with which dictatorial North African regimes fell at the beginning of 2011 in the Arab Spring is the result of information age technology and strategies for change that overtook the abilities of repressive governments to respond.

New problems, such as the digital divide, are the direct result of information technology. Older problems, such as environmental degradation or use (such as the desire to drill for oil in the protected area of the Arctic National Wildlife Refuge or to build the Keystone XL pipeline from Canada to Texas to transport oil) continue to play out within the confines of political parties developed in an industrial age. One major political movement, the Green Party, is the only political party that has developed in response to changes in the world in the information age era although its influence in the United States is very limited. Still, the threat of its appeal to voters has led other parties to try to co-opt some of its positions so as to attempt to capture voters who are interested in information age political problems.

A similar example on the right is the Tea Party which burst upon the political scene in America in the 2010 elections. The energy of the Tea Party movement (although not yet a political party itself) has led the Republican Party to embrace many of its positions. This is one way that the American two-party system endures—by adapting to the expressed desires of voters.

Questions for Discussion

1. Reading the positions of the various political parties, which do you most agree with? Which do you think best represent the values of the social work profession, as you understand them? Is there a difference between these two?

2. Is it acceptable for different social workers to have different political philosophies and belong to different political parties? What are the implications for the profession if they do agree, or if they don't agree?

Exercises

1. Choose a country other than the United States. Study the government in power and place it somewhere along the philosophical continuum described in this chapter. How does this influence the types of policies that are in that country?

2. Between the time this chapter was written and when you read it, some positions of major political parties may have shifted somewhat. Can you find examples from around the globe of this happening?

Websites

The Democratic Party (United States): http://www.democrats.org

The Republican Party (United States): http://www.gop.com

Visual Media

Made in Dagenham (2010). Directed by Nigel Cole. This movie tells the story of a strike by female Ford employees in the Dagenham car plant.

Mandela: Long Walk to Freedom (2013). Directed by Justin Chadwick.

Further Reading

Baradat, L. (2011). *Political ideologies: Their origins and impact* (11th ed.). Englewood Cliffs, NJ: Prentice Hall.

Heywood, A. (2007). *Political ideologies: An introduction* (4th ed.). New York, NY: Palgrave Macmillan.

Chapter 6

Policy Analysis: Tools for Building Evidence-Based Social Policy

It is clear from the preceding chapters that policies can have a substantial impact on human well-being and social stability. It is important for decision-makers to have the best information before they commit to a course of action. Although political considerations occasionally trump data and analysis, better information often influences political considerations.

Policy analysis is a tool that allows people to anticipate the results of a potential policy or compare a potential policy to current policies or other proposed policies (Bardach, 2011; Chambers and Wedel, 2008; DiNitto, 2010; Dunn, 2011; Karger & Stoesz, 2009). Policy analysis is a form of policy research. It is a rational process that often involves quantitative methodology. Policy analysis is often done at the state, national, and even international level, but smaller agencies and other organizations conduct policy analysis as well (Flynn, 1992). This chapter will discuss how to conduct a limited policy analysis and provide some foundation for future work in the area. Policy analysis is an important part of policy practice and there are social work positions that require policy analysis skills.

Policy analysis looks at policies rationally and scientifically. It does not determine which policies are morally best but it can provide data to support conclusions about which alternatives have the best technical chance of success. Value questions can only be answered by normative analysis. What rational policy analysis can do is to present decision-makers with a complete or relatively complete view of the options before them and the possible consequences of those alternatives. Policy analysts do not make policy decisions. Those decisions are made by political leaders, administrators, boards, commissions, and others (Dunn, 2011). Those decision-makers consider not only the objective information that policy analysts provide, but the perspective of politics and other value considerations.

Doing a policy analysis involves evaluating a proposed policy or program against an alternative policy, be it the status quo, a proposed or existing policy, or the option to do nothing. The knowledge that people develop in the course of performing the policy analysis can help them avoid mistakes and craft better policy proposals.

Many policies have enormous consequences for large numbers of people. Even simple changes in eligibility requirements or funding levels can have devastating effects on very vulnerable populations. As policies become more interdependent, changes in areas unrelated to social welfare become important. Changes in energy or transportation policies can have direct and substantial impacts on the people served. A change as simple as moving a bus route or eliminating a subway stop can throw an entire community of the working poor into unemployment.

Policy analysis occurs at many levels in the human services system. At the highest levels, policy analysis involves sophisticated methods that support both national and international analysis and decision-making. This work is done in national agencies such as the General Accounting Office and the Congressional Budget Office, as well as in major agencies, nonprofits, and think tanks. This work can affect decisions that can affect millions of people.

State and local analysis is often less complex (Flynn, 1992). The methods used are frequently less sophisticated and the analysis is more limited. This does not mean that analysis at this level is less useful or important, but it often reflects lower levels of training and desire on the part of decision-makers to use the information from analyses.

Policy analysis has two basic components: the policy context and the policy analysis process. The context includes the problem or issue, the policy goals, and the institutions that govern the policy arena in question. The process describes how policy analysis is undertaken and what information is developed and used. This determines how useful it is to decision-makers.

DISCIPLINARY ROOTS OF POLICY ANALYSIS

Policy analysis draws most of its roots from economics and political science. Information from sociology, anthropology, geography, and even psychology is also useful.

Economists study the way that people make choices and whether those choices are optimal, given scarce resources (McConnell, Brue, & Flynn, 2011). Although there are qualitative economists, most use statistical analysis as the basis of their work. They develop elegant, mathematically based models of choice and utility. These models are based on assumptions of human behavior that are specified by economic theorists. At least some of those assumptions are difficult for those with training in the other social sciences to accept. Some of this comes from the economist's view of the world, but much comes from ignorance of what these assumptions actually mean. The economic conceptualization of rationality, for example, does not mean that people make the best choices, only that those choices are reasonably related to goals that the person pursues. If your goal is what might be called irrational for a reasonable person, but you go about it in a reasonable way, then you are still considered rational.

Economists tend to favor solutions that use the market as a way to allocate resources. Buyers and sellers come together in the market and an optimal price is created. By seeking the best price for a good or service, buyers try to advance their interests while sellers, for the same reason, try to advance theirs. In a perfect model, this clash of interests leads to the best possible price for both. In an imperfect market there is no way to guarantee such an outcome. Although very few professional economists believe that the market always makes the best choices, most believe that market decisions are better than decisions made other ways such as by governmental edict. This leads to policies that provide incentives for desired action rather than regulation against undesired actions. These systems occasionally lead to perverse incentives, situations where unintended consequences are realized. For example, putting only a small fine on pollution can create an incentive to pollute, if profits made from the polluting process are higher than the cost of the fine.

There is also recognition by economists that there are situations where markets do not work at all. These are situations where market failure comes into play and the provision of public goods is needed. These public goods are often provided by nonprofit organizations or government. Roads, national defense, and the needs of the poor and disabled are public good situations.

Economists talk about maximizing utility rather than meeting needs. Utility is the ability of some good or service to fulfill wants. Economics assumes that most people will do what gives them the most utility.

One thing that tends to irritate social workers and others is the practice of reducing all things of value to money. This seems materialistic and negative. Economists argue that, although money isn't everything, it does provide a means to compare different things by providing a common metric. For many things (cars, buildings, textbooks) there is a market price. There are also things that don't have a market price and for those, there is a system called shadow pricing. A shadow price is one that you create through logical analysis. What is a life worth? It is, of course, priceless. If you had to put a value on it, how would you do it? Two of the major ways are lifetime earnings and replacement cost of services. This means the value of what you earn in life or what value your services have to your family is what you're worth. Most economists understand the limitations of that kind of analysis. Sadly there are some who lack the training but use the analysis in a thoughtless way. This happens often when people with minimal training use techniques such as benefit-cost analysis.

Economic theory provides a range of useful concepts that make decision-making more successful. The idea of sunk costs, for example, suggests that when individuals or organizations have already invested a great deal of time or money in a project, they are reluctant to give it up even if the results are not what are wanted. There are two competing impulses here—"Try, try again!" and "Don't throw good money after bad." It is frequently difficult to get people to change their mind about past decisions. If you have to shut down a program because it is not providing benefits to clients, it is admitting that the decision was a mistake in the first place.

Opportunity costs are the costs of not doing an alternative activity with the resources. If you go to a movie and don't like it you incur not only the costs of the movie but the value of what else you could have done with the time and money. If society spends its resources on an enhanced military, it cannot use those resources to build or repair infrastructure such as roads, bridges, and communications facilities or for the production of consumer goods. This is known as the "guns versus butter" dilemma. Whenever there are limited resources (and resources are *always* limited) then decision-makers must confront questions around opportunity costs.

An externality happens when someone making a decision does not pay all of the costs of that decision (a negative externality) or does not receive the full benefit from the decision (positive externality). Negative externalities create an incentive to do too much of something, because the creator of the problem doesn't have to worry about the full effects of the decision—some of the costs are passed on to others, such as society in general. Air and water pollution, for example, are side effects of industry. If a manufacturer can make a product more cheaply by polluting the air and water of a community at no cost to itself, but with the benefit of making more profits, it will probably do so. The costs of increased health care services, or higher infant mortality, are paid by individuals in the community or by society. It is a cost to the people who live around the factory or downwind, not the company. In this case, government regulation to require the factory to clean up its pollution is a way to reduce the negative externalities. On the other hand, a positive externality can lead to decision-makers not investing enough in a given activity. For example, a community that invests a great deal of resources in its educational system may see that many of the graduates of the schools leave the community. That community then does not realize the benefits of having well-educated young adults living there and so may begin to cut the amount spent on schooling. The benefit to society as a whole is being paid disproportionately by the people in one school district.

Given the range of useful tools for understanding decision-making that economics offers, it is unfortunate that social workers have been reluctant to use this analysis in dealing with social welfare policy. This is not only regrettable; it is professionally dangerous given the substantial influence that economics has in the conduct of public policy. Economics had a substantial role in the creation of the profession. The first dean of the New York School of Philanthropy was an economist and Simon Patten, an economist at the University of Pennsylvania's Wharton School of Finance, coined the term "social work" (McNutt & Austin, 1990).

Political science also has much to add to policy analysis. Political scientists add knowledge of political institutions, policy processes, and political culture. These tools fill out much of the analysis that economics ignores.

POLITICAL INSTITUTIONS

Political institutions are the decision-making structures that are the skeleton, or framework, for all political decisions. Extensive knowledge of political institutions such as the United States Senate, the House of Representatives, the presidency, and the judicial system has been amassed. Such information is also available at the state and local levels of political institutions. All this information is important for social workers interested in policy practice to comprehend. At the very least, policy analysts should understand the level of government to be addressed, which of the many potential actors could be involved and will be active, and the structural aspects of the situation.

As a simple example, an analyst who is examining a topic relating to a state government should know not to contact a U.S. senator's office or a local official, such as a county commissioner. Once having located an appropriate level of government, another step is to determine if the topic is best addressed by the legislative, executive, or judicial branches. Assuming that one is not involved in a court case, the judicial branch can be eliminated. Within the legislative and executive branches, however, there are many actors who might want the information that you are developing. Deciding which members of the legislative branch to approach, for example, you would want to understand the legisla-

US Capitol

ture's committee structure, who the leaders of the relevant committees are, and such structural questions. If the analysis will be provided to a member of the executive branch (someone writing a regulation for a new law, for example), you will need to know which department within the executive branch is involved and how to provide your material within what is a complex environment.

Policy Processes

In the past, students learned about policy processes through diagrams explaining "how a bill becomes law" which showed the path an idea must take before it can be passed and possibly signed into law by the president (or governor, at the state level). If one thinks of political institutions as the skeleton of government, one can visualize policy processes as the circulatory system, with pathways leading from one part of government to another, nourishing them with new ideas, or blocking what are perceived to be "diseases" that are bad for the body politic.

Examples of policy processes include the functioning of members of legislatures in terms of negotiating the details of bills, voting for or against bills, interacting with constituents, running for office, and so on. Other processes include the executive branch, such as writing regulations, appointing people to higher level positions (including judicial appointments), and implementing programs and policies. The judicial branch has its own set of policy processes to understand, including the ways that judges decide guilt or innocence, how appellate courts (including the Supreme Court) decide which cases to accept, and the ways that courts work to keep their decisions enforceable when they do not have many direct ways of enforcing their decisions.

Interest groups, social movement organizations, and political parties also have an impact on the policy process. Interest groups, like the Sierra Club, the Children's Defense Fund, and the National Rifle Association try to change policy with a variety of tactics (Berry & Arons, 2002: Child & Gronbjerg, 2007; Hoefer, 2000a, 2000b). Social movements, such as the civil rights movement, the women's movement, and the peace movement are also influential in the policy process, often using a different set of methods that may be more confrontational. Finally, political parties influence policies by helping to select candidates with certain beliefs and values. A similar function is performed by political action committees.

The bureaucracy is a creature of the executive branch and is largely made up of career civil servants who work for administrative agencies. Each of these organizations is led by political appointees. The civil service is intended to be apolitical. Many of the people who work in the agencies have definite ideas about how things should be done. These ideas occasionally clash with the current administration. Situations such as this can delay policy efforts for a substantial amount of time. Organizations develop cultures that can last for many years and are difficult to change.

Political Culture

A state's political culture refers to its inhabitants' orientations toward key objects of the political system and toward the individual's role in that political system (Almond & Verba, 1965; Silver & Dowley, 2000). Political culture consists of political views, characteristics, and the core values that are shared by individuals within a society, and it influences the social and legal policies of a society (Fisher & Pratt, 2006; Mead, 2004; Shock, 2008).

To continue the analogy to the human body, the political culture might be seen as the skin, as all the other factors affecting the policy process are contained within the political culture. In the United States, for example, the political culture shows a strong bias towards individualism, or the idea that each individual is responsible for his or her own condition. The Constitution, which lays out all the governmental institutions, has a Bill of Rights (the first ten amendments) aimed at protecting individual liberty. Political processes are often described in ways that emphasize the power of individuals to change policy, based on their position within the structures of government. Even if there are some more collectivist ideas in the United States, the overall political culture stresses individualism, and thus all actors must take into account this prevailing view of the world when acting as policy analysts or advocates.

Daniel Elazar (1972) found three main political cultures, with mixtures of these pure types, in the fifty states. A state could have a traditional culture, an individualistic culture, or a moralistic culture (or some mix of these three). States with traditional cultures tend to believe that the purpose of government is to maintain the current social order, which is often controlled by a small segment of the population. This type of political culture was seen as dominant in the "Deep South" and mixed with other cultures in the other states along the southern edge of the United States and border states of the old Confederate States of America.

The individualistic political culture sees government in very utilitarian terms—the purpose of government is to solve problems. According to this view, the way that problems are solved is less important than that they are solved. Thus, as long as streets are kept clean, a bit of corruption in the awarding of the contracts to a particular street cleaning company is acceptable. The individualist view is strongest in the Middle-Atlantic states, and, when combined with the moralistic culture, extending through the Middle Plains up to the Northwest.

The moralistic culture sees government as a force for good, taking action to improve society, placing the good of all above the good of a few individuals. Government officials are expected to place service to the people above personal loyalties or profit. This culture is dominant in Upper New England and the Upper Midwest, as well as Colorado, Utah, and Oregon. It is mixed with an individualistic culture in other Midwestern and Western states.

These cultures are mentioned here because they have a large impact on how people in different states view government, and the types of policies that are acceptable within those states. Zimmerman (1992) for example, shows how a state's political culture has a definite impact on the types of family policies that social workers must work under. Erickson, McIver, and Wright (1987) indicate that an individual's state of residence (and thus his or her political culture) has a very large impact on a person's partisanship and ideology, independent of that individual's demographics. State political culture has also been found to be a significant determinant of policies relating to the death penalty (Fisher & Pratt, 2006), the stringency of voter identification laws (Hale & McNeal, 2010), educational policy (Louis, Thomas, Gordon, & Febey, 2008), the implementation of the Temporary Assistance for Needy Families program (Mead, 2004), and the agenda-setting impact of newspaper coverage (Tan & Weaver, 2009).

The information from political science can be of utmost importance to social workers as they conduct policy analysis and advocacy. It provides another way of examining problems and issues.

HOW TO CONDUCT A POLICY ANALYSIS

Conducting a policy analysis is a professional activity, not only in social work, but in a number of different professions. There is clearly some disagreement about what a policy analysis is and what is involved. Some authors argue that if you take a checklist and compare the items included to a current policy, then that constitutes a policy analysis. Although this might be defensible in the abstract, it is certainly not the same type of policy analysis that professional analysts who advise policy makers would do. On balance, much of the highly statistical policy analysis would be too in-depth for agency decision-making, especially at the local level.

This book's approach takes a middle ground. It endorses the approach taken by Patton and Sawiki (1993) in advocating for a limited but still adequate approach. Their approach, called quick analysis, aims at developing information that is useful to policy makers but is within the reach of smaller organizations and for decisions with briefer time frames.

This method is a modification of quick analysis. It is a six step model:

- Understanding the problem in context
- Setting goals and defining criteria
- Developing alternatives to meet the criteria
- Comparing alternatives and arriving at a policy decision
- Implementing the decision
- Evaluating the results

Similar to what Patton and Sawicki (1993) describe, the process is a cycle that allows for continuous improvement. (See Figure 6-1.)

Figure 6-1
The Cycle of Policy Analysis

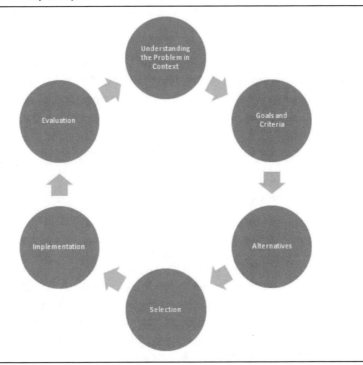

This approach parallels Patton and Sawicki's (1993) approach but diverges from it in important ways. It puts more emphasis on developing the context of policy decisions. Social welfare policy making often ignores globalization, the developing information economy, and the environment. This leads to significant side effects (what economists call externalities) that are often unintended and surprising. In today's world, serious problems promise to become overwhelming without immediate action. Such problems are the result of policy making that does not consider context.

Understanding the Problem in Context

Most problems look relatively simple and straightforward until you understand the context and how it affects both how the problem developed and what can be done about it. Why is there unemployment? Is it because there are too few jobs or because people don't want to work? Or is there a considerable mismatch between the skills that are needed and the skills that are available among job seekers? Maybe unemployment in one location is because another locale has a comparative advantage—some jobs can be done more effectively or less expensively there. In some areas, there is high unemployment because resource depletion has led to job loss. High fuel prices, for example, led to unemployment in the automobile sector and higher prices for many commodities. You need to look at five context areas to make good decisions:

- Economic
- Political
- Sociocultural
- Environmental
- Global

These areas are, of course, interrelated. Unless you understand the larger context, it is impossible to respond intelligently to social problems. Unfortunately, in the search for cheap and quick solutions, policy makers often substitute what is expedient for what will solve the problem in the best way possible. This process, known as satisficing, entails adopting the first "solution" that meets minimal criteria, rather than expending additional effort to create a more fundamental and effective response to a problem.

Collecting Information about the Problem

No problem is addressed, much less solved, without information. The process of understanding the problem or issue begins with appreciating the aspects of the

---

Box 6-1

Sources for Learning about Policies and Programs

Midgley, J., Tracy, M., & Livermore, M. (Eds). (2008). *The handbook of social policy* (2nd ed.). Beverly Hills, CA: Sage.

Mizrahi, T., & Davis, L. (Eds.) (2008). *Encyclopedia of social work* (20th ed.). New York, NY: Oxford University Press.

The House Ways and Means Committee (2004). *The green book: Background material and data on programs within the jurisdiction of the House Committee on Ways and Means.* Available at http://www.gpoaccess.gov/wmprints/green/index.html.

problem, looking at the theories, and collecting data about the problem. The data collected are analyzed and used to inform policy decision-making. This provides the analyst with a foundation that can be used throughout the process. Naturally, the information gathered will differ by the nature of the problem.

John Friedman (1973) differentiates between processed information and personal information. Processed information is professionally developed information. Personal information is the information that people obtain through their day-to-day lives. Both types of information are critical to understanding the problem. The experiences of people who are dealing with situations created by the problem are important. They put a human face on an abstract issue. This information can be obtained through survey research, interviewing, and other methods.

Processed data are also important for developing a comprehensive view of the situation. You can use existing statistics, research results, and research developed specifically for the analysis. You can also use sources such as review articles, article databases, and other materials. Once you have gathered all of the information that you need, it must be organized in some fashion to make it useful.

Box 6-2
Sources of Policy Statistics

- *U.S. Census* (www.census.gov) offers extensive statistics on nearly every social problem or issue. Much of the data are available online and can be downloaded quickly and easily.
- *Bureau of Labor Statistics* (www.bls.gov) has a wealth of statistical information on labor, work, the workforce, and unemployment.
- *Data.Gov* (www.data.gov) provides access to a wide variety of government datasets.
- *National Center for Health Statistics* (http://www.cdc.gov/nchs/) has wide-ranging data on health and disease.
- *National Center for Educational Statistics* (http://nces.ed.gov/) offers data on schools, educational attainment, educational finance, and so forth.
- *Environmental Protection Agency* (http://www.epa.gov/) has information and statistics about environmental conditions, problems, and trends.
- *Federal Election Commission* (www.fec.gov) has statistics on voting, registration, campaign contributions, and so forth.
- *World Bank* (http://data.worldbank.org/) has excellent data on international and comparative issues.

Analyzing the Data

Analyzing data can mean using statistical analysis, but it encompasses other techniques as well. At its core, data analysis helps to organize and understand the data. For some issues (such as understanding the current distribution of day care facilities or where agency field offices should be located), a mapping system using Geographic Information Systems (GIS) could be most helpful. For other issues, more qualitative information can help. Statistical analysis, of course, is a part of many policy analysis situations. The point is that data analysis is supposed to facilitate understanding the data and ultimately help you to comprehend the situation as comprehensively as possible.

Most policy decisions are conducted in a short time frame so the amount of data that can be gathered and analyzed is limited. Although you might be able to gather terrific information with a specially crafted survey, it might not be possible in the time before information is needed. The key here is to get the best information that is available in a timely manner.

It is important to build your analysis on a substantial base of information. This will allow you to confidently work toward solutions for solving the problem.

Setting Goals and Criteria

Once you know where you are (that is, data have been collected and analyzed), it is a relatively straightforward process to formulate a set of realistic goals for where you want to be in the future. Goals are long-term outcome statements. They tell you where you're going, but not how you plan to get there. It is important at this stage to separate ends from means. Deciding that Policy A or Service B is what is needed is the end of the process, not the beginning.

The other part of this process is the creation of criteria. You can use criteria to decide which potential policies are desirable or undesirable. There are several types of criteria that a policy analysis would address. First, there are the criteria that directly address the problem. If the problem is, for example, a high infant mortality rate, then one logical criterion would be reducing the number of babies who die (infant mortality). In most cases, there are a number of criteria that are logically related to the problem at hand. In addition to these, you will have other criteria that speak to cost, feasibility (technical and political), and acceptability. Chambers and Wedel (2008), DiNitto (2010), and Gilbert and Terrell (2009) all have lists of possible generic criteria.

Developing Alternatives

There are many ways to address most problems. Each of these ways to tackle a problem will have assets and liabilities and a different chance of success. As Patton and Sawicki (1993) note, doing nothing is always a possibility. The concept of opportunity costs, described earlier, comes into play here. If you choose Alternative A, you will also be choosing *not* to choose Alternative B, if it is financially impossible to do both.

Each alternative should be a viable way to address the problem. This means that only realistic alternatives should be examined rather than straw person alternatives that can be easily dismissed. Every alternative needs to specify what the basic assumptions are, how the alternative will work, what interventions will be used, and what social science findings attest to their effectiveness.

You can learn about alternatives from a variety of sources. Certainly what you hear at meetings, what you learn in your professional reading, and what other programs are doing are important sources of ideas. Also important are the creative ideas of you and other stakeholders. Because change is a part of everyone's life, it is important to keep your eyes open for new policy solutions. Sometimes they come from unexpected places.

When you have developed a reasonable list of alternatives, it is time to evaluate your alternatives against your criteria. If you have done a reasonably good job with the first part of the process, this should be a straightforward process.

Considering Alternatives and Deciding on the Best Alternative

The next step is to compare the alternatives according to the criteria. Which is most effective? Which costs less? Which will be easiest to implement? This is where analysis comes into its own.

Say that you need to have a policy about drinking on campus. Say your criteria are as follows:

1. Reduce student drinking
2. Respect student privacy
3. Keep costs low
4. Prevent alcoholism

These are fairly simple and direct criteria. Next, look at some possible alternatives. One alternative would be to double the budget for campus police to apprehend excessive drinkers. Another might be a voluntary treatment program through the student health center. A third alternative might be slightly better enforcement coupled with a referral program for problem drinkers.

Now compare the three alternatives against the four criteria. The campus police strategy would probably reduce student drinking by making it more difficult. It probably wouldn't reduce alcoholism or respect student privacy. The treatment option would fall down on the first criterion because it would depend on motivation to get students to treatment. Both this possibility and the one above are likely to be expensive. The third or hybrid model would have police to bring people in, so case finding would not be a problem. It would do treatment by referral, thus lowering costs.

You might quantify these alternatives by creating a rating scale to compare the alternatives on each criterion. You might decide that a score of one means marginal achievement of the criterion, two is average, and three is high. This gives you an easy way to make comparisons over multiple criteria. Some criteria are more important than others so you might weight some criteria. For example if cost is most important to you, you might double the score for cost. When you have a score on each criterion, you add up the scores for each alternative. These scores are then compared, as in Table 6.1.

The mixed strategy comes out on top in this analysis. If you add criteria or weight some of the criteria, that can change. For example if you weight "reduce drinking" at triple the points (that is, it is the one criterion that is three times as important as any other criterion), the police strategy comes out on top (12 points for it, compared to 8 for treatment and 11 for mixed). As long as the assumptions are known to all, the process provides a reasonable way to support decision-making.

Table 6.1
Comparison of Alternatives

Alternative	Reduce Drinking	Protect Privacy	Cost	Prevent Alcoholism	Total
Police	3	1	1	1	6
Treatment	1	2	1	2	6
Mixed	2	1	2	2	7

In some cases, the individual doing the decision-making is the person doing the analysis. In other cases, the analysis is done by a staff person, and an administrator or political decision-maker makes the decision. Although the analysis must be rigorous in both cases, the way that the analysis is presented can be different.

The product of analysis comes to decision-makers in different ways. The most comprehensive analysis comes in white papers or other major policy documents. Some of these reports are book length and are the work of many policy practitioners. On the other hand, some are brief memoranda of a page or less.

There is often a presentation that accompanies the report. This may be a short briefing for a single decision-maker or a formal presentation to a group of decision-makers such as a committee, a board, or a governmental body. In an advocacy group situation, the report may be released at a press conference.

This presentation should be well organized and informative. Stories about how the problem affects individuals are useful. Attractive charts and graphs are also useful, if they serve to illustrate the major points in the study. It goes without saying that charts and graphs that are misleading are not used.

Clear communication is essential in both the report and the presentation. This means a number of things that are often different from academic presentations. Certainly having a solid argument that is well reasoned, fair, and complete is important. Poor grammar, spelling, and proofreading are apt to give the reader a negative impression of your abilities as a professional. On balance, academic audiences have to make different decisions than other decision-makers. Be careful about the use of profession-specific language (jargon) and advanced statistical techniques. These are areas that may mean more to people in the field than people who do not have the years of training and socialization that professionals have. If consumers of your analysis don't understand the words or the techniques you use, it will be difficult to persuade them using your work.

Another issue is that reports need to speak to the decision being made. This means that information that is relevant to the decision should be emphasized and ought to be easy to find, preferably in an executive summary, which is a one or two page summary of the analysis that is the part of the report that is read first. Given the time pressures on decision-makers, the executive summary may be the only part of the report read, so it needs to be created with care.

The final part of this process is a decision by the appropriate person or persons. The decision-makers will often use information that is not part of the analysis. This is to be expected and will bring in many of the political and values issues that are generally left out of a formal study. When the decision is made it is time to move forward on other fronts. This leads to the process of implementation.

Implementing the Decision

Implementation is the process of taking a plan or policy and making it into a real program. Many programs and policies are never implemented properly even though a decision to go forward has been made. This is unfortunate because many valuable ideas never get the opportunity to prove their worth. They remain promises of what could have been. On balance some policies are unworkable and others are bad ideas from the beginning. In those cases, non-implementation is beneficial.

Implementation means creating the setting where the decided-upon policy can be put into practice. For some policies, the process is quick, easy, and relatively painless. For others (and this is common), implementation is a long, drawn out, and often difficult process.

Implementation success depends on the skills of the administrator and the change theory used. In a classic book, *The Planning of Change*, Bennis, Benne, and Chin (1985) argue that there are three types of change strategies: the rational empirical strategy, the normative reeducative strategy, and the power coercive strategy.

The rational empirical strategy operates on the assumption that those people with the best data and the best arguments win the day. This assumes that people are essentially rational and that, shown a better way, they will embrace it. Implementers who prefer this strategy will provide participants with data and research. Many mass communication strategies are based on this model. In certain systems, this strategy is clearly the best. Often scientists, engineers, and medical practitioners are much more easily swayed by data than other approaches.

The normative reeducative strategy operates on the idea that people resist those things that are inconsistent with their view of the world. This system attempts to resocialize people to new ways of looking at reality. In essence, people are reeducated to the policy and what its benefits might be. This strategy is often used in primary prevention, drug abuse education, and some types of community development.

The power coercive strategy is the third and final approach. In this strategy, force is applied to guarantee compliance. This is either the force of authority or actual legal force. Although this might seem like the easiest solution, it is often difficult to implement and the side effects are often highly unpleasant. When people are simply ordered to do something, they frequently resist coercion efforts, whether overtly or covertly. The use of a power coercive strategy can be counterproductive when large amounts of resistance are created. There are clearly times that this is the strategy of choice such as when a crisis looms. In most other cases, however, this is the strategy best saved for last.

These three general strategies can also be used together. The threat of legal action or executive power is often enough to motivate resisters—so change implementation leaders can use the two less severe strategies, knowing that they have the power to force change in reserve.

Evaluating the Results

Evaluation is the final stage but it is also the beginning of a new process. Evaluation can answer many questions about how a program is working, how it can be improved (formative evaluation), and what strategies are effective (summative evaluation). It can also tell you if the intended policy has been implemented in a manner that is something like the original plan (fidelity assessment). There are basically three operations that evaluation can perform in the policy analysis realm. The first looks at the policy implementation and the extent to which policies are implemented correctly. This is often called ongoing monitoring (Hoefer, 2012a) and is an important part of administration and policy oversight. As you might expect, agencies differ in their interest in fulfilling the goals of policies. Some are actively supportive, others indifferent, and a few outwardly hostile. If they want, agencies can sabotage a policy's implementation. Ongoing monitoring (using the techniques of fidelity assessment) can help prevent this situation. It can also prevent well-intentioned mistakes that can frustrate the intent of the policy process.

A second type of evaluation, one that Scriven (1991) referred to as formative evaluation, aims at making policies or programs more effective. This process makes the policy more effective by helping program management to perfect the program.

The last type asks if the policy or project worked. Scriven (1991) calls this summative evaluation and its aim is to help you understand whether the program worked and what was responsible for the results. This type of research is what most people equate with program evaluation. Evaluators will typically look at effort (what the program did), process (how the program worked), outcome (whether the program met its goals), impact (what effects the program has on the population), and efficiency (if the program was cost effective).

Although program evaluation is very useful in its own right, it also provides the policy analyst with information to further understand the problem and potential policies. This makes the process a circular one with the information developed in the evaluation feeding back into the problem and policy decisions (Hoefer, 2012b).

CONCLUSION

Policy analysis is an accessible skill and one that can be an important tool in the quest for social justice. The tools of policy analysis can create better policies and more effective programs. Policy analysis makes evidence based policy making possible.

Not every idea works. Over the years, there have been a number of programs and policies which have been shown to be either ineffective or in some cases destructive. Many of these efforts could have been improved or the resources that they used gone elsewhere if a proper policy analysis was conducted.

This is clearly an area where social workers can afford to "kick it up a notch." A lot of what the profession has settled for is less than what is needed. The approach described here is an important step in the right direction.

Policy analysis is a useful skill and one that is likely to be in demand in the future. As an important component of policy practice, it is essential material for social workers in all roles, but especially for those who want to create policies, work on social change, and practice social administration. This is an excellent practice career for those who want to make a difference in their world.

Questions for Discussion

1. Why are there conflicts between a rational model of decision-making and a political model of decision-making?
2. Does policy analysis really help people make better decisions?

3. Is it possible to "load" the criteria in a policy analysis to reach the decision that you desire? Is this ethical?

4. Where should you draw the line in considering which outside factors to allow in a policy analysis?

Exercise

1. Analyzing Class Policies: Take the class attendance policy. Conduct a policy analysis using the model presented in the chapter. What are the pros and cons of the current policy and of the possible alternatives?

Websites

American Association for Policy Analysis and Management: www.appam.org/

American Evaluation Association: www.aea.org

Congressional Budget Office: www.cbo.gov/

U.S. General Accounting Office: www.gao.gov/

Visual Media

Ben Willington, "How We Found the Worst Place to Park in New York City—Using Big Data": http://www.ted.com/talks/ben_wellington_how_we_found_the_worst_place_to_park_in_new_york_city_using_big_data

Further Reading

Bardach, E. (2011). *A practical guide for policy analysis: The eightfold path to more effective problem solving* (4th ed.). Washington, DC: CQ Press.

Blank, R. (1997). *It takes a nation: A new agenda for fighting poverty.* Princeton, NJ: Princeton University Press.

Blank, R., & Haskins, R. (Eds.). (2001). *The new world of welfare.* Washington, DC: Brookings Institution Press.

Della Porta, D., & Mosca, L. (2005). Global net for global movements? A network of networks for a movement of movements. *Journal of Public Policy, 25*(1), 163–190.

Chapter 7

Advocacy in the Information Age World of Social Policy

Advocacy is a core concern of social workers dealing with social policy. Social workers are not content with only understanding current policy, the forces that shaped it, and what its effects are. Such analysis and understanding is but a first step in assisting clients with their situation. Indeed, because policy shapes what social workers can do to assist their clients, and how they can practice social work, the importance of understanding and being able to conduct effective advocacy is vital to all social workers.

DEFINING ADVOCACY

The term "advocacy" has been defined in multitudes of ways (Schneider & Lester, 2001). The *Social Work Encyclopedia* defines advocacy as "the act of directly intervening, supporting or recommending a course of action on behalf of one or more individuals, groups, or communities, with the goal of securing or retaining social justice" (Mickelson, 1995, p. 95). Advocacy is thus an application of a set of tools and processes to assist clients live better lives. Other people and professions use the same techniques of advocacy that social workers do. What makes advocacy in social work different from similar activities by others is that social workers should always have the goal of securing or retaining social justice as the primary motivation for their advocacy.

Two types of advocacy are sometimes said to exist, case and cause. The difference between them is the level of intervention: case advocacy is related to individuals or families, such as in assisting them to receive benefits or services for which they are entitled; cause advocacy is related to larger groups or social movements, such as an effort to guarantee civil rights to the lesbian, gay, bisexual, and transsexual (LGBT) population.

Although dividing advocacy into these two categories is useful for some purposes, it also runs the danger of ignoring the commonalities of advocacy, no matter what level of client system is addressed. This chapter presents a unified model of advocacy, based on the generalist approach to social work.

THE UNIFIED MODEL OF ADVOCACY (ADVOCACY PRACTICE)

As you may recall from introductory classes in social work practice, the generalist model of social work provides a problem-solving approach to client issues. Although different authors present the steps of the generalist model slightly differently, substantial agreement on the overall approach exists. Figure 7-1 shows the steps in the generalist model of social work as presented by Kirst-Ashman and Hull (2011) and the corresponding steps in the unified model of advocacy (also known as advocacy practice) (Hoefer, 2016).

The first step in the generalist social work process is "engagement," where the social worker gets to know the client system and builds rapport. In advocacy practice, the first step is called "getting involved." When social workers "get involved" it means that they are willing to expend time, energy, and other resources on behalf of a client, with the ultimate goal of promoting social justice.

Kirst-Ashman and Hull's (2011) second step is "assessment," when social workers determine the extent of their clients' problems, what their strengths are, and what their goals are. Getting to know the situation is essential to planning how to move beyond clients' starting positions (step 3). Similarly, in advocacy practice, the second step is "understanding the issue." Social workers at this stage are working to know what the issue is and to define it in a way that is mutually agreeable for key stakeholders, including the client system. Social workers also strive to understand who benefits from the current situation and who suffers. Advocates strive to generate possible solutions. The final action in

Figure 7-1
Comparing Generalist Social Work and the Unified Model of Advocacy

Generalist Social Work (Kirst-Ashman & Hull, 2011)	Unified Model of Advocacy (Advocacy Practice) (Hoefer, 2016)
Engagement	Getting Involved
Assessment	Understanding the Issue
Planning	Planning
Implementation	Advocating
Evaluation	Evaluating
Termination	
Follow-up	Ongoing Monitoring

understanding the issue in the unified model of advocacy is to assess the possible solutions according to how well each one promotes social justice. Only after the issue is understood to this extent do social work advocates move on to planning their advocacy effort. In essence, the second step in advocacy practice is to conduct a policy analysis as described in the previous chapter. The purpose of advocacy is to bring knowledge to decision-makers to influence the choices that are selected.

Planning is the third step in both generalist practice and advocacy practice. The advocacy planning process has five aspects:

- identifying what is wanted
- determining the targets of advocacy
- assessing when to act
- understanding what to do
- gathering the appropriate information and incentives to bring the target to adopt the advocate's position

Step 4 of the generalist model consists of implementation of the treatment plans developed in the previous step. The same is true in advocacy practice—the actual advocacy that was planned in the previous step is put into effect. After the implementation of the plans (treatment or advocacy), step 5 is to evaluate the progress made. In the generalist model, evaluation will usually consist of measuring clients' gains to solve their problems, whether at the individual, family, group, or larger level. In advocacy, evaluation is the process of comparing expected changes in clients' conditions with what actually occurred. Social workers also judge the extent to which they were able to implement their plans. If barriers arose to putting their plans into effect, it is reasonable to expect that fewer desired outcomes will be achieved.

Kirst-Ashman and Hull's (2011) model of generalist social work includes a step labeled termination. This step exists to provide a formal exit for the social worker and to provide a way for clients to resume their lives on their own. In this regard, social workers are constantly trying to work themselves out of their job (at least with the currently engaged clients). The unified advocacy model doesn't have an analogous step. Although social work advocates may indeed move away from certain clients who have attained their immediate needs and now understand how to advocate on their own behalf, the struggle for social justice is never-ending. There is always something else to do, another case to take on, and, it is hoped, many more victories to celebrate. Termination of caring for the overall cause of social justice is not part of social workers' approach to advocacy.

The final stage in the Kirst-Ashman and Hull (2011) generalist approach to social work is follow-up (not all models of generalist social work include this concept). Social workers periodically check back with former (now terminated from regular contact) clients, to ensure that they continue to function better than before, and, it is hoped, function well. Advocacy practice has a final step called ongoing monitoring. In this step, social work advocates continue to watch for social injustice to reappear or look for ways to improve conditions or policy even more. Monitoring provides additional information upon which new planning, advocacy, and evaluation of efforts may occur.

This brief overview of advocacy practice shows that it is similar to other types of practice that you may be familiar with and that it uses the same generalist problem-solving approach pioneered in social work many years ago. Although the techniques may be different than in direct or other types of macro practice, many of the skills you learn elsewhere are important and can be applied. Social work advocates must be good listeners; be able to reflect back to others what is said; build on others' strengths; gather information from many sources; move discussions to solutions; and act in ethical ways to achieve client goals.

The remainder of this chapter provides additional details on the advocacy practice process. The idea is to take each stage in turn, even while realizing that advocacy may take steps out of order, return to stages you thought were completed, and not always end up where you thought you were going when you first began. In these ways, and many others, advocacy practice is like all social work practice. Helping human beings change themselves and the world around them is not an exact science, so you must always be ready to develop and implement Plan B, Plan C, and even Plan D in order to achieve something akin to what you really are striving for.

STAGE 1: GETTING INVOLVED

Research indicates that social workers are at least as active in politics (and thus advocacy) as are other professionals (Ezell, 1993; Wolk, 1981). Political science literature describes the characteristics of people active in politics and social workers, by training and inclination, tend to have many of the attributes of politically active people. The research shows that certain personal values are important in that they increase a sense of professional responsibility to correct injustice and also increase a person's level of interest in engaging in advocacy (see Figure 7-2). Educational level also has a direct impact on the amount of advocacy a person will engage in. Participating in other organizations affects a person's skill level and also has a direct impact on advocacy because it provides more opportunities to become an advocate. Finally, the amount of time a person makes available for advocacy is important. These are the vital variables of advocacy engagement. The more of these factors a person has, the more likely that person will engage in higher levels of advocacy work.

All of these factors leading to increased advocacy are, to some extent, changeable. Individuals can make changes on their own but it is important to understand that the values and practices of organizations that employ social workers have an impact on their employees. If advocacy is talked about, and staff members are provided with training on effective forms of advocacy, it is likely that more advocacy will be conducted than if supervisors never discuss

Figure 7-2
The Seven Vital Variables of Advocacy Practice

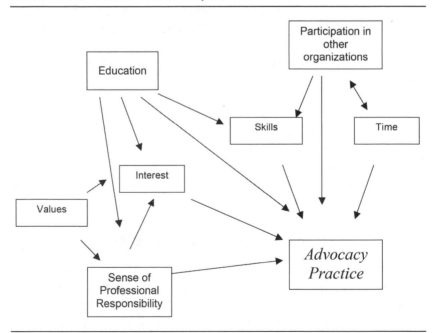

Source: Hoefer, R. (2016). *Advocacy practice for social justice* (3rd ed.). Chicago: Lyceum.

the topic, no time for advocacy is built into a worker's schedule, or no training opportunities relating to increasing advocacy skills levels are provided. The underlying decision to become involved, however, is up to each individual social worker, no matter what organizational incentives may or may not exist. It is important to understand, as well, that social workers may be even more passionate and involved in issues outside of their job than those associated with their job. For example, a social worker who has a child with problems in school may become more active on the school front than in assisting clients of her agency, no matter how much care and concern she has when helping her clients.

A final thought relates to clients. If these factors are changeable in you, the social worker, they are also factors you can work on with clients. In the spirit of empowerment (a strong social work value prominently displayed in the National Association of Social Workers' Code of Ethics), your effort to assist clients to become advocates on their own behalf is not only ethical practice on your part, but a sure-fire way to enhance social justice, the ultimate goal of all social work advocacy practice.

STAGE 2: UNDERSTANDING THE ISSUE

Once people decide to become involved in something, they usually want to move to the action stage right away. It is perhaps the same psychological mechanism as when a person buys a new gadget. A strong temptation exists to start using the new tool without reading the instruction manual thoroughly. The whole point of having the new tool, after all, is to use it, not to study it! Later, when and if problems arise, the owner looks through the instructions book or goes online to find a fix. There is nothing really wrong with this approach to new gadgets, but when it comes to advocacy, this tendency should be set aside. The tools for policy and advocacy practice you are learning work well but you really should read the full set of instructions before jumping in. After all, you are dealing with people's lives and their well-being, not just another device that promises to make your life easier or more fun.

Thus, before moving along in the advocacy process, it is important to truly understand the issue you are getting involved with. The process of understanding an issue involves five steps. They are to (1) define the issue; (2) decide who is affected and how they are affected; (3) decide what the main causes of the issue are; (4) generate possible solutions to the issue (based on what the causes are); and (5) review the proposed solutions to determine their impact on social justice. By going through all five steps, you can be certain you have a grasp of not only what you are trying to fix (the problem) but also on what appropriate solutions are to increase social justice in the world.

Defining the issue seems like a very easy thing to do but it is frequently a contentious process. For example, when faced with a hungry homeless person, some would say that the problem is obvious. But there are actually many different ways to understand what is going on, and different interpretations should lead to different paths being taken. Suppose you define the issue here as "A man is hungry and homeless." As soon as you try to address the issue, however, you run into difficulty. Should you give the man food? Although a short-term fix, will the longer-term problem be addressed? Do you even care about the longer-term issue, or are you content knowing that the man has had food for one meal? If you care about what happens tomorrow, and how to help the man become self-sufficient, then giving the man a sandwich now is not an adequate response. Is it important to dig deeper to understand how the man is affected by homelessness and hunger and how they may be related? Of course it is. Perhaps a different issue causes both of these presenting problems. The possibilities are many: Substance abuse may be the root cause, as all the man's income is consumed by alcohol and drug purchases. Perhaps the twin problems are caused by an untreated mental illness. Maybe the high cost of housing or having his home foreclosed by a bank has put the man on the street, and, once there, his life spiraled downward to where his job was lost and hunger began. Is this his problem alone, or are many others also hungry and homeless, thus indicating that advocacy is needed beyond assisting this one person? In short, until you understand this man's context and the other factors that play into his current situation, you should refrain from beginning your advocacy planning.

The point of determining who is affected, and how, is that, in almost all situations, even when there are one or more people suffering as a result of the situation, at least one person is benefitting. Those who benefit may have a vested interest in maintaining the current situation and could lead the opposition to your advocacy efforts. It is thus important for you to determine ahead of time who they are and what they see as their interests. Who benefits from a hungry homeless man? If the person is a substance abuser, the seller of his preferred substance gains his money. People who hire day workers at low wages may benefit, if the man is able to work, by having a cheap source of labor. Then, whoever receives the benefit of the homeless man's labor (such as a suburban homeowner who pays less for landscaping work) also receives a benefit. If this sort of work is widespread, the city and school districts may ultimately benefit from having higher status and more costly homes in their jurisdictions, resulting in more tax money being collected on the higher value homes. Of course, benefits and costs are almost never equally shared. Some businesses near where homeless people gather complain about such people scaring off customers. Taxpayers who foot the bill for repairs to public property or for homeless shelters may feel an unfair burden has been placed on them.

Each situation is unique and requires careful thought as to who is being harmed and who is being helped by any one problem. It can be quite interesting to follow this line of thinking to determine who is on what side of the benefits equation and how the different stakeholders are involved. Once this has been done, the advocate decides what the main causes of the issue are. It is frequently easy to say that the problem is an individual one and the client bears all or nearly all of the blame for being in the situation. Social workers, however, are trained to look at systems and their impact on individuals. Homelessness may be due to substance abuse on the individual's part. Even homeless people with current substance abuse issues once were not addicts. What occurred to start the client down that path? A divorce? A job loss? Eviction from a home or apartment? Here you see the connection between case advocacy, which focuses only on assisting this one client, and cause advocacy, which looks at patterns that affect larger numbers of people. By determining earlier who was affected, and how, you have information to help you decide the nature of the problem.

Knowing the cause of the problem leads you to have good ideas about how to solve the problem. Reversing the causes, or finding ways to work around them, are the most typical approaches to generating possible solutions. In the case of a hungry homeless man, one may surmise that the addiction, although it occurred after homelessness began, is keeping the client in homelessness because all available financial resources are being used to support his habit. Thus, it is not a viable solution to provide food and short-term housing, unless treatment for the addiction is also provided. On the other hand, if addiction is not involved, but a lack of job skills is, then you would want to find a way to increase the man's employability level. If you have found that many homeless people have been left behind by the job market, or that the job skills possessed are not in need by employers accessible by workers, additional or different solutions may be called for.

The final aspect of understanding the problem, once a number of potential solutions have been developed, is to rate the degree to which each solution affects the attainment of social justice. All other things being equal, you should prioritize possible solutions that increase social justice by larger, rather than smaller, amounts.

In keeping with empowerment practice, the process of understanding the issue must include client input and decision-making. Because clients frequently will assist in the planning and implementation of the advocacy effort, they should be included in this preliminary work, as well, so that they will be "co-owners" of whatever comes next. It isn't surprising that social work advocates may have a different understanding of issues than the people they are working with—and this different understanding may be considered "wrong" or "misguided" by the very clients who are supposed to be being helped! Clients' understanding of their situations may not always seem correct to you but their beliefs should be acknowledged and worked with. For example, a client may believe that he alone is responsible for his situation, whereas you see many organizational or societal factors that affect his situation. By presenting your ideas to the client, you may make it easier for him to move forward by changing his thinking that he alone is responsible. On the other hand, a client who accepts no responsibility may find it helpful to see how she can assist in her own recovery from the negative aspects of the situation.

STAGE 3: PLANNING

The planning stage of advocacy practice is fun, exciting, and a bit challenging. In stage 2, you developed at least one proposed solution and judged it according to how well it would promote social justice. In this stage, you determine the steps you are going to take in order to implement the solution chosen. You can think of the planning stage as mapping out how to get from "here" (the current situation) to "there" (where the client wants to be). Just as you might use a map (or Google Maps, if you want to rely on the Internet) to determine a good route to take on a journey, you must plan your advocacy effort to find a good way to make progress with your client.

The first thing to do in any journey is to decide where you want to go. For working with clients on an advocacy project, the first thing is to determine what you want to achieve, that is, how you want the world to be after the advocacy effort is completed. For example, for the hungry homeless man referred to earlier, the goal might be to have stable employment, no addiction, and a roof over his head. These are really three different outcomes, and the process of achieving each one will require many steps (and probably a few missteps) along the way. But by laying out the long-term goal and the short and intermediate term outcomes that must be achieved along the way, you have created a map with milestones that show progress achieved on the overall journey. It's like starting in San Bernardino and having the ultimate goal of being in New York City. You know that you have to travel through several towns along the way, even if you are flying from California to New York. Naturally, your "advocacy roadmap" may not be completely correct, or you may run into a few road closures and detours along the way. If (or when) that occurs, you will need to revise the itinerary, but will likely keep most of the desired or expected outcomes intact.

In addition to this advocacy roadmap, one of the important elements of advocacy planning is to determine who the decision-makers are who can get you where you want to go. After all, if it was within your power to decide, you wouldn't need all this advocacy effort—the decision would already have been enacted! Which specific individuals or decision-making bodies (such as a city council, a legislature, or a nonprofit board of directors) have the power to grant your request or withhold approval? Once you determine who has the authority to move your case forward, you know who your target is. Without knowing who the target of your advocacy effort is, you may make many mistakes and will certainly waste a great deal of time.

STAGE 4: ADVOCATING

At last you and your client have an understanding of the issue, and a plan to put into effect. Now all you have to do is get the decision you want from your target. Naturally, this may be a long-term process, as when a new law or change in policy is the desired outcome of your advocacy efforts. Still, this is the time to gear up for the actual education, negotiation, and persuasion processes that advocacy entails.

Education

In clinical work, you might use the stages of change model (Prochaska, Norcross, & DiClemente, 1994) to get a client to think about changing a behavior that is a problem or potential problem. For example, although "everyone knows"

Boston demonstrators against the war in Iraq in 2003. This was one of many protests worldwide over the U.S. decision to invade Iraq after a confrontation between the Bush administration and Iraqi strongman Saddam Hussein.

that smoking is a dangerous habit, that does not necessarily mean that all smokers are thinking about quitting. So, someone trying to change that person's behavior has to introduce the idea of smoking cessation in a way that assists the smoker to consider stopping. The client is in what is known as the "precontemplation" stage and the change agent wants to move the smoker to the next stage, called the "contemplation" stage, where he or she is actively considering a shift in thinking pattern or behavior. This requires overcoming the defenses of the client.

How is this relevant to advocacy? There is a direct correspondence to an advocate bringing a new issue to the target. It is often the case that the target you have chosen is not informed about the issue that you are passionate about. The target may not ever have thought about the topic and so can be considered to be in the precontemplation stage in terms of being willing to act as you desire. You will need to overcome the target's defenses to obtain action.

Here's a rather simple example of local advocacy. Suppose you purchase a new home and discover that the lamppost right next to your driveway is too bright for your comfort and also an impediment to getting in and out of your garage, due to the driveway's unusual shape. You know that the previous owner of the house once knocked the lamp over when exiting the garage. So, you want to have the city move the lamppost to another location. This will get it away from the house where it is too bright, and also eliminate the danger of it being knocked down. You make an appointment to meet with your city council representative, Ms. Lovelace. When you present this totally new problem to her, you may encounter the following "reasons" that she doesn't want to support your position:

- Denial and minimization: "I've never heard of anyone else having problems with the lamppost in their yard. It can't be *that* bad!"
- Rationalization: "City policy says the lampposts have to be placed just so. Moving that lamppost would be against regulations."
- Projection and displacement: "This is not the city's problem. Perhaps you really need better shades on your front windows. And just be careful when backing out!"
- Internalization: "I'm sure this is a problem for you, but I just don't know what to do for you. Lamppost regulations are beyond me!"

Before you can get your preferred solution adopted, you need to move Ms. Lovelace from precontemplation to contemplation. Two empirically supported techniques to use in this process are consciousness raising and social liberation (Prochaska et al., 1994).

Consciousness Raising (CR)

Before being able to change, the precontemplator needs to realize the damage being done by current behavior or conditions. Sometimes, this is simply a matter of not having accurate information, and all an advocate has to do is to present the information collected in earlier steps of the advocacy process. The information may be so compelling that the target quickly converts to wanting to take action. At other times, you must confront the defenses of denial and minimization, rationalization, projection and displacement, and internalization. If the defenses are not removed, the target may not hear the information you are presenting.

The first step in the consciousness-raising process involves building a relationship with the target. Only then can you get beyond the defensive walls blocking the information from getting through. Sometimes you can make a connection quickly, though developing a relationship may take longer. Important aspects of the advocate role in consciousness raising include:

- Don't push someone into action too soon—he may seem to comply, but he may also "push back" and refuse to engage in further discussion with you.
- Don't nag—have other concerns to discuss and at least sometimes provide positive feedback on things you and your target agree on.
- Don't give up—presenting accurate information over time, in different ways, and in different contexts can help get past defenses as the target learns more and sees your determination.

Social Liberation

Social liberation is a process of "creating more alternatives and choices for individuals, providing more information about problem behaviors, and offering public support for people who want to change" (Prochaska et al., 1994, p. 100). Examples of successful advocacy efforts revolving around social liberation include no-smoking sections in restaurants, wheelchair accessible public facilities, public awareness campaigns regarding drinking and driving, or the dangers of using drugs. Three techniques have been identified as being helpful in using the social liberation approach:

1. Ask "Who is on the target's side and who is not?" In other words, who gains and who loses if the target supports the advocacy effort? What benefits accrue to the target?

2. Ask "Whose side is the target on?" Is the target on the side of the problem and/or the side that benefits from people having the problem? Or is the target on the side of people wanting to improve the situation and make the world a better place?

3. Seek and welcome outside influences who already have the target's ear and who support the advocacy effort's desired outcomes.

The main objectives of education are to get the target knowledgeable about the topic and to develop a relationship if you have not yet done so. You also want to move the target from not even thinking about the topic to wanting to take action. If you are lucky, you may find your target is completely on board with what you are advocating for, simply by hearing the facts from you. Other times, you may need to engage in the processes of negotiation and/or persuasion.

Persuasion

Persuasion is another approach to resolving differences between actors. In persuasion, however, one side gets what it wants and so does the other side. How is this possible? It is possible only when one side changes its mind about what it wants. When both parties now want the same thing (because one side changed its view of what it wanted), the result is a very positive outcome for everyone. To put it in personal terms, think about choosing where to eat dinner. In a negotiation, you might start off wanting to eat at a fancy, expensive restaurant, while your partner wants to eat frugally and prepare dinner at home. Perhaps in the end, you "split the difference" and eat at a moderately priced diner. Neither of you got what you wanted, but you reached an acceptable compromise. In persuasion, though, imagine that your partner reminds you that you both want to go on a cruise to the Bahamas. If you both agree to take the money that would have been spent on the expensive dinner and place it in the vacation savings account, you might decide that you didn't want the fancy dinner after all. You have been persuaded, and feel that you are getting what the two of you both want.

Persuasion has a great deal of scientific study that shows how best to be convincing. Although there is not enough space in this chapter to cover the topic fully, experts agree that persuaders must pay attention to four factors: the context, the message, the message sender, and the message receiver (see Figure 7-3). Each factor plays a vital role in the persuasion effort.

Figure 7-3
The Communications Approach to Persuasion

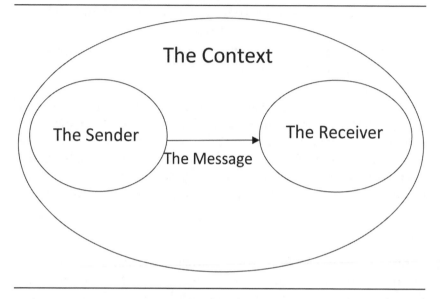

Context

Context is the way that the people involved in the persuasion effort (both the person doing the persuasion and the person or people being persuaded) view the situation. One of the key elements of any advocacy issue is the way it is seen. In other aspects of social work practice, practitioners sometimes talk about "reframing" a situation, that is, changing the way the situation is seen. Advocates should make every effort to have their view of the situation (their frame of reference) become adopted by the others involved because this starting point frequently leads to a more easily agreed on solution. For example, Kingdon (1995) describes the debate about transportation policy for people with disabilities as a struggle over which frame would be adopted. Is it a policy dispute about transportation (in which case the emphasis is on the most efficient and easiest to use method of getting from one place to another) or is it a struggle about civil rights for people with disabilities (in which case the emphasis is on making having a disability irrelevant to being able to move from one place to another without any more hindrances than non-disabled people)? Different policies may ensue from the different frames used to create policy in this area. For example, in Sweden, people with disabilities were provided with vouchers to use to ride in a taxi for the same price as taking a bus. The emphasis was on quickly and easily providing transportation. Taxi transportation is usually more comfortable, pleasant, and convenient than bus travel, with door-to-door service from your home to your destination. This pragmatic approach, particularly in Sweden, where the winter weather lasts a long time, was also combined with environmental changes, such as curb cuts and crosswalk lights that made faster ticks to indicate how much time was left to cross the street. In the United States, on the other hand, the view that was adopted aimed to make public transportation easier for people with disabilities to use, such as with wheelchair lifts, and to make curb cuts and other structural changes in the environment. This approach made everyone more equal, in that everyone used the same public transportation system. Although it is expensive to retrofit buses and make other changes, the ongoing costs are relatively low, once the initial investment is made. Such environmental changes also assist others in the community who might not be labeled as "disabled" by eliminating transportation barriers for all.

If your advocacy effort does not seem to be gaining ground, you may want to try to reframe the issue to something more beneficial for your side. Popular frames for advocates of a cause include:

- It isn't fair (to have things this way or to make this proposed change).
- It won't work.
- It can be done in other ways.
- It costs too much.
- It will hurt the public (or clients, or some other identified group).
- It will help the public (or clients, or some other identified group).
- The benefits outweigh the costs.
- If it saves one life, it will be worth it.
- After what they've been through, they deserve it.

When you are in an advocacy situation, be sure to analyze what frame for the issue is best for your position. Also examine the other party's words to uncover how they see the situation. Their frame may be very different, and not acceptable to you and your clients.

Message

Your message is the information that you intend to communicate to your target. According to research (Booth-Butterfield, 2010), six elements of the message are important in persuasion: intent, organization, sidedness, repetition and redundancy, rhetorical questions, and fear appeals.

Announcing your intention to persuade someone is frequently counterproductive, as the target quickly raises walls for defense. This generality is not true in two specific situations. When you merely want to ask for minor changes in a proposal that all parties basically agree on, it is best to be up-front about wanting to make small changes. Your forthrightness should put the target at ease, knowing that you do not want large changes. Also, when the target expects you to be trying to be persuasive (as when you are talking to an elected official) there is no point in acting coy. Admit what you are trying to do (which is what the target will believe you are trying to do whether you admit it or not) and press forward.

It is always better to be more organized than less. Take the time to plan what you are going to say, the order you wish to say it, and how you want to close the discussion. You may not get to deliver your message just the way you have it planned, but being organized and to the point demonstrates respect for your target and never hurts your case.

Sidedness refers to whether you should present only your viewpoint or also discuss "the other side's" perspective. Research indicates that presenting both sides comes across as being "fairer" to listeners, but for it to be effective in promoting your cause, you must not only mention the other side, but also attack it. Otherwise, you merely give that other position more credence (Cialdini, 2000). Repetition (saying the same thing over and over) and redundancy (sending similar, but not identical, messages) are important in persuasion. When done well, as long as you have sufficient time to engage in both processes, you can be more persuasive. Repetition is important because people often do not tune in to your message on your first effort and redundancy is important because people quickly grow used to hearing your arguments if they are always phrased the same way. Both of these principles are clearly in view with advertising campaigns.

Rhetorical questions are effective, aren't they? Of course they are because they make a statement that is hidden in the guise of a question. People who are not actively listening will often accept the embedded implied information within a rhetorical question without seriously thinking about it (Cialdini, 2000).

Fear appeals are effective—if people are scared, they tend to take action to ease their fears. An important point behind using fear appeals, however, is that you must not only scare your target into action, but you must also provide a feasible solution to calm the fears you have aroused.

Sender

According to communications research, no matter how well-crafted the message is, a great deal of persuasiveness is dependent upon aspects of the sender. The most important element that you should strive to create and maintain is your credibility. You must be believable in order to be persuasive. Credibility is composed of three aspects: expertise (you must know what you are talking about), trustworthiness (you must come across as honest and lacking bias), and likeability (you won't be believed if you are not liked) (Cialdini, 2000). All of these three aspects also have details that are important, but the basic concepts behind expertise, trustworthiness, and likeability are not difficult to grasp. You must know what you are talking about, be sincere, and do your best to get along, even if you disagree with what your target supports.

Receiver

This is the final piece of the persuasion puzzle. Persuasion takes place within a relationship (even if it is a short-term relationship). You can't be persuasive if the receiver doesn't choose to listen to you. So, you, as the advocate, must tailor your topic's frame, your message, and even yourself (to some degree) to meet the desires of your target. Bedell (2000) argues that you must fulfill some need of the target (such as the target's need to win, to gain security, or to be accepted). You also must evaluate how much the target seems to care about the issue. Someone who doesn't care much won't likely pay much attention to your presentation, but will probably be easier to persuade to your viewpoint. People who are not much involved with the topic are more likely to be persuaded by emotional presentations. People who are more involved and knowledgeable will only be convinced with strong arguments and a well-researched point of view (Booth-Butterfield, 2010).

This section has covered a great deal of material, skimming over a topic that has a great deal of research associated with it. If you are curious about those details, you can look for the latest research on the topic by the authors listed in the references. In the end, you will see that advocates can greatly increase their chances of advocacy success with even a bit of knowledge of the best ways to persuade.

Negotiation

The process of negotiation, when done well, can be quite structured. It can require a planning process all its own, particularly involving research about what your target's current stance on the issue is, what he or she hopes to gain from future decisions about the issue, and areas of agreement and disagreement between yourself and the target. The more research you can conduct ahead of time, the more you can build on areas of agreement and the more you can counter probable objections to your plan.

You should have a negotiation plan that includes the best possible outcome you can imagine, the worst possible outcome you can accept (your limit), and various outcomes in between these two extremes that you can accept, even though they are not as good as you would like (fallback positions). When negotiations first begin, you will present your well-thought-out initial position, working from that to come to an agreement with the target of your advocacy. A common approach to negotiation is to have the other party begin by describing its initial position. In this way, you know if you can agree to some things that you didn't think you could achieve without a struggle. But the other party will be trying to get you to reveal your initial position first as well, so even this becomes part of the negotiation process.

An important point about advocacy negotiation is that advocates are often working with collaborations or in coalitions. In these cases, negotiation is with their allies, not an opponent. The negotiation process is to decide what the joint position of the collaboration or coalition will be. Some partners may want to advocate for less, some may want to advocate for more. Each member of the coalition should come to the table just as prepared when negotiating with friends as with adversaries.

In almost all cases where both sides to a negotiation are working hard for their position, none of the parties comes out with their initial position intact. Each party gives in on some points in order to achieve others. Because of this, a prepared negotiator will prioritize the various positions within the larger array of possible positions. When you can achieve a higher priority point at the cost of a lower priority item, it is usually a trade worth making. In the end, however, you didn't get everything that you wanted, and most likely, neither did anyone else.

STAGE 5: EVALUATING ADVOCACY

Once the advocacy is actually completed, it is tempting to say that the fun (or work) is over and it is time to go on to something else. But this would be like playing a game and not keeping score. Sure, you can play just for the fun of it, but usually you want to know how well you did, and you know that by looking at a score. In order to improve in any skill, after the effort is over, it is important to review what went well and what could have been done better. Advocacy is an activity that has a purpose beyond just doing advocacy—you are trying to improve the state of the world for your clients and yourself. Thus it is crucial that you find a way to "keep score" or evaluate your efforts and the outcomes you achieve. Although many ways exist to evaluate your advocacy efforts, the one suggested here is to compare your actual progress to the roadmap you developed earlier in the advocacy process during the planning stage. You can fairly easily determine which milestones you reached and the extent to which you achieved your planned outcomes. Also evaluate the processes by which you got there—what connections you used, how smoothly the planning went, to what extent your advocacy work involved clients and their empowerment, and so on. All of this information will be important for the next advocacy effort you are part of.

STAGE 6: MONITORING

The final stage of the unified model of advocacy is monitoring the results of your work on a longer-term basis. Evaluating advocacy (as in the previous stage) is necessary to get better at the planning and implementation of advocacy. But most policy change is slow and once the new policy is ratified, the hoped-for results may take a while to occur. Thus, advocates should devote themselves and some resources to keeping track of policy change and evolution. This entails three aspects. The first is to try to influence the regulation-writing process, the second is to influence agency budgets, and the third is to affect the implementation process.

Regulations are written to interpret laws and to put the details into what are often vague legislative phrases. For example, Congress passed a law permitting Medicare reimbursement of social work services, although no definition of that was provided, nor was it clear exactly who was and who was not a social worker. Without this type of detail, it would be impossible to put the law into effect. So the executive branch agency in charge of implementing the law needed to develop an operational definition so that it could ensure that social workers are paid for providing social work services, but also that non-social workers do not get paid for providing social work services and that social workers do not get paid for providing non-social work services. (You can read the definitions developed by the Centers for Medicare and Medicaid Services, Department of Health and Human Services by looking in the Code of Federal Regulations, Title 42, Volume 2, 42CFR410.73. This text is available online at http://a257.g.akamaitech.net/7/257/2422/16nov20071500/edocket.access.gpo .gov/cfr_2007/octqtr/42cfr410.73.htm.)

Federal law provides a process for interested parties and individuals to keep track of proposed regulations and to provide input concerning how the regulations are written. In the case of Medicare reimbursement for social workers, the National Association of Social Workers was able to provide written and oral testimony as to how a clinical social worker should be defined. Now this definition has the force of law, just as if Congress had passed that definition itself. Although it is not necessarily easy for individuals to monitor this process, organizations should certainly have at least one person on staff that keeps track of such concerns.

The second way to monitor policy is to keep track of how much funding an agency receives or how much money is set aside to implement and oversee any particular policy. An oversight or compliance office can be starved for personnel or other resources if the legislature does not allocate funds for the process. One example is the decrease in the number of inspections for workplace hazards that occurred between 2000 and 2008. No laws or policies were changed that were designed to make the workplace less safe, but because the budget for oversight was cut, the number of people who did inspections dropped, and the number of inspections declined. It should thus come as no surprise that workplace safety worsened.

The final way to monitor progress (or lack of progress) regarding achieving policy goals comes from influencing the implementation of a program. Even after a fine law is passed, good regulations are written, and adequate funding is allocated, it is possible that a program can be implemented in a way that decreases, rather than increases, social justice. Social workers or others in charge of providing benefits to clients, or of improving community resources, may not actually do so. Benefits may be provided in such a way as to benefit one group of people and not another or certain areas of town may receive more than their "fair share" of community resources. Social work advocates must be sure to insist on the equal, non-discriminatory, and just implementation of programs.

All of these steps require practice and a considerable amount of effort. Yet, not only is advocacy an ethical imperative for social workers, it has great value to society and to the people who engage in it. With a well-conceived plan in place, the chances of getting more of what you want increase tremendously. The next section describes how advocacy is being affected by what Friedman (2007b) calls the "flat world."

ADVOCACY IN A POST-INDUSTRIALIST WORLD

The previous portions of this chapter outline an approach to advocacy that is rooted in a problem-solving, generalist-model perspective to social work practice. The key to using this unified model of advocacy is to systematically think through what you want and how you can persuasively put forward your information to the correct target. The model and its stages approach to advocacy have great validity whether you are living in an industrialist society or an information society. Still, living in an information society does mean that you have some great advantages compared to advocates in an earlier time period.

The foremost advantage is that you have easy access to the World Wide Web. This brings several benefits to you. First, in a few minutes of artful searching, you can find information that could have taken weeks or months to find looking through paper records in a large library or government repository. Huge volumes of government documents and the latest in scientific research are, literally, at your fingertips. News reports, historical information, and opinions of millions of other people can be searched and downloaded within seconds, perhaps giving you just the bit of information or compelling story that can drive your point home as you advocate for social justice.

A second benefit the Web brings to you is the easy ability to connect with like-minded individuals from around the world. One such group is called the Doe Network. Its tagline is "International Center for Unidentified and Missing People." Members of the Doe Network use their Web savvy to "give the nameless back their names and return the missing to their families" (Doe Network, 2011). They do this by working on cases of unknown people who are dead: "giving the cases exposure on our website, by having our volunteers search for clues on these cases as well as making possible matches between missing and unidentified persons and lastly through attempting to get media exposure for these cases that need and deserve it" (Doe Network, 2011). The Doe Network is made up entirely of volunteers, many of whom had worked on their own, individually, to identify the unidentified deceased of their community. Through the power of the Web, however, not only can these people find otherwise obscure information that might lead to an identification years after a person's death, but they can share tips, provide encouragement, and celebrate successes as part of a community of interested advocates for a forgotten group.

A third benefit of the Web is the ability to garner publicity in ways that are otherwise beyond the scope of most individuals or small groups. A strategically promoted, entertaining YouTube video may be the start of an advocacy campaign that shakes the foundations of a corporate giant. Friedman (2007a) discusses how plans of TXU, a huge supplier of energy and electricity in Texas, to build eleven new coal-fired, carbon dioxide spewing power plants were drastically altered due to the intervention of environmental activists who developed a Web-based plan to stop TXU. The Natural Resources Defense Council (NRDC) created a dedicated website, wrote regular email alerts to a wide audience of policy makers, mainstream journalists and editorialists, environmentalists, and others in a successful effort to change the terms of the debate. In the end, TXU was purchased by another company but only on the condition that the NRDC approved of the plans for expanded production of electricity. Among other concessions that NRDC received before giving its approval were a cut in "the number of new TXU coal plants from eleven to three," support for "a federal cap on carbon emissions," a commitment by TXU to "plowing $400 million into energy-efficiency programs," and "doubling its purchase of wind power" (Friedman, 2007b, p. 491). Friedman (2007a) summarizes this episode in an editorial in the *New York Times*:

> Message to young activists: If you do your homework, have your facts right and the merits on your side, and then build a constituency for your ideals through the Internet, you, too, can be at the table of the biggest deal in history. Or as Mr. Krupp puts it: the TXU example shows that truth plus passion plus the Internet "can create an irresistible tide for change."

Before leaving the topic of the Web, it is important to think about the differences between one-way communication (advocate to public via website) and two-way communication (advocate to public and public to advocate using Web 2.0 features). Although it is beyond the scope of this chapter, tools that allow readers (or viewers) of a website the ability to respond, leave comments on blogs or videos, take polls, and so on, are becoming more expected among the Web-savvy population. A few of the currently important tools for advocates include YouTube and Vimeo (video sharing), Slideshare (PowerPoint and Document presentation sharing), Twitter (short messaging), Flickr (photo sharing),

Facebook (information and status sharing),and LinkedIn (professional relationship building) among other potential tools.

Technology has also altered the way that advocates create and use media. Rocha (2007) discusses how desktop computer programs make the production of newsletters and brochures much easier than in earlier times. These materials can be quickly made, and handed out. Distribution of these media can also be done at no cost through email or by being placed on a webpage. With the wide use of laptop computers and the advent of tablet computers, creating such media products is even more portable. Smartphones are not yet able to be used for easily producing finished products such as brochures (at least not yet, simply due to size constraints) but people with smartphones can almost always read information on their handheld mobile devices and people are increasingly using their phones and tablets rather than a desktop or laptop computer to access the Web.

This chapter could list many more examples of successful advocacy using the tools known to ancient Greeks and Romans who studied rhetoric and speech in order to make the most persuasive case they could; we could also list advocacy efforts that occur via use of smart cell phones, instant messaging, Web 2.0 tools, and other technological marvels. There is not room for an encompassing list of successful advocacy efforts through the ages and any description of using technology in advocacy will be out of date before it is printed.

The challenge for all advocates in an information age is to understand and use all the tools (old and new) available to make their most persuasive case, promote their views to opinion leaders, interested stakeholders, and the public, and to gain access to the correct target. This is done, not for personal gain or public glory, but to ensure social justice. When information age social workers do this, they join and provide future examples for a distinguished history of the profession.

ADVOCACY IN A GLOBAL VILLAGE WORLD

The advocacy practice approach to change is not unique to the United States, nor is access to the tools of the information age. The spring of 2011 demonstrated the power of advocacy efforts yoked with technology to bring new regimes to power in a number of Arab countries. Although this was exciting enough to happen in one country, the use of Web 2.0 tools such as YouTube and instant communications solidified opposition movements in several countries, all leading to new leadership after decades of tyrannical rule. Although it is true that military forces provided the backbone of armed resistance, tens of thousands of citizens in these countries risked their lives through organizing demonstrations and demanding changes for themselves and their countries. Meanwhile, those in the United States were able to see the action unfold almost in real time.

Such instantaneous communication is a positive side of technological advances which lead to globalization of information production. You can learn wonderful things from people who you will never see in person nor meet. You can learn from them the lessons of courage in advocating for freedom, steadfastness in the face of overwhelming odds, and strength in numbers. When you look at what others around the world have done and continue to do to advocate to make their part of the world a better place, it makes some of the reluctance about being advocates for addressing human needs in the United States seem rather overblown. In addition to praising social workers who in previous years set the stage for the world of today, you can also draw upon the vigor of your own time to renew your determination to leave the world a better place for those who come after you.

Questions for Discussion

1. Why is advocacy an important function of social work?

2. What skills and abilities do you feel make for an effective advocate? Which do you currently possess, and which ones need additional training or practice?

3. What are the important differences between education, negotiation, and persuasion? Choose an example and apply each technique to a topic of interest to you.

4. How can living in the information age add to advocacy practice? What problems might emerge from living in this age?

Exercises

1. Find out the mailing address of two of the elected officials who represent you. Choose a topic that interests you and develop two letters, with each one using a different approach to framing the issue. Send the letters and compare the different responses you get.

2. Speak with a person in your community who is an advocate. Ask him or her about the information in this chapter and describe the advocate's reactions. Does this advocate tend to agree or disagree with what you have been taught as effective advocacy methods?

3. Research an advocacy effort in another part of the world. How is advocacy similar to and different there from what is described here? What lessons can you learn from what was done in another country?

Websites

International Federation of Social Workers: http://www.ifsw.org/p38001792 .html. Gives an international viewpoint on human rights issues.

National Association of Social Workers: http://www.naswdc.org/advocacy/ default.asp. Provides excellent information for U.S.-based advocacy and legislative issues.

The Advocacy Net: http://www.advocacynet.org/. The Advocacy Project partners volunteers with community advocates to assist "marginalized communities to tell their story, claim their rights and produce social change" around the globe.

Visual Media

Norma Rae (1979). Directed by Martin Ritt. The story of a woman's journey as a labor organizer.

Further Reading

Hoefer, R. (2016). *Advocacy practice for social justice* (3rd ed.). Chicago, IL: Lyceum.

Rocha, C. (2007). *Essentials of social work policy practice*. New York, NY: Wiley.

Schneider, R., & Lester, L. (2001). *Social work advocacy: A new framework*. Belmont, CA: Brooks/Cole.

Chapter 8

Poverty, Inequality, and Income Maintenance Policy

Poverty is the most significant challenge facing the social welfare system and the most substantial barrier to social justice. Poverty affects every aspect of a poor person's life. Simply put, poverty is about deprivation—the lack of sufficient material resources to live a full and comfortable life. Poverty is often a potential threat for those who are not currently poor. Poverty is always a serious concern and one that influences almost every other area of social welfare. Poverty is a world wide problem with significant consequences.

In the United States, as in almost all nations, wage employment is the means that most people use to secure their income. It is also the source of many of the benefits that individuals and families receive. The latter is often referred to as occupational welfare (Titmuss, 1974). These benefits include health insurance, retirement income, paid leave, and other important supports.

Social welfare systems create a series of income support or income maintenance programs to deal with the problem of poverty. Although these are primary interventions, there are few, if any, programs and policies that do not deal with some aspect of poverty. This chapter discusses poverty and the programs that are designed to deal with poverty and its side effects. Poverty becomes more complex in an information economy. Information poverty becomes an issue and the changing nature of the economy becomes another factor. Another layer of possible causes is added to that for poverty in the industrial or agricultural economies. This has major implications for antipoverty efforts.

WHAT IS POVERTY?

Poverty and inequality are facts of life for much of the world's population. They are separate but interrelated concepts. What do they mean?

Poverty

Poverty is usually defined as deprivation of a meaningful or significant level. Poverty is often divided into absolute and relative poverty (Todero, 1985). Absolute poverty means lacking the very minimum of material goods and services to sustain life. Relative poverty means that you are deprived relative to others in your society. Unfortunately, for many of the world's poor, absolute poverty is a fact of life and starvation is a very real threat. In the United States, although some people clearly experience absolute poverty, relative poverty is usually the focus of social policy discussions. Although the U.S. social safety net is certainly not what it once was, fewer people face food insecurity in the United States than in much of the world.

Inequality

Poverty is not the same as inequality, although there are similarities and they should be considered related concepts. If everyone is starving but has the same level of income, everyone is poor but no one is unequal. By the same token, one can have substantial inequality without anyone being poor. Inequality has its own consequences however. Inequality offends social justice; it makes social cohesion more difficult and creates barriers to the development of social capital (Putnam, 2000). It has also been shown to have negative implications for health (Wilkinson & Pickett, 2006).

Redistribution of income is one of the goals of a progressive tax policy. At one time, the federal tax rate for the wealthiest group was much higher. In the mid-1980s this changed. The amount of inequality in American society has increased substantially in recent years (Luhby, 2011).

As the recent economic downturn has demonstrated, the potential for poverty is widespread. Many Americans are close to the threshold where poverty can be a reality in a very brief time. The idea of being "one paycheck away" from poverty is reality for many Americans. At the same time, the United States is becoming an ever more unequal society.

HOW POVERTY IS MEASURED IN THE UNITED STATES

There are many ways to measure relative poverty and the one that is officially used in the United States is the poverty line or, more correctly, the poverty threshold. (See Cellini, 2008.) This is the official measure of poverty. The poverty line was constructed by Social Security Administration economist Mollie Orshansky in 1965. Reasoning that food was one third of a typical household's expenses, she took the cost of the USDA's Emergency Meal Plan and multiplied it by three. The resulting number separated families (later households) who were poor from families who were not. This is the method that current antipoverty policy uses to define benefits, coverage, and other factors. The current (2015) poverty threshold for a family of four with two children is $24,250 (U.S. Department of Health and Human Services, 2015). The Department of Health and Human Services has a competing standard that is based on other metrics.

There are clear limits to this system of measurement. If a family has one dollar less than the poverty threshold they are defined as living in poverty. Give them one additional dollar, however, and they are now not poor. This one dollar clearly makes no true difference in their ability to take care of themselves, but statistics would show successful movement out of poverty for this family. The poverty threshold approach to measuring poverty is controversial. Conservatives charge that it distorts the number of poor by failing to include the value of program benefits such as housing subsidies, nutrition programs, and cash benefits. Liberals argue that the poverty threshold doesn't tell very much about how poor you are or whether you are likely to be poor for a long time vs. a short time. Someone experiencing absolute poverty will look like everyone else under the poverty threshold. The issues experienced by people at different levels under the poverty threshold are diverse.

There have been many attempts to replace the poverty threshold with something less problematic. In the mid-1990s the National Academy of Sciences convened a panel to discuss the issue and a number of suggestions were made. This did not result in a significant change in practice, however. The problem really isn't methodology or opinion or even ideology; it is politics. There are serious political consequences to potential change in the poverty rate. Economists have developed a number of metrics to capture poverty throughout the world (Todero, 1985). Although these measures are not part of American poverty policy they very well could be in the future.

One encouraging way to look at poverty is to evaluate the level of development as a substitute for a purely income based measure. These approaches use social indicators to assess the population status. An early approach, the Physical Quality of Life Index (PQLI), which was created from life expectancy at age one, infant mortality rate, and adult literacy rate (Morris, 1976), became influential in international development circles. Its simple model gave each area a score from 1 to100 (higher is better). The United Nations developed a more complex Human Development Index (HDI) that encapsulates a more sophisticated picture of deprivation. Table 8-1 presents the highest and lowest nations in 2011. This work continues to evolve and develop.

These approaches demonstrate that poverty is more than income-related factors. Poverty is being deprived of the opportunity to live a positive and ful-

Table 8-1

Highest and Lowest Scoring Nations on the Human Development Index

Highest Scoring Nations	Lowest Scoring Nations
1. Norway	1. Democratic Republic of the Congo
2. Australia	2. Niger
3. Netherlands	3. Burundi
4. United States	4. Mozambique
5. New Zealand	5. Chad
6. Canada	6. Liberia
7. Ireland	7. Burkina Faso
8. Liechtenstein	8. Sierra Leone
9. Germany	9. Central African Republic
10. Sweden	10. Guinea

Source: Human Development Index (HDI)—2011 Rankings. Retrieved from http://hdr.undp.org/en/media/HDR_2011_EN_Tables.pdf.

filling life. Looking only at income paints a skewed picture. The measurement of poverty is not just a technical matter. There are serious emotional and political issues. Policy often gets made on emotion and spin rather than being based on rational discussion.

Inequality is measured in a number of ways, but the most common is to use the Gini Coefficient (World Bank, 2011). The Gini Coefficient is a scale that can be between 0 and 100, with a lower number indicating more equality. In 2011, the Gini Coefficient for the United States was .45, which was one of the most unequal distributions of wealth in the industrialized world. A few other countries that have a Gini Coefficient between .45 and .49 are Mexico, Sri Lanka, and China. Sweden, Australia, and Russia have lower Gini Coefficients (and thus have greater equality), while South Africa, Chile, and Papua New Guinea have higher Gini Coefficients (less equality).

CONSEQUENCES OF POVERTY

Poverty is a problem that has consequences for almost every aspect of human life. Among the disadvantages of being poor for the individual are the following:

- Your chances of being incarcerated are higher. Almost any interaction with the criminal justice system will be more severe if you are poor. You are more likely to be a victim of crime if you are poor. The likelihood of dying violently is higher.

- Your chance of dying of a preventable illness is higher. The poor have less access to primary care and are more likely to use emergency rooms as their physician. The types of testing and preventative care are much more difficult in such a setting.

- Your chances of getting a good education are lower. Educational opportunities in poorer neighborhoods are often of lower quality. Poor homes are less likely to have the types of resources needed to promote early and consistent learning.

- Your chance of suffering from a mental illness is higher. Poverty is stressful and that stress makes you a much better candidate for mental illness.

- Your chances of going to college, becoming an elected official, having a professional job, and so forth are much lower if you are poor. You also lack the connections to make these careers a success.

- Your chance of exposure to noxious chemicals and hazardous materials is considerably greater. Your chances of living near a toxic area are more substantial and you have a higher risk of working in a dangerous area.

Poverty is heavily stigmatized in American society and the poor are often blamed for their own fate. Poverty is a serious issue and it has consequences for everyone in society. Because poverty prevents the actualization of human potential, the results of that potential are lost to everyone. If a poor child were to discover a cure for HIV/AIDS or a way to make gasoline from water, it is much less likely that he or she would get the chance to make that contribution. Everyone is thus denied the possibility of what could have been. Poverty and inequality are dangerous to social stability. They add to the complications of modern society by polarizing parts of the population. Poverty is clearly an issue that must be addressed forcefully in order to have a just society and a just world.

Relationship to Environmental Issues

Poverty is inherently tied to environmental destruction and depletion. The relationship between the economic system and the environment has been well documented (Brown, 2009; Hoff & McNutt, 1994). Given that poverty is related to economic system performance, any disruption in the economy will affect poverty rates. Poverty is related to environmental issues because resource

Beach in Mumbai, India, demonstrating the consequences of urbanization.

depletion and destruction lower the level of possible economic system performance. When the economic "pie" is smaller, the poor tend to get less.

One only has to look at the current situation with energy to see how an environmentally based issue (resource depletion) can lead to shortages and rising prices. Although these situations stress everyone, they are much more stressful for the poor. The move toward using agricultural products (such as gasohol which is made from corn) as fuel will be even more serious for the nearly one billion people worldwide who lack sufficient food.

The issues of environmental justice and environmental racism are additional concerns that complicate the relationship between the environment and poverty (Bullard, 2005). If you are poor, you are more likely to live in an area with air pollution, groundwater contamination, and so forth. This fact is an integral part of discussions about environmental racism and environmental justice. More affluent communities are often able to shift the location of noxious facilities to poorer areas. They exercise their political clout, hire lawyers, and engage in the policy process whereas poorer communities might not have those resources. This is often called the NIMBY (Not in My Backyard) syndrome. The consequences for human health can be serious and can persist through generations. This can include genetic issues and long-term mutations.

The penalty of environmental destruction and depletion can be witnessed in the third world to a larger extent. Activities that can no longer be legally conducted in the United States and other advanced societies often find homes in developing nations.

Social Justice Implications

Poverty is a serious affront to social justice, especially when basic needs are not met. Fairness is a principal concern of social justice (Rawls, 1971). Basic needs should be met before preference needs are addressed. Because poverty implies deprivation, it also suggests that basic needs are not being met at the level that society expects. How many people are affected, however? Is this really such a serious issue?

STATISTICS ABOUT POVERTY

Statistics cannot really portray the human issues that poverty creates nor can they convey the suffering of the poor. They are useful in demonstrating how great the problem is and who suffers from it.

National Statistics

In 2013, there were about 45.3 million poor people in the United States (DeNavas-Walt, Proctor, & Smith, 2014) for a poverty rate of 14.5. Children have the highest rate of poverty of any age group. See Table 8-2.

Poverty rates are higher for nonwhites, but most of those who are poor are white. The highest poverty rates are for African Americans and Latinos. About 10.7 million of the poor in 2010 worked at least part time during the year. The South is the area with the highest poverty rate. There are areas that are historically poor, such as Appalachia and the Mississippi Delta.

Table 8-2
Number of U.S. Children in Poverty 2009–2013

2009	2010	2011	2012	2013
14,657,000	15,749,000	16,387,000	16,397,000	16,087,000

Source: KidsCount datacenter (http://datacenter.kidscount.org).

Poverty affects many Americans in profound ways. There are ethical and moral issues but there are also practical issues for the economy. Poverty is also connected to race, age, and education.

The picture that these statistics paint is not a pretty one. Poverty is a reality for far too many people in our society. Even minor economic reversals can throw many other Americans into poverty. Levels of inequality are also worrisome and sparked the Occupy Wall Street protests across the country in 2011.

Global Statistics

Poverty in the United States is a very serious matter. The United States has substantial resources and could deal with poverty more directly. In much of the world, poverty is an emergency.

The number of people living in extreme poverty around the world has fallen in the past two decades, but the global challenge from poverty is still formidable. The World Bank's world poverty threshold is $1.25 a day or less for extreme poverty. Using this standard, over 1.9 billion people were extremely poor in 1990. Despite world population growth, this statistic has improved, with 1.3 billion people living at or below this level in 2008 (World Bank, n.d.-b). Although the problem of global poverty is far from solved, the percent of the world's population in such dire straits has dropped from 43.1 percent in 1990 to 22.4 percent in 2008. Clearly, too many people around the earth live at an unacceptable level of income. Every day, people continue to starve in nations throughout the world.

Many developing nations have extremely high poverty rates. Countless children die each year and life expectancy is low. But the fact that considerable progress has been made can provide hope that global poverty rates can be improved even more.

Against this backdrop, the world community is beginning to come together to address the issues. One of those efforts is the development of the Millennium Development Goals.

The Millennium Development Goals

In 2000 a world conference set a series of eight goals for the nations of the world to attain by 2015. These are the Millennium Development Goals. They are (United Nations Development Program, n.d.):

- Goal 1: Eradicate extreme poverty and hunger
- Goal 2: Achieve universal primary education
- Goal 3: Promote gender equality and empower women
- Goal 4: Reduce child mortality
- Goal 5: Improve maternal health
- Goal 6: Combat HIV/AIDS, malaria, and other diseases
- Goal 7: Ensure environmental sustainability
- Goal 8: Develop a Global Partnership for Development

Although progress has been made, the world is a long way from meeting these goals (Brown, 2006). It is unlikely that any, let alone all, of these goals will be met by the target date or in the near future. Global poverty has improved in parts of Asia (India and China for example) but parts of Africa (such as Darfur) continue to experience serious challenges.

The available statistics demonstrate that poverty is a serious problem in the United States and a more serious problem worldwide. It is a challenge that stands in the way of hopes for a better future but one that can be successfully addressed.

THEORIES ABOUT POVERTY

Before creating new policies, it is important to review the major theories about the problem. These are generally grouped into conservative, liberal, and radical theories.

Conservative Theories

Most conservative theories of poverty look for issues in poor people themselves, their community, or some type of defect in the economic system. Classical and neoclassical economic theorists look at the motivation of the individual as a function of incentives. If people are just as happy collecting welfare as having a job, they will collect welfare. If not, they will find work. This is supported by an analytical technique called indifference curve analysis. This means that society should set up a system that makes it unlikely that people will want to be on welfare such as by stigmatizing welfare receipt, having unpleasant conditions to be on welfare, and having rude personnel working with clients.

On the other hand, conservative classical economists argue that government interference creates poverty. In a perfect market, poverty will be eliminated by the action of market forces. Government efforts such as transfer payments, the minimum wage, and so forth interfere with the operation of a free market and thus create poverty. A similar argument is made by Charles Murray (1984), who concluded that social programs create poverty by changing the culture to reject the work ethic and by encouraging other behaviors that lead to moral problems.

A related approach is taken by the culture of poverty theory, which argues that the poor develop a culture that prevents them from achieving. Formulated by anthropologist Oscar Lewis (1961), culture of poverty theory argues that in order to survive, the poor develop a culture that is functional for survival. This includes traits like present orientation, an inability to defer gratification, fatalism, and so forth. Although the culture of poverty makes it easier to survive, it makes achievement much harder. The solution for poverty is to change the culture of the poor through education, psychotherapy, and so forth. Ryan (1976) points out that this amounts to blaming the poor for their poverty.

Liberal Theories

Liberal theories tend to look at a combination of individual and systems issues. Human capital theory (Becker, 1964) argues that people can compete in the labor market based on how much human capital they possess. Although much of human capital is composed of education and skills it can also include health (illness reflects negatively on human capital) and other factors. The cause of poverty is insufficient human capital and the cure is to allow people to develop more human capital. This type of strategy looks principally at education and training interventions.

Other liberal theories look more at structural issues. The dual labor market theory (Piore, 1974) is one of these approaches. It argues that there are two labor markets, the primary labor market (where the good jobs are) and the secondary labor market (where low-paying jobs without benefits are). Workers in the secondary labor market find it very difficult to move to the primary labor market. This barrier is due to factors like education, social class, and, in some cases (like skilled trades), union membership. Thus, there are few avenues out of poverty, even for people willing to work hard to do so. Possible solutions to poverty suggested by this approach include education, apprenticeship programs, job training and coaching, and other ways to improve the skills and habits of people otherwise destined to be in the secondary labor market. One of the obvious questions here is what changes in the economic system due to theories like this one. Many formerly unionized skilled trades have been eliminated or automated by change in the economic system.

Radical Theories

Radical theories of poverty rely on structural explanations. Marxists have always seen poverty as the result of one class oppressing another. This has played out in critical theories of social welfare. In fact, some radical thinkers have argued that social welfare programs prolong the suffering by delaying the eventual revolution. Piven and Cloward (1971), for example, argue that capitalism is inherently unstable and must maintain a pool of labor through periods of unemployment. The role of social welfare is to maintain this labor pool by maintaining and regulating the poor. Piven and Cloward offer as evidence changes to welfare rules when more or less labor is required. When there is a labor shortage, rules are tightened to drive former welfare recipients into the job market. When unemployment is high and fewer workers are needed, rules are relaxed. Although this approach has critics, it remains influential. Radical theories suggest that the structure of society and the economy must be changed if poverty is to be eliminated. The type of change varies from the creation of alternative structures (the strategy in the War on Poverty) to overthrow of the capitalist system of economics.

All of these theories assume a larger system that is not quickly changing and is based on the characteristics of an industrial order. In the information society, many of the assumptions that support these theories will no longer be tenable. They need to be replaced with theories that reflect these new realities. One of the emerging ideas is the power of networks over other forms of organization, such as markets. Theories that use these new assumptions, such as Benkler's (2006) wealth of networks, will prescribe different interventions. Issues such as the digital divide and international competition for labor are rarely addressed. Many of these approaches specify an internal labor market that is relatively free from international competition. This doesn't mean that these theories are useless, only that their explanatory power will decline as time moves forward.

These are the theories used to build the system that America has today. Each theory tends to prescribe certain interventions and those are the ingredients of social welfare policy. Figure 8-1 looks at this relationship.

Figure 8-1

Selected Theories of Poverty and Associated Policy Strategies

This is a general overview of some of the major ideas about poverty and the approaches that policy makers can use in addressing poverty within the context of these theories. Understand that these are general descriptions rather than rigorous reviews of the theories in question.

Theory	Assumptions	Mechanism	Strategies
Neoclassical Economics	Markets are self-regulating and will eliminate poverty and unemployment if left unfettered	Remove barriers to a free market/Some people will still need help—Residual Social Welfare. Others choose to be poor for refusing to work at the equilibrium price of labor	Deregulation/ Some support for dependent population
Human Capital Theory	Workers' ability to compete in the labor market depends on human capital (education, health, etc.). Poverty results from low levels of human capital	Help people develop human capital and they will obtain employment	Build more human capital. Education and health care programming
Dual Labor Market Theory	There are two separate labor markets, the primary labor market with the good jobs and a secondary labor market where the not so good jobs are. Moving between the two markets is difficult or impossible	Help people in the secondary labor market obtain primary labor market jobs	Create training programs and apprentice programs
Culture of Poverty Theory	In order to survive in a poverty environment people adopt a lifestyle that makes it difficult to pull themselves out of poverty	Essentially change the culture of either the currently poor or the children	Counseling/ reeducation
Opportunity Theory	People will seek opportunities through pathways in society. If legitimate pathways are blocked then they will take illegitimate pathways such as crime and violence	Create pathways to opportunity	Build parallel structures and break down unfair structures Legal efforts/ Negotiation
Geographic Mismatch Includes Internal Colonialism, Central Place Theory, Etc.	There is a mismatch between where workers are located and jobs. This might be because of economic change or changes in the terms of trade	Relocate people or economic units, move capital, change terms of trade	Regional planning, microenterprise. Community economic development/Legal Efforts/ Negotiation
Information Poverty & Digital Divide	Access to information technology and networks places workers at risk of being excluded from the information economy. Education also plays a role here	Provide access, training, and education	Community technology grants and efforts for universal access/broadband
Social Welfare as Creator of Poverty	This school discusses the role of social policy in creating poverty. 1) Poverty is created because antipoverty programs reduce motivation and change morality (Charles Murray) 2) Poverty is essential to provide a surplus labor force to compensate for the boom-bust cycle of capitalism (Piven & Cloward)	1) Social welfare programs change the moral fiber of the poor 2) Social programs maintain and regulate the poor	1) Eliminate or change social programs 2) Socialism

This is not to say that the political system relies only on academic theories and research. Using this research, people have created a social welfare system with a number of identifiable programs and policies. This is where the discussion turns next.

CURRENT INCOME MAINTENANCE POLICIES

The American system of income maintenance is an incrementally created hodge-podge of programs that were created for a range of reasons. They reflect much about America's industrial order and its values. In general, programs are divided into social insurance programs and public welfare programs. (See Figure 8-2.)

Social Insurance Programs

Some of the most generous public programs are social insurance programs. They are tied to the workforce and generally require some contribution. As the name implies, they are handled more like insurance programs. People feel entitled to them and they are not considered charity. They also have less stigma than other programs.

Figure 8-2
U.S. Income Maintenance Policies

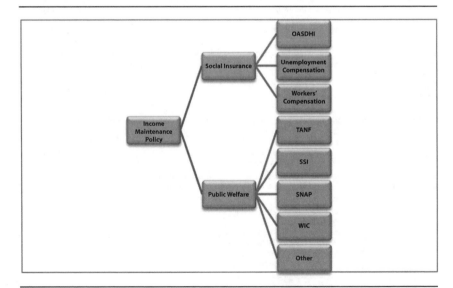

Social Security (OASDI)

What people usually call "Social Security" is actually a program called Old Age, Survivors, Disability, and Health Insurance (OASDHI). This was the central piece of the Social Security Act of 1935. Old age pensions were added first, followed by survivors' insurance and disability insurance. Health insurance (proposed in the 1930s) didn't become law until Medicare (Title 18 of the Social Security Act) was passed in 1965. Social Security provides a modest, though relatively comprehensive, income support system for workers.

If you are a worker in a covered industry (almost all are covered today) you are entitled to receive a monthly payment at retirement provided that you have contributed for the prescribed number of quarters and have reached retirement age. If, before that, you become disabled, you are entitled to a monthly payment for that. If you die and leave survivors, your survivors may be entitled to a monthly payment.

Social Security is funded from a combination of employee and employer contributions. This money is deposited in the Social Security trust fund and much is used to pay current claims. There is considerable political debate as to how long the Social Security trust fund will have sufficient funds to pay retirees using current law. According to the Social Security Administration (2012a), the funds will not be exhausted until at least the years 2036 to 2041, using intermediate estimates of economic and demographic shifts.

Social Security addressed a real need when it was created. Few jobs offered pensions and the extended families that had previously taken care of the aged were breaking down. Poverty among the elderly was a serious problem. The degree to which Social Security is still relevant is open to debate.

Unemployment Compensation

The Unemployment Compensation program provides benefits for those who lost their jobs due to economic dislocations and are actively seeking other employment. The benefits are short term (usually six months) and are administered by the states. Funding is obtained through a tax on employment. The Department of Labor provides an emergency fund in cases where the state exhausts its funds. This occurred a number of times in major recessions and some legislation provided more benefits for workers who lost their jobs as a consequence of trade agreements. In times of serious economic stress, the benefit period can be extended.

Workers' Compensation

Workers' Compensation is a social insurance program that protects the worker who is injured on the job. It is administered by states and by private insurers. States require that all employers have workers' compensation coverage. Employers either get the coverage from the state pool or private insurers. The latter is usually far less expensive. The cost of coverage is usually based on the employer's loss experience so more dangerous workplaces will have higher rates.

Public Welfare Programs

These are programs that are far less generous than social insurance programs. They are not tied to the workplace and are generally stigmatized. There is usually a means test which looks at an individual's or family's economic resources to determine if they should receive assistance.

Temporary Assistance for Needy Families (TANF)

TANF is the largest public welfare program. The TANF program was created by the Personal Responsibility and Work Opportunity Reconciliation Act of 1996 (P.L. 104-193) (see Coven, 2005 for an excellent review). This block grant program replaced Aid to Families with Dependent Children, an entitlement program that could be traced back to the Social Security Act of 1935. This program is the centerpiece of what was referred to as welfare reform in the 1990s. States were given wide latitude to develop their programs.

The TANF program provides a limited amount of cash for a limited amount of time (usually two years). There are work and child support requirements. Some states have more requirements while others require less.

TANF is administered by the states under the supervision of the Department of Health and Human Services. Funding is jointly provided by the federal government and the states. TANF differs from the earlier AFDC program in that it is not an entitlement. Once the appropriated funds are expended, then benefits can be discontinued.

This program has been reauthorized a number of times since its inception. Each reauthorization brings potential changes.

Supplemental Nutrition Assistance Program (SNAP)

SNAP is the latest version of the food stamp program and provides nutritional provisions to needy Americans. This program is administered by the states and the U.S. Department of Agriculture.

The food stamp program is an outgrowth of federal efforts to support the agricultural sector. When agricultural surpluses occur, farmers tend to lose quite a bit of money as the price of food falls. Unlike other goods, food has what economists call inelastic demand (there is a limit on how much you can eat) and when prices drop people do not buy more food. This is called the "farm problem" and the policies designed to support farm prices are an important part of our economic policy. In essence, the government buys all of the surplus farm products. This food was, in the past, distributed to the needy through the commodity foods program, which was eventually replaced by food stamps. Another avenue has always been the Food for Peace Program (P.L. 480) which provides surplus food to the hungry in other nations.

Supplemental Security Income (SSI)

SSI is designed to meet the needs of the disabled who have not been in the workforce long enough to receive Social Security disability payments. There are three types: SSI-A (aged), SSI-B (blind), and SSI-D (disabled). This program was created out of the Aid for the Permanently and Totally Disabled (APDT) which was a state run program. The program provides cash payments and usually access to Medicaid. The program is administered by the Social Security Administration with the assistance of the states.

Women, Infants, and Children (WIC)

WIC is a nutrition and health care program for mothers and their children. Benefits are also provided to expectant mothers. The benefits include health screening and medical care and food subsidies. This program attempts to prevent many of the nutrition-related problems of poverty.

Other Public Welfare Programs

Most states have a program called General Assistance or something similar that provides very limited aid to those who do not qualify for other programs. This money is often from state and local government and can be very different from jurisdiction to jurisdiction. Low Income Energy Assistance is often provided through a number of efforts. This program took on a substantial importance when energy prices spiked.

When the new millennium began, the income maintenance system in the United States consisted of relatively well funded and stigma free social insurance programs and much less well supported and stigmatized public welfare programs. Most of these programs can trace their roots to the programs of the New Deal. Society is changing however and you can begin to see gaps in the social welfare system.

There are also a number of private programs that provide aid to the poor. Large nonprofits like Catholic Charities or the Salvation Army work with poor families, as do a host of smaller agencies. Churches also provide help to the poor in their communities.

WORK, INCOME, AND WELFARE IN A CHANGING ECONOMY

The one area in social welfare that will be most immediately changed by the information economy is the relationship between work and income. The connection between work, income, and poverty is the nexus on which our income

Occupy Wall Street demonstrations, New York City, 2011. This was the original OWS site a few blocks from Wall Street in Zuccotti Park. Occupy Wall Street was a movement created to protest rising inequality in the United States and throughout the world.

support programs are based. When American income maintenance programs were designed, the relationship was based on industrial models of work and income. The nature of work changes radically in an information economy and the relationship between work and income is also altered (see Bridges, 1994; McNutt, 2005). This means that many of our programs do not fit well with the emerging needs of society and will become hopelessly out of touch as society proceeds.

Industrial Social Welfare

Our current income maintenance programs are based on what the industrial society saw as the traditional pattern of work, employment, and lifestyle. In this scenario, you went to work for one employer, stayed with that employer throughout your whole working life, and retired at around age sixty-five. At that point you left the workforce. You might become occasionally unemployed or possibly disabled. Thus, the system was designed to cover you for retirement, temporary unemployment, and the possibility of disability. The system also planned for your family in case of an early death. This is what was incorporated into what you might call America's premium social welfare system. This system was created by the Social Security Act of 1935.

There is also a system for those who do not fit the model. Although there are some better benefits for the disabled, most of those who do not fit into the model are given stingy, stigmatized benefits. These are the benefits offered by Temporary Assistance for Needy Families (TANF), food stamps, and a host of other programs offering benefits that are arguably inadequate, definitely stigmatizing, and frequently lacking in any real connection with a good future outcome. The former programs are our social insurance programs while the latter are public welfare programs.

It is inevitable that society would change and many of the assumptions that underpinned earlier policy are no longer supportable. One example is the norm of lifetime employment by a single employer. That was true for many people who were employed up until the 1970s. Many people discussed the idea of the social contract in the workplace where employers "took care" of their workers in exchange for loyalty and labor peace. Then rounds of economic restructuring led to massive layoffs in the manufacturing sector and the idea of a social contract no longer seemed reasonable or workable. Larger numbers of people became contingency or temporary workers and many business organizations made it clear that they were no longer recruiting people for the long haul. Training and benefits became harder and harder to get.

The concept of having a job was an industrial idea made necessary by Fordism and the development of the assembly line (Bridges, 1994). This meant that having a stable, dependable employee was critical. Now, employees can often be hired for short contracts and let go when the task is completed. Companies no longer keep workers on the payroll if they are not fully used—maintaining surplus capacity is a serious competitive disadvantage.

Information work, on the other hand, can occur at multiple locations. This book, for example, was written in South Carolina, Texas, Delaware, and Spain. Although not true for all workers, the tie between location and economic activity has become more tenuous and opportunities are becoming more global. Capital however, is usually far more mobile than labor.

The work model that many information workers will be moving toward is often called a theater model of employment, which this book has discussed previously. Although this model might open up new possibilities for information workers, it also creates enormous insecurity for them and others.

Gaps in Current Policies

When Social Security was created, the most serious point of economic vulnerability was at the end of your working life. This time of risk was eventually covered by Social Security, and the rate of poverty among the retired dropped dramatically. Other programs addressed the limited vulnerability that could occur for disability, layoffs, and other eventualities. A combination of employment and social insurance saw to the needs of the average American despite some disparities between racial and ethnic groups and between men and women.

Now people live in a time where many are experiencing multiple episodes of unemployment and employment that cycles between full and part time status. This creates massive insecurity and considerable family and individual stress. None of America's existing programs addresses this issue directly.

An additional dynamic that is shifting is the quickly changing workforce and the need to switch careers. Earlier, most people kept the same job and had the same career for a lifetime. The need to readapt and retrain takes substantial financial resources that were once absorbed by employers. This is complicated by the growing importance of information technology. In terms of the digital divide, the development of technology-oriented work skills becomes very problematic for many who once had employment in the industrial sector.

The Organization for Economic Co-operation and Development (OECD) (2002) offers this definition:

> The term "digital divide" refers to the gap between individuals, households, businesses and geographic areas at different socio-economic levels with regard to both their opportunities to access information and communication technologies (ICTs) and to their use of the Internet for a wide variety of activities.

This is a concept that has evolved. Initial research looked at network or computer access (McConnaughey, Everette, Reynolds, & Lader, 1999; McConnaughey, Nila, & Sloan, 1995; van Deursen & Van Dijk, 2014). This was later extended to a greater range of factors that looked at the capacity to use technology.

As long as the digital divide is an issue, people who lose existing employment will have a much more difficult time finding comparable employment. More important, their ability to retrain themselves may not exist (Luhby, 2011). In addition, globalization is putting pressure on middle class workers who are being required to decrease their standard of living so that their companies can avoid or emerge from bankruptcy. Workers are threatened to have no job at all if concessions on wages and working conditions are not made.

FUTURE POLICIES

Given that there are real differences between the current system and the one that is needed, where should social welfare policy be going? One type of policy that is clearly needed is a lifelong economic support system to take the place of the social contract in the workplace that once prevailed. This should include the training and other benefits that were once available from the employer. This will allow workers to survive without regard to the occupational welfare system which is quickly unraveling.

This should begin with a merging of most of our income support systems and health care systems to address needs of every age group. New approaches are needed. Just creating a massive social security program will be both politically unfeasible and economically prohibitive.

Network and community approaches are likely to be part of the new income maintenance policies. In an information economy, wealth flows through networks and through cooperative behavior. Networks can pool productive efforts and make them financially viable. A strategy based on social enterprise might be the welfare system of the future. This could build on community and asset-based strategies. It could also bring in our global and environmental concerns.

Social enterprise and micro finance strategies have been effective in reducing poverty in the third world. These strategies allow the poor to develop their own business strategies and turn them into income generating efforts. Organizations like Ashoka (www.ashoka.org) have been successful in promoting these types of efforts.

Certainly, education is important in preparing people for the digital economy. This has been a particularly tough nut to crack from a policy perspective. Although there are many reasons for this, the United States could find itself in the unenviable position of lagging behind much of the developed world. Changes at multiple levels are needed to make the education system competitive.

As time goes on, traditional strategies will work less and less well. A new system based on the information future is called for. This new system might become the developmental social welfare that was once envisioned.

CONCLUSION

Poverty is a serious problem, both in the United States and in the world today. It has implications for the stability of society and the health of democracy as well as safety in the world. From an individual perspective, being poor is costly in terms of both life chance and potential contributions. As this chapter has shown, industrial age poverty and income maintenance programs and policies are inadequate for protecting people in an information society.

As the transition from an industrial economy to an information economy continues and the environment deteriorates, the nature of poverty will change and the actions that are necessary to deal with poverty will also evolve. This will provide interesting challenges for social workers, advocates, and policy makers.

Questions for Discussion

1. Why is it important that social policies evolve to fit new realities?
2. Social welfare programs fill other needs in addition to helping people. Discuss these other uses.
3. How would global climate change affect global poverty?

4. What are some of the things that social welfare can do to address the environmental crisis?

5. Will poverty be better or worse in the future?

Exercise

1. What are the poorest areas in your state? Look at the county by county data in the U.S. Census. What patterns do you see? Why do you think they exist? Apply the different theories described in this chapter to make testable hypotheses. Try to find data to support each theory. Which theory has the most support?

Visual Media

Bono, "The Good News on Poverty (Yes, There's Good News)": http://www.ted .com/talks/bono_the_good_news_on_poverty_yes_there_s_good_news

Further Reading

Bullard, R. (2005). *The quest for environmental justice: Human rights and the politics of pollution.* San Francisco, CA: Sierra Club.

Davis, M. (2006). *Planet of slums.* London, England: Verso.

Piven, F. F., & Cloward, R. (1971). *Regulating the poor: The functions of social welfare.* New York, NY: Vintage.

Chapter 9

Physical and Mental Health Care Policy

Physical and mental health care is one of the most basic needs that people have. It speaks to ultimate survival and quality of life. Good health is essential to a happy life and efforts to maintain health are vital. The health care industry in the United States is enormous.

Health and mental health are major areas for social welfare policy and primary employment areas for social work. Health care spending affects many other areas of government and many areas of social welfare policy. Mental illness has strong impacts on health care costs so it is important to consider the overlapping issues of both arenas of social policy.

The United States spends the most per person on health care but does not have the healthiest residents on most measures. Other OECD nations spend between $2,000 and $4,000 per year. But the United States spends two to four times that amount annually, nearly $8,000 (Sauter & Stockdale, 2012). Despite spending the most per person, the United States has the eighth lowest average life expectancy among industrialized nations.

What do the American people get for their money? Medical miracles fill our TV screens daily and many Americans live with the wonders of modern medicine. According to the World Bank, the United States spent 17.9 percent of GDP in 2012 on health care (World Bank, n.d.-a). With that amount of money expended and the talent of our medical practitioners, you would think that Americans should be the healthiest people on earth. Unfortunately that isn't the case. Americans' life expectancy is less, America's infant mortality rate is higher, and Americans die of more preventable diseases than the populations of many nations that make much more modest health care investments.

It is not completely fair to charge the health care system with these outcomes. Environmental and lifestyle factors certainly play a part. (You might expect, however, that the American health care system would make a difference in the overall results.) It is also important to note that America's health care system provides care for medical issues that other nations cannot.

It's not that America has poor quality medical facilities or that Americans are unconcerned about health. There are many reasons for the crisis in American health care. The system does not make the best use of the resources available. Many Americans do not have access to health care for a number of reasons (Adler & Rehkopf, 2008). The system stresses cure (also known as tertiary health care), not prevention. The structure is strongly privatized and the profit motive runs counter to ideas about altruism and caring. The public policies for health care are a fragmented mess, full of duplication and with important coverage gaps. The medical system is highly oriented toward tertiary care. As in many nations, environmental contamination adds to the health care burden, and the stress of the American lifestyle could be a contributing factor. Without a doubt, the health care system can do far better in terms of how it takes care of people. Part of that will be how policies are designed.

The cost of health care in the United States is a huge policy problem for the federal government, for state government, and for employers. It makes for difficult choices in the public arena. It can be a serious issue for individuals and families and there are equally difficult choices to be made. This is a very complex policy enterprise and a situation that promises more conflict as time goes by.

Health care is also an incredibly contentious political topic going back to at least the Franklin Roosevelt administration (Starr, 1995). The passage of the Medicare and Medicaid laws in 1965 continued the long-standing debate around government involvement with health care. Most recently, when the Patient Protection and Affordable Care Act (P.L. 111-148) (otherwise known as Obamacare) was introduced, the stage was set for an incredibly antagonistic debate in Congress and the media about the proper role of government. That debate continues even today. The bill was passed in 2010 but engendered a great deal of opposition, including an appeal of its constitutionality in 2012 and again in 2014. As this book is going to press, the Supreme Court announced that the Affordable Care Act was constitutional in the case of *King v. Burwell*. This is the second Supreme Court decision upholding the Act's constitutionality.

Along with physical health, this chapter addresses issues of mental health. Although there are many reasons for mental illness, research continues to find physical precursors (particularly in brain chemistry) correlated with cognitive, emotional, and behavioral maladies. This strengthens the hand of people who believe in a medical model of mental illness. Thus, the line between physical and mental health is blurring even more than before. Other people emphasize the social environment as a reason for mental illness and argue that the medical model too often ignores the larger picture of continual stress and environmental factors that affect individuals' ability to be mentally well.

WHAT IS HEALTH?

In general, there are two conflicting views of health (both physical and mental). One view sees health as the absence of disease. If you are not sick, then you are healthy. This tends to be the view of many in the medical community and leads to a system that puts curing disease ahead of preventing disease.

The other view looks at wellness—how well you are. This is the state of optimal physical and mental health. These are obviously very different ways to look at health and health care. One direction looks at disease and its cure, perhaps with some attention to prevention. The other looks at prevention first and curative approaches only when needed. These two basic positions define how the system will be defined and what policies are likely. Most health care systems fall on a continuum between these two ideal types (see Figure 9-1).

America's health care system is clearly closer to the curative model than the wellness model. This has real consequences for policy making and for the outcomes of health care. This type of health care system also costs more than a preventatively oriented health care system. Other aspects of American society have real impact on our health care system and its performance. Things such as social stress, culture, social class, environmental issues, and so forth are also important determinants of health care needs and levels of care provided.

Disease is generally divided into two types: acute and chronic. Acute diseases are short term and may be severe. Chronic diseases are long term. In some cases an acute disease can lead to a chronic condition. There is also an interplay between mental health issues and physical health. Physical problems and imbalances can lead to mental illness; mental illness often exacerbates physical distress.

Figure 9-1
Approaches to Wellness

THE HEALTH CARE SYSTEM IN THE UNITED STATES

Health care in the United States is a complex mix of governmental, nonprofit, and profit-making entities. Although there are national health care programs and policies, much of the effort is state or industry-based and many of the providers are either nonprofit or profit-making.

Some of the largest players are health insurance companies that finance much of the physical and mental health care system. Health insurance is purchased by individuals or groups (including employers) and provides a defined set of benefits for a certain level of costs. These plans are regulated by state insurance commissions.

Although the difference is often difficult to detect at the organizational level, some of these companies are Health Maintenance Organizations or HMOs that not only fund treatment but manage your health care. In general, an HMO assigns you to a primary care person, or gatekeeper, who manages your referrals for medical services and authorizes payment. This is how many managed care schemes work. Managed care can also mean capitation. Capitation means putting a cap on how much money can be spent on health care by a person in a given period. Although this idea of managed care began with HMOs it is now part of most insurance structures, including those run by the government.

Managed care can often be difficult for patients and providers. Decisions about what procedures can be approved often seem based on some other metric than the patient's best interests. This isn't always true. Not all medical care decisions are evidence-based (this is especially true for mental health interventions) and managed care can protect patients from this kind of ill-informed practice.

Some employers are self-insured, which means that they pay claims from organizational revenues. They generally use insurance companies to administer their programs. Most of these are for-profit companies but some are nonprofits. Self-insured companies are regulated by the U.S. Department of Labor unless they reside in Hawaii. They are not generally regulated by state insurance commissions.

Federal and state programs round out the funders of health care. The most important of the federal programs are Medicaid and Medicare (administered by the Department of Health and Human Services), the Veterans Administration, and the Department of Defense.

On the provider side, there is a bewildering array of possibilities. Starting at the largest level is an array of general and specialty hospitals under private, nonprofit, federal, and state auspices. Many larger cities and counties also sponsor hospitals. Some of the hospitals are for specific purposes (such as rehabilitation, neuropsychiatric treatment, and specific diseases such as coronary or respiratory care), while others are for general needs. The Veterans Administration operates a large number of facilities for veterans including 151 hospitals (U.S. Veterans Administration, 2011). Churches also sponsor hospitals. There are also a number of large, for-profit networks of hospitals.

Clinics and outpatient facilities are another level of services. These facilities include community clinics, community mental health centers, specialty outpatient treatment centers, and so forth. These are also under a range of auspices and funded by a range of entities.

Nursing homes and assisted living facilities provide services ranging from full, inpatient care to help with normal living in a familiar environment. Many of these facilities are for-profit but there are some nonprofit and governmental units.

Individual and group providers are another level of service. Many medical and dental practitioners (and not a few social workers) work on their own or in group practices. Allied health professionals have also gravitated to this type of system.

Health departments and public health efforts are aimed at the prevention and management of disease at the national, state, and local levels. This includes health education, public health preventative care (like inoculation clinics), the management of disease outbreaks and epidemics, public health inspections, and the maintenance of public health records. The U.S. Public Health Service Commissioned Corps provides medical personnel to underserved areas. In general, most of these units are operated directly by the federal government.

The health care system is large and complex. This tends to make any policy changes difficult and contentious. By and large, that summarizes America's experience with reform since 1935.

MEASURING HEALTH AND HEALTH CARE

The importance of health care and the portion of the nation's economy devoted to health care mean that monitoring the system's outcomes is important (Dobrow, Goel, & Upshur, 2004). A highly developed statistical system is available that evaluates many of the key factors.

Several indicators are important benchmarks for the health care system. The infant mortality rate is the number of children who are born, live, and die in the first year of life per 1,000 live births. Because infants are the most vulnerable part of the population, their experience is an important indicator of health care performance. Life expectancy at age one is another indicator. How long you live is an important outcome of health care and the health of the population. These are the central indicators but there are others.

Mortality is the cause of death. Was it preventable? Morbidity is the cause of an illness. These things can tell you a great deal about the health of the population. Much of these data come from a series called Vital Statistics that reports health care events. In the United States these statistics are reported by practitioners to local health departments. These are sent to state health departments and then to the National Center for Health Statistics (http://www.cdc.gov/nchs/), which is a part of the Centers for Disease Control. International statistics are available from the World Bank and the World Health Organization, which generally obtain them from national governments.

Although important, these statistics do not even begin to scratch the surface of the huge body of health care data available. There are many additional official statistics, epidemiologic studies, surveys of health-related behavior, and an entire range of studies on health care providers and institutions.

CONSEQUENCES OF HEALTH AND HEALTH CARE

The consequences of health and health care at the individual level range from situations involving minor discomfort to those whose effects are immediate, severe, and life threatening. It is difficult to overestimate how important these consequences are at the level of communities, nations, and global systems. The health of a population is critical to the function of the economic and political system, to social stability, and to national survival. It is no wonder that chemical and biological weapons are so feared in modern society.

The consequences to a nation's economy can also be relevant. An unhealthy workforce is generally not a productive workforce. Physical and mental health care interventions can improve health status and boost productivity and profitability. This is one reason that some employers are willing to fund amenities such as smoking cessation programs and provide Employee Assistance Programs, which grant easy access to counseling for personal problems.

The cost of health care can place a significant drain on the national economy and on the federal and state governments. State governments struggle to deal with the cost of caring for an aging population within the context of Medicaid. In general, care of the elderly is far more costly than the care of younger people. Inpatient care is more expensive and more prevalent among aging populations. Because other sources of funding do not always cover this care, it is left to the states to fund these needs via Medicaid. The United States, like most other developed nations, is facing the aging of its population. This means that the cost of health care will continue to rise.

Employers also face the cost of health care in both their benefits for current employees and, in many cases, retirees. This can make a company uncompetitive in a market against those opponents who reside in nations where health care is provided by public policy.

ENVIRONMENTAL ISSUES

The relationship between human health and the environment is one of the best developed bodies of research, due partly to already existing efforts within public health (Brulle & Pellow, 2006; Bullard, 2005; Hoff & McNutt, 1994, 2008; Rogge, 2000). Environmental depletion, with its relationship to poverty, is clearly a factor in the health of the population. Poverty is a driver of both poor health and inadequate health care. Poverty leads to improper nutrition, higher levels of stress, poorer housing conditions, and higher levels of exposure. The state of America's food system (Brown, 2005) is also a concern (often called food security) for a variety of reasons, many related to environmental destruction and other issues.

At the same time, environmental destruction has a direct impact on human health. Brownfields, areas despoiled by years of groundwater and soil pollution, often have immediate health consequences for local residents in terms of acute and chronic diseases. Longer term, birth defects, cancer, and other serious conditions are related to these chemicals. Air pollution can lead to respiratory diseases such as emphysema, lung cancer, and asthma. These diseases are painful and expensive to treat. Occupational exposure is also a threat with a long history of destroying the health of workers. The interaction between poverty and environmental exposure is a contribution that cannot be ignored.

Although efforts have been made to deal with these issues in developed nations, many underdeveloped nations have been the recipient of many of the same industries that have created the problems at home. This is a very difficult issue to deal with because many of the nations that are home to these activities need the economic benefits to feed their people.

Environmental problems are a substantial threat to human health (Hoff & McNutt, 2008). In order to have a healthy society, the health of the environment is crucial. This means that policies to protect the environment are especially crucial.

SOCIAL JUSTICE ISSUES

There are very few things that are more basic than the right to live a healthy life. In the United States, physical and mental health care are considered a consumer good rather than a right. This leads to situations that offend social and economic justice.

Because health care is a basic need, social justice requires everyone to have a minimal level of health care before other needs are met. In the United States, poor children go without basic primary care while medical resources are invested in treatments to reverse normal aging. Such anti-aging treatments include face lifts, wrinkle removing, and other cosmetic procedures that are not necessary to preserve health or repair disfigurement.

The distribution of health care resources in rural areas and inner cities is a problem. In a number of areas in the United States, a doctor is not available. At the same time, the supply of doctors in some areas exceeds the demand. Many developing nations lack a number of the health care resources Americans take for granted. This accounts for serious health challenges in these nations.

All of these issues lead to a situation that offends social justice. Redressing these problems is a moral imperative (Brown, Grootjans, Ritchie, Townsend, & Verrinder, 2014; Bullard, 2005).

STATISTICS ABOUT HEALTH AND HEALTH CARE

The cost of health care continues to increase every year. According to the National Center for Health Statistics (2014), health care expenditures in the United States in 2011 were about $2.7 trillion. The World Bank (n.d.-a) put U.S. health care costs in 2012 at 17.7 percent of GDP. Although health care is expensive anywhere, this is a major issue for health care in the United States. Unfortunately, the high costs don't necessarily equal the best results in the world. In fact, despite having the most expensive health care system in the world, residents of other countries often have better outcomes (Davis, Schoen, & Stremkis, 2010).

On the plus side, out of seven countries, the United States ranks first on preventive care and is also strong when examining results for specialist care and nonemergency surgical care. On the negative side, the United States ranks worst in patient safety, efficiency, and equity. Access to primary care is also relatively weak. Countries with systems that work better include the Netherlands, Australia, and the United Kingdom (Davis, Schoen, & Stremkis, 2010).

About 42 million Americans did not have coverage in 2013 (Smith & Medalia, 2014). This means that they cannot pay for expensive treatments and that they do not have regular access to a doctor or health professional. This also means that they are far less likely to get preventative care and important screening procedures. For some, the choice used to be theirs. Some young people chose to go without insurance because they were young and healthy and they felt that they could spend the money that they would pay for the employee share of health insurance for other things. The Affordable Care Act has largely eliminated that choice. For others, there is no choice. They are either in employment situations that cannot or do not offer affordable health insurance or they are self-employed and cannot afford health care. For those, there are options to extend health insurance coverage.

There is also evidence that Americans who do get care often get either the wrong care or less than complete care. In some cases accidents and illnesses reduce the quality of health care. Nosocomial illnesses (those caused by exposure to the health care system) continue to be a problem in many health care facilities and have caused or contributed to 99,000 deaths in the United States (Pollack, 2010).

When you compare the health care that Americans receive with care in other developed nations, the comparisons are not always flattering. Still, people in many nations experience far less desirable outcomes than in the United States. Medical care is nonexistent, at least for the poor, in many nations. The plight of children is especially worrisome, as child survival can be a day-to-day struggle. More than five million children under the age of five died around the globe in 2010. The most common causes are considered highly preventable: pneumonia, diarrhea, and birth complications (United Nations Children's Fund, 2012). Nations with the highest and lowest infant mortality rates are shown in Table 9-1 (Central Intelligence Agency, 2012).

The United States is ranked 174 out of 222 countries in terms of infant mortality. Monaco has less than one-third the infant death rate, but Afghanistan has over twenty times the infant mortality rate as the United States. Relatively speaking, the United States is losing ground. In 2008, it ranked 180 among all nations, which means six countries have improved their position compared to the United States in the past few years.

There are a number of issues that are illuminated by these statistics. First, there is the huge cost of medical care. Although the United States seems par-

Table 9-1

Nations with the Highest and Lowest Infant Mortality Rates 2014

Nations with the Highest Infant Mortality Rates				Nations with the Lowest Infant Mortality Rates			
Rank	Nation	Rate	Year	Rank	Nation	Rate	Year
1	Afghanistan	117.23	2014 est.	215	Iceland	3.15	2014 est.
2	Mali	104.34	2014 est.	216	Macau	3.13	2014 est.
3	Somalia	100.14	2014 est.	217	Hong Kong	2.73	2014 est.
4	Central African Republic	92.86	2014 est.	218	Czech Republic	2.63	2014 est.
5	Guinea-Bissau	90.92	2014 est.	219	Sweden	2.60	2014 est.
6	Chad	90.30	2014 est.	220	Singapore	2.53	2014 est.
7	Niger	86.27	2014 est.	221	Bermuda	2.48	2014 est.
8	Angola	79.99	2014 est.	222	Norway	2.48	2014 est.
9	Burkina Faso	76.80	2014 est.	223	Japan	2.13	2014 est.
10	Nigeria	74.09	2014 est.	224	Monaco	1.81	2014 est.

Source: CIA World Factbook (https://www.cia.gov/library/publications/the-world-factbook/rankorder/2091 rank.html). Defined as "Infant mortality rate compares the number of deaths of infants under one year old in a given year per 1,000 live births in the same year." The U.S. rate is 6.17.

ticularly troubled in this regard, the idea that health care is cheap anywhere in the developed world is a misperception. Next, there is the large number of people who lack basic access to the system because they lack health insurance. Even those who have health care may find that it doesn't cover enough. Of course, having insurance means very little if you cannot find a doctor or a hospital. All of this doesn't address the larger issue of the wellness-cure debate.

Mental health statistics paint a dark picture, too. According to the Centers for Disease Control, the prevalence rate for mental illness in the previous two weeks in the United States is about 16 percent (Centers for Disease Control, 2011). About 25 percent of Americans experienced mental illness in 2003 and half of Americans will suffer from mental illness sometime during their life (CDC, 2011). In 2002, the cost to the economy of mental illness was estimated at $300 billion.

Between 2005 and 2008, for example, 11 percent of Americans aged twelve and over took anti-depressant medication (Pratt, Brody, & Gu, 2014). This rate was 400 percent higher than during the time span 1988 to 1994. According to this same report, females are more likely to take anti-depressant medication than men, and non-Hispanic whites are more likely to use these medicines than are Mexican Americans or African Americans. Despite this high rate of use, however, only about one-third of people with severe depressive symptoms take anti-depressant medication (Pratt, Brody, & Gu, 2014).

One impact of mental illness is the exacerbation of physical illness; thus it is logical to treat both issues in one chapter. As stated by the Centers for Disease Control (2011):

> Mental illness exacerbates morbidity from the multiple chronic diseases with which it is associated, including cardiovascular disease, diabetes, obesity, asthma, epilepsy, and cancer. This increased morbidity is a result of lower use of medical care and treatment adherence for concurrent chronic diseases and higher risk for adverse health outcomes. Rates for injuries, both intentional (e.g., homicide and suicide) and unintentional (e.g., motor vehicle), are 2-6 times higher among persons with a mental illness than in the overall population. Mental illness also is associated with use of tobacco products and alcohol abuse.

Theories about the Problem

Health care and mental health care are important areas of social policy and different groups offer different explanations of how the system works and what is likely to result in effective policies.

Conservative Theories

Most conservative social welfare theorists see the market system as the key to solving the health care crisis. Health care is a commercial service like any other commercial service. The market will allocate health care resources in the most efficient way possible. They also see current third party pay systems as misallocating health care resources by removing any incentive to economize. If your insurance company is paying for that test, procedure, or service, why should you decide not to have it done? This is known as the problem of "moral hazard" whereby people are enticed to accept services that are unneeded or undeserved because the costs are borne by someone else, such as an insurance company or governmental agency. This theory operates whether it is physical health care being discussed or mental health services.

Conservatives almost always see mental illness as an individual problem. Mental illness is still sometimes seen as the result of sin or other moral, personal, or familial failure (Barusch, 2011), especially in cases of addiction or criminality.

Some conservatives see the cost of health care rising due to unnecessary litigation. They point to malpractice judgments as an example of this type of intervention and argue for tort reform to address it. Conservatives favor medical savings accounts, which provide the incentive to economize.

Liberal Theories

Liberals see health care as contributing to social well-being and consider widely available health care as a desirable outcome. Human capital theory (Becker, 1964; Pronk, 2015) argues that health care can contribute to economic development by maintaining the productive edge of the workforce. This means that an investment in health care should lead to a healthier and more productive workforce.

A liberal analysis also holds that physical and mental health care is a right and government's role is to enforce that right and provide care when other mechanisms fail to do so. This argues for health care planning and utilization review. This is designed to cover gaps in access and to prevent costly duplication of services that can drive the price of health care forward. Managed care can fit into this model if it is aimed at controlling cost rather than protecting profits. Government should, according to a liberal viewpoint, force insurance companies to cover mental health services to the same extent that they cover physical health services. This was the idea behind the National Mental Health Parity Act of 1996, although the law covers only employers with more than fifty employees and their insurance companies.

Radical Approaches

Radicals see health care as a right. They also see many of the threats to health and health care as arising from the capitalist system. Radicals see the crisis in health care as a byproduct of the profit-making system in health care. The profit motive pushes out the altruism that should guide health care. This analysis holds true for both physical and mental health policy.

The conditions that create many health problems are the result of economic activity. Dangerous working conditions and the externalities of industrial activity are responsible for many illnesses.

In the area of mental health, a position called radical therapy or radical psychiatry has emerged. This approach looks at the role of oppression in the development of mental illness. Building on the writings of Thomas Szasz (1974) and R. D. Laing (1983), radical therapists look for the roots of psychopathology in the oppression present in society. Creating mental health means consciousness raising and redressing oppressive situations. Mental health activity leads to systems change activity and therapists and patients work together to make the system less oppressive.

CURRENT POLICIES

As is true in most of the American social welfare policy enterprise, the health care policy area is a series of policies with gaps and duplication. Until 2010, the United States was one of the few developed economies without a national health insurance plan. In that year, the Affordable Care Act (dubbed "Obamacare" by opponents) was passed. This is actually two pieces of legislation: the Patient Protection and Affordable Care Act (P.L. 111-148) and the Health Care and Education Reconciliation Act of 2010 (P.L. 111-152). This law has been under legislative, legal, and judicial attack from the very beginning. Part of our health care policy framework deals with public funding of health-related activities and part deals with oversight of private health insurance. There are several issues in this policy framework that need to be discussed including who is covered, for what, and how secure that coverage is. Insurance of all types operates on the idea of spreading risk throughout a larger population. This means trying to plan a group so that the people who cost the plan money are balanced by those who do not. Groups that contain a great deal of risky people are charged a higher rate by insurance companies with the expectation that they will have to pay out more in claims. This makes it harder for people who are at risk to get insurance in the first place and their premiums are much higher.

An additional consideration is what is covered. Many insurance plans exclude certain illnesses from coverage or cover them at a very low level. This is what the parity debate is all about. Some insurers do not provide coverage for mental health services or provide very minimal coverage. Some limit coverage to psychiatrists and other physicians. This, of course, has the effect of excluding social workers and other mental health providers. Professional groups, such as the National Association of Social Workers (NASW), have tried to prevent this by introducing required content or mental health parity legislation that requires mental health care coverage. The barrier here is self-insurance plans, which are not regulated by the states. This is why federal parity legislation is so important and why the profession pushed so hard for its passage.

Public Health Care Insurance

There are three major programs to provide coverage for health care: Medicaid, Medicare, and SCHIP. Many minor programs exist and some programs aimed at other needs (like Workers' Compensation) also provide coverage.

Early in President Clinton's administration, a task force was created to study the creation of a national health care plan (see Starr, 1995). Chaired by First Lady Hillary Clinton, the commission issued a report proposing a model called managed competition. This would have replaced federal health care programs with a system of competing health maintenance organizations. This effort was halted by resistance from the health care industry and others. Hawaii had an early comprehensive health care program. In the past few years Massachusetts has begun to implement a program with some promise for covering many, if not all, of the state's population (Kline, 2008).

Medicaid

Medicaid is Title XIX of the Social Security Act. It is a partnership between the states and the federal government to provide health care for the poor. Medicaid is a means-tested program that covers many low income people, but excludes a good portion of the working poor. Medicaid is also a fantastically expensive program, costing nearly $431 billion in FY 2013 (General Accounting Office, 2014). It provides much of the care for the elderly and disabled and for long-term care.

"Medicaid is the single largest payer for mental health services in the United States and is increasingly playing a larger role in the reimbursement of substance use disorder services" (Medicaid.gov, n.d.). Medicaid, through state plans that vary from one state to the next, pays for services such as "counseling, therapy, medication management, psychiatrist's services, licensed clinical social work services, peer supports, and substance abuse treatment" (Medicaid.gov, n.d.). For recipients of Medicaid, the Early Periodic Screening Diagnosis and Treatment (EPSDT) benefit provides comprehensive mental and physical health care for children and adolescents under the age of twenty-one.

Medicaid is administered by the states under the supervision of the Department of Health and Human Services. Each state submits a plan for Medicaid and the federal government matches the state share according to a formula. Medicaid pays for both physical and mental health care. Reimbursement levels to practitioners are often low, and some professionals do not accept Medicaid.

Medicare

Medicare (http://www.medicare.gov/) is Title XVIII of the Social Security Act. Medicare covers all persons over age sixty-five and people who participate in the survivors' and disability categories of traditional Social Security. Medicare is a social insurance program and income is not a factor in determining eligibility. You become eligible for Medicare when you become eligible for other Social Security programs or when you reach age sixty-five. Medicare is a program that covers a wide swath of people but has limited benefits and a large amount of co-insurance (co-pays and deductibles). Medicare Part A is Hospitalizations, Part B is Major Medical, Part C is the Medicare Advantage program, and Part D is the Prescription Drug Program. These changed under the recently passed health care reform law.

Medicare's coverage isn't adequate for the needs of most people so consumers usually purchase some type of supplemental insurance program. In some cases that supplement is Medicaid or some other public program. Medicare is administered by the Department of Health and Human Services. Day-to-day operation is contracted to insurance companies that process claims and make determinations about what and how much to pay.

State Child Health Insurance Program (SCHIP)

This program was created in 1997 under Title XXI of the Social Security Act to cover children who are not covered by Medicaid. This program was reauthorized in 2009 by the Children's Health Insurance Program Reauthorization Act. SCHIP is a state-federal partnership. It was the single largest increase in health insurance coverage for children since Medicaid. In fiscal year 2010, more than 7.7 million children had ever been enrolled in the program (Centers for Medicare and Medicaid Services, 2011).

Management of Private Coverage

State insurance commissions regulate health insurers throughout the United States. Depending on state law, they can require private insurers to modify coverage in such a way as to address problem areas such as content and coverage. Unfortunately, many larger employers are self-insured and the federal presumption clause in the Employee Retirement Income Security Act (ERISA) puts those programs under the jurisdiction of the Department of Labor.

The Health Insurance Portability and Accountability Act (HIPAA) was passed in 1996 and it protects health care coverage for people who move from job to job. It prevents many of the problems that were experienced by job changers even after the implementation of COBRA (which allowed workers changing jobs to maintain health insurance, at their own cost) in the 1980s. Other titles were designed to protect patient privacy and the security of medical records. The Employee Retirement Income Security Act (ERISA) (P.L. 93-406) was designed to regulate and protect employee pensions. It also included a limited oversight of health care benefits, particularly those offered by self-insurance plans.

Mental health care is provided in a fragmented system that varies greatly from one state and jurisdiction to another. Private psychiatric hospitals have been a growth industry in recent years, funded largely by private insurers who prefer to authorize short stays (Barusch, 2011). Public hospitals tend to be where people with long-term care needs, such as treatment for schizophrenia, go. Barusch (2011) notes that the deinstitutionalization of people with mental illness from public hospitals during the 1970s and 1980s has led to many more mentally ill people in other institutions, such as nursing homes and jails and prisons. Mental health treatment in such institutions is often not of very high quality.

The Obama Administration and Health Care

Early in 2010 Congress passed and the president signed the Patient Protection and Affordable Care Act (P.L. 111-148) into law, fulfilling a long held goal of progressives to broaden the health insurance coverage of all Americans. This policy (commonly called Obamacare) was not what progressives had hoped for. There was no public option and many of the provisions that different groups had advocated were not included. Health care would still be controlled by private insurance companies, for example. Because of the many compromises necessary to gather enough votes to pass the bill, some thought the law was not a very large step forward. Proponents argued that it was the best bill possible at that time.

Strictly speaking the law is health insurance reform. It changes and broadens existing policies and creates new requirements and capacity. It requires all Americans to have health insurance and this has caused considerable controversy, leading to the law being challenged as unconstitutional. This legislation resembles in many ways the program developed in Massachusetts by then governor Mitt Romney (see Kline, 2008). Changes in the system mandated by the bill are phased in over a series of years with some provisions not taking effect until 2018.

Early challenges to the legislation have included vitriolic media attacks, lawsuits, and threats by the 2010 Republican majority in the House of Representatives to "repeal and replace" the policy. The Tea Party movement has advocated its repeal (Zerike, 2010).

In the early days of the program, there was a lot of misinformation about what the bill does and what it means. The charge that there were "death panels" that would prevent senior citizens from receiving care is false but the rumor seems to have its own life. Supporters of the law show that it will provide insurance coverage for millions of people who do not have their own insurance, many because they have preexisting conditions. Young adults up to the age of twenty-six may stay covered by a parent's insurance plan. Advocates also say that the legislation cuts waste by ensuring that at least 80 percent of premiums are spent on patient care. Lifetime caps on insurance payments have been eliminated, and more preventative care is included.

Mental health care is affected by these same provisions. Young adults up to age twenty-six will be eligible for mental health treatment under a parent's coverage, and insurance cannot be denied due to preexisting mental health problems.

Opponents claim the law is unconstitutional because it requires individuals to buy health insurance. The Supreme Court, however, found that it was within Congress's power to do so in *National Federation of Independent Business v. Sebelius* (132 S. Ct. 2566). They also assert that the reform law extends government reach too far into the doctor-patient relationship, creating a socialistic medical system. It is difficult to foresee how the policy will evolve over time but it represents a move forward in providing affordable health care to all.

Funding and Delivery Issues in Health Care

States receive federal funds for mental health and substance abuse treatment through block grants from the federal government and a small number of categorical funding programs. Most of these are administered by the Department of Health and Human Services. States also receive Block Grants for Child and Maternal Health, for General Health Services, for Rural Health, and other health related matters. The Social Services Block Grant also provides funding for at least some of these activities.

Nonprofit hospitals and clinics are another large pillar of the health care delivery network. The network of charity hospitals includes those run by reli-

gious organizations and by philanthropic organizations. At one time these organizations provided a great deal of charity care but this has become much more
difficult as the health care financing system changed. Some state governments
have challenged the nonprofit status of these hospitals, arguing that they do
not provide any more charity care than commercial hospitals. This would mean
that they no longer merited the tax advantages of a nonprofit entity.

The general trend is for states to deliver a small number of services directly
and to manage others through purchase of services contracting and other
means. This has created a situation where governmental mental health services
are delivered by third parties who are reimbursed by the government.

The commercial sector is a significant player in health care. Many of the insurance companies are profit-making and virtually all of the pharmaceutical manufacturing and medical equipment providers are profit-making corporations.
There are many individual commercial hospitals, clinics, and nursing homes. More
important, there are huge profit-making health care corporations that manage
chains of hospitals, nursing care facilities, assisted living centers, and so forth.

One massive group of commercial actors is private practitioners in medicine, dentistry, nursing, and social work. This group includes both sole practitioners and smaller group practices. This group is often stressed by the
managed care system with little clout to deal with the huge entities that finance
health care.

Of concern is the blurring of boundaries between the traditional three sectors. There were once sharp distinctions between public, nonprofit, and commercial organizations but there have been changes in these boundaries over
time. Nonprofits are becoming profit-making corporations and some nonprofits have commercial side ventures. Because each sector is thought to have a
specific role to play in the larger scheme of things, this blurring of the boundaries creates problems.

The role of information technology in health care is a substantial one and
growing every day. Not only does information technology operate in the area
of accounting, financial management, and clinical record keeping, but services
are beginning to emerge online. Starting with the modest investments in
telemedicine that began in the past four decades, information-technology-
based services have included online counseling and psychotherapy, health
information, and online self-help groups (Mallen,Vogel, Rochlen, & Day, 2005;
Slack, 1997). Lucas (2008) argues that these technologies could be very useful
in addressing the needs of the poor in underdeveloped nations. The lack of doctors and other types of health care professionals in many third world nations is
a serious issue.

Before leaving the funding of health care, it is important to note that most of what has been discussed in this chapter so far is in the formal sector. There is also a huge informal health care sector. This sector is made up of local helpers, self-help groups like Alcoholics Anonymous, support groups, and culturally relevant traditional helpers. The relationship with the formal health care system is sometimes complementary, occasionally hostile, but frequently nonexistent.

Gaps in Current Policies

Current physical and mental health care policy shares the assumptions of current income maintenance policy about the relationship between people and the workforce. Most health care funding is part of the occupational welfare system and is postulated on lifetime or at least long-term employment. The system still expects that you will have health insurance from your job until you retire, although the Affordable Health Care Act takes a step towards acknowledging modern realities. After retirement, you will qualify for Medicare. If poverty strikes, you have Medicaid and SCHIP. When Medicare and Medicaid were created in the mid-1960s this was still very much the case for most people. This was before the dislocations of economic restructuring in the 1970s and 1980s. A lot of people lost their health insurance during these times. Part-time and contract employment often comes without benefits and even in regular employment the escalating cost of health care makes health insurance beyond the reach of smaller employers. This fact was addressed by the Patient Protection and Affordable Care Act (Obamacare) through the use of tax credits, but does not solve the problem entirely.

As jobs move toward a theater model of employment the situation worsens. Even more people will need private coverage. This will create real problems for people with chronic illnesses or risk factors that can lead to higher costs.

Many people receive their health care from their employers, a system Titmuss (1974) described as occupational welfare. When jobs are not permanent, many employers do not provide these benefits because they do not wish to invest the funds in temporary employees.

Clearly, there isn't a good fit between the current policy framework and the changing face of employment. What is needed is coverage for all and a management and financing system that will make it affordable for both the nation and individuals.

America's current system, in most cases, makes it difficult to reimburse for preventative care. Although this is consistent with our curative model of health care, it also means that health care will continue to become more expensive. Organizations find it difficult to conduct activities that cannot be reimbursed. That means that people devote fewer resources to prevention, which also means that problems will be dealt with when they are most expensive.

The current system is very much tied to the idea of fee for service. There are strong professional norms and a professional subculture. There is also considerable concern over risk and legal liability. This culture makes it difficult to engage the informal sector and make use of those capabilities.

There is another issue that haunts America's health care system. The current system of financing health care is endangering America's global economic competitiveness. The United States competes against industries in nations with national health coverage. American products include a portion of the price that goes to pay for the manufacturer's health care coverage. It's actually cheaper to make a car in Canada and ship it over the border to the United States because the cost of health insurance paid by the manufacturer is part of the price tag of the American-built car, but not the Canadian one.

Keeping the American population healthy is an important task but the United States is not isolated from the health concerns of the world. With quick and easy air travel, health concerns in Asia and Africa can be translated to health care concerns in the United States in a matter of hours. This strongly suggests that the health of the world must be a priority.

For many reasons the current system of policies and the structure that they create is problematic. As America moves forward, a new structure must be considered.

FUTURE POLICIES

One issue is undeniable. The United States cannot continue as the only major world economy without national health insurance. The country needs a system that provides coverage for everyone. It also needs a system that makes the best use of our national physical and mental health care capabilities. This won't be politically or technically easy. Still, it has to be done if America is to move forward. Although the Obama administration's policy may not be the best of all possible worlds, it represents positive change.

The type of national coverage that the United States will eventually choose is unclear. There are many models and each has certain assets and liabilities. Canada, for example, has a single payer plan. Other nations have other models and some make use of a number of approaches.

As the nature of employment changes and people find themselves responsible for many of their own benefits, it is difficult to see how health insurance can continue the way it is now. Although some occupational groups do provide insurance pools, this is more of a stop gap approach than a viable policy instrument.

The use of technology to improve the management of health care is a movement that will not stop. Technology can help to root out waste and corruption and can add to efficiency. It can also be part of a heavy burden of reporting for health care providers so policy makers must be careful not to require more than is necessary. Some worry about the security and privacy of client records as the sophistication of computer hackers increases.

The telemedicine movement has also shown that technology can extend the range of physical and mental health care to inaccessible areas. This means both domestic underserved areas and those in other nations. Although it is still unclear what the ultimate impact of this approach is, the future looks very bright. At least some telepsychiatry interventions have excellent potential for social workers. This may be the growth job market of the next decade but one must acknowledge that legal issues are as yet unsolved in areas such as cross-state licensing requirements.

Technology has also allowed public health organizations to monitor and predict outbreaks of various diseases using tools that aggregate search engine activities. By watching who searches for various symptoms and where they are located, health care workers can predict and track potential epidemics much more quickly than with traditional techniques.

Health care policies must be preventive and wellness oriented. The United States needs to stop ignoring the state of the environment and move toward protecting itself and the world from environmental destruction. Ignoring the environment will have the dual effect of weakening the economy and destroying people's health.

Preserving the environment is a huge task that will have to be shared by many if not most of the organizations in American society. The consequences will affect people's health and will also affect their livelihoods and ultimately their survival.

CONCLUSION

America's physical and mental health care system faces a number of very serious challenges in the years going forward. Internally it faces issues of cost, coverage, effectiveness, and adequacy. Externally, the aging population, a smaller world, and a more damaged environment are issues.

There is also the problem of moving an industrial institution into the information age. Technology, new organizational forms, and an appreciation of the changing landscape can help move the system in the right direction. Health outcomes cannot be achieved through the health system alone. Managing the environment and the economy is also needed.

Questions for Discussion

1. What is the relationship between poverty, environmental damage, and health? How does this relationship change in a move from an industrial society to an information society?
2. Are more Americans uninsured because of the policy choices that American society makes?
3. How does America's physical and mental health care system affect the nation's economy?
4. Disease outbreaks in other nations can be in the United States in a matter of hours. How can people prepare?
5. Mental health care is becoming more focused on genetic and biological interventions. How will this affect social workers' involvement in providing assistance?

Exercise

1. Assume that you are a planner for your state's health agency. Make a list of the things that you expect will affect the health of the people in your state. Create a plan for dealing with these factors.

Websites

American Telemedicine Association: http://www.americantelemed.org

The Commonwealth Fund: http://www.commonwealthfund.org

HealthCare.gov: http://www.healthcare.gov/law/introduction/index.html

Kaiser Family Foundation: http://www.kff.org/

World Health Organization: http://www.who.int/en/

Visual Media

Philadelphia (1993). Directed by Jonathan Demme. The story of a lawyer fighting for a victim of the AIDS epidemic.

Further Reading

Fuchs, V. (1974). *Who shall live?* New York, NY: Basic.

Israel, A. B. (2011). *Using the law: Practical decision making in mental health*. Chicago, IL: Lyceum.

Mackelprang, R. W., & Salsgiver, R. O. (2015). *Disability: A diversity model approach in human service practice* (3rd ed.). Chicago, IL: Lyceum.

Moniz, C., & Gorin, S. (2014). *Health care policy and practice: A biopsychosocial perspective*. London, England: Routledge.

Chapter 10

Social Services for Children and Families

Care for children is one of the cornerstones of American social welfare policy. The importance of children and their families is central to many of our policy arenas. The sad reality is that for many children, the actual care that they receive is frequently inadequate and sometimes damaging. Part of our culture cherishes children while another part treats them with indifference and contempt. Similar things can be said for nations all around the world. Some nations are much better to their children than the United States. Others are much more severe. Rights for children vary widely in the United States and around the world.

Although many policies aimed at other issues have an impact on children, the children and family or child welfare system is perhaps the most direct expression of concern for children (Kadushin, 1980; Laird & Hartman, 1985). Social services are provided for a variety of human problems that are experienced by children and their families. The range of interventions is extensive and growing constantly.

All of these services are delivered within a policy context that can often be contradictory and confusing. In addition to lacking a well thought out framework for health care, the United States lacks a coherent family policy. Some of the value streams that guide policy and law conflict in serious and profound ways. This situation makes both policy making and child welfare practice a challenge and accounts for some of the negative outcomes experienced in this policy realm.

American family law evolved from the English system and defines the rights and responsibilities of children and their parents. Parental rights, once nearly absolute, have weakened though they are still substantial. They include custody, consent to military service, consent to medical treatment, and so forth. Interfering with parental rights is a serious matter but it is clear that children also have rights. The balance between the rights of the child and the rights of the parents is often difficult to navigate.

This chapter will discuss how social services are provided for children and families. It will talk about the policies that govern this practice and what gaps are present. It will also discuss implications of the societal transition to an information society on children, their families, and their communities.

WHAT ARE SOCIAL SERVICES FOR CHILDREN AND FAMILIES?

Most social workers are very familiar with child welfare as a policy field. It is one of the core areas of human services practice where state governments try to balance the rights of parents with the rights of children. Decisions about whether to remove children for their own safety due to allegations of abuse or neglect or leave them with their family are not at all easy to make. But it is incorrect not to recognize the context within which issues of child welfare are intertwined with the issue of parental functioning and the family living situation. The vast majority (81 percent) of child abuse and neglect perpetrators are the mother and/or father (Children's Bureau, 2011, p. 76), so clearly services to families belong within the same frame as children's services. Discussing these two areas of policy in the same chapter keeps the link between children and their families.

According to Kahn and Kammerman (1976), defining social services is an uncertain business, but they focus on "those public and private-sector benefits, goods, services, entitlements and policies which are informed by other than market concerns and which are not included in the categories of income maintenance, health, housing, education and employment" (p. 7). Included in this arena, then, are services such as child welfare, family services, community and protective services for the elderly, homemaker and home assistance programs, residential programs for youth and people with disabilities, and so on. This chapter focuses on the sub-sector of social services aimed at children and families, including the senior population, which have the goal of keeping families together or people safely in their own homes, when that is possible. This chapter also looks at the alternative services available when it is not possible.

Provision of and financing for this group of services are frequently separated, with federal, state, and local governments often paying for services that are contracted out to private entities, both for-profit and nonprofit, to conduct. The major federal funding for social services comes from Social Services Block Grants (Title XX of the Social Security Act). Only states, the District of Columbia, and territories may apply for these funds directly; these governmental bodies then pass the funds to localities or directly to service providers. In FY 2012, $1.7 billion was allocated to states and territories (Administration for Children and Families, 2012b). These funds may be used for services that include but are not limited to the following:

daycare for children or adults, protective services for children or adults, special services to persons with disabilities, adoption, case management, health-related services, transportation, foster care for children or adults, substance abuse, housing, home-delivered meals, independent/transitional living, employment services or any other social services found necessary by the State for its population (Administration for Children and Families, 2012a).

Many other programs exist as well, paid for by individuals and by insurance companies. In all, this is a large sector of services, one that is difficult to capture.

HOW IS THE NEED FOR SOCIAL SERVICES MEASURED?

Each state and territory that receives Social Services Block Grants is required to have a plan to use the funding. The process for deciding how to spend the funds is left up to the state so that it can best serve the recipients of services. State authorities may delegate the decision of how to spend the funding on county or local jurisdictions. Oftentimes, community assessments are conducted to determine which needs are most pressing. These are frequently conducted at the city or county level, rather than at the state level, to ascertain which problems are most pressing. State governments, however, do determine the budgets for state programs such as Child and Adult Protective Services.

Social indicators are frequently used to determine the extent of social service needs. For example, the rate of child abuse helps policy makers understand the extent of that problem. Other social indicators include infant mortality, Food Stamp coverage, and poverty among single parent families.

An ideal social indicator is a statistic that is timely, has a fixed and frequent reporting schedule, gives a sense of direction (better or worse), and informs a routinized intervention (Miringoff & Opdycke, 2008). Unfortunately, many social indicators do not meet these criteria, particularly that of timeliness, because of the difficulties of conceptualization and collection of adequate measures.

THE CHILDREN AND FAMILY SERVICES SYSTEM

The child and family service system in the United States is a complex system that has developed and evolved over almost two centuries. It is one of the oldest social services systems in the United States and one that is intimately involved with the development of social work as a profession. As the system evolved, public views of children have also changed from the sense that children were the property of adults to the feeling that they were very important and perhaps even central to our culture. Laws to protect animals predated laws to protect children. Our legal system has evolved to address these changing understandings but often seems unable to keep up.

Structure and Dynamics

America's current system is often called a mixed economy of care. It consists of a robust public system and a fairly large nonprofit system. There is a growing for-profit system, mostly in the areas of day care and institutional care. Much of the funding comes from state and federal sources, although a growing amount comes from insurance payments.

Privatization has had a major impact on children and family services. Many of the services that were once delivered by public agencies are now delivered by nonprofit organizations via purchase of services contracting (Collins-Camargo, McBeath, & Ensign, 2011; Smith & Lipsky, 1995) and funding under Medicaid and other health insurance programs. This has important implications for the way that services are delivered and evaluated. In theory, privatization could make services more efficient. Competition could bring out the best in all service providers. In practice there have been quite a few problems with this arrangement.

The children and family services system touches the edges of many other systems. It interacts regularly with education, law enforcement, health and mental health, income maintenance, and housing. It is also a regular contact to juvenile, family, and probate courts.

The child and family services system serves children and families who for whatever reason are not providing adequate care to their children. This can be due to abandonment, neglect, abuse, or some other condition that prevents adequate care. Child abuse can be physical, emotional, or sexual. There is often a fine line between child abuse and child neglect, a fact that has caused some to use the term "child maltreatment" as an alternative to the phrase "child abuse and child neglect." It is worth mentioning that the criminal justice system also has jurisdiction here as many of the issues dealt with by child and family service workers could also constitute criminal activity.

In general, the system delivers care to children and their families in their homes and communities. If that isn't possible, children can be moved to tem-

A Real Birmingham Family sculpture by artist Gillian Wearing in Birmingham, UK. The statue portrays an actual family demonstrating the variety of family forms. This sits on the green in front of Birmingham's Public Library.

porary or permanent situations elsewhere (Barth, Lee, Wildfire, & Guo, 2006). The system has a number of major components divided into those efforts aimed at keeping the child in the home and those that place children elsewhere.

In-Home Care

In-home care is the first category of child and family services. Removing people from their home is an eventuality to be avoided if possible. Preventative services work to retain people in their homes if that can be done in a safe and secure manner. There are four types of services that address preserving the family or individuals in their home. They target different populations but have that common goal. The first, Child Protective Services, aims to keep families together in the long run when there are allegations of child maltreatment. Second, homemaking services assist people with disabilities and the elderly with tasks of life that may be too difficult but for whom institutionalization is an extreme solution. Third, day care and respite care are designed to allow caretakers a break from their duties and also to let persons being cared for have an alternative place to go or person to care for them. Finally, there are other prevention programs, such as Adult Protective Services, which seek to provide safety and alternatives to institutionalization.

Child Protective Services (CPS)

The lynchpin of the children and family services system is child protective services. Child protective services units investigate reports of child abuse and neglect/child maltreatment (Cicchetti & Toth, 2005) and, if the report is substantiated, provide the appropriate intervention. Such interventions might include providing supportive services, making referrals, monitoring the situation, providing case management, and removing the child. In many cases, families are overwhelmed by the stresses that they encounter (Hopps, Pinderhughes, & Shankar, 1995).

Every state has a mandatory child abuse reporting law that helps to identify potential cases of abuse and neglect. A large number of professional groups (such as doctors, teachers. social workers, nurses, etc.) must report cases of suspected child abuse or neglect. Anyone can be a permissive reporter, that is, report on a voluntary basis. State laws often shield people who make reports from liability if the report is made in good faith. These reports are cataloged in a central registry so that if the family moves outside the jurisdiction of the local agency, the information will be available to child welfare workers in other areas. Still, just because people are mandated to report child abuse doesn't mean that all maltreatment is actually reported. Because child maltreatment often happens in private, this should not be surprising.

The report is investigated by a CPS worker, who interviews the family and collects evidence. How quickly this is done depends on the urgency in the report and may be influenced by the workload of the agency. If the child is in immediate danger, the child can be removed and placed in emergency care. This usually requires the involvement of the court system. The final report is posted to both state and national registries. According to the United States Department of Health and Human Services (DHHS) (2010), about 3.3 million reports were received in 2009, involving over six million individual children. The estimated cost of child abuse was $124 billion in 2008 (Fang, Brown, Florence, & Mercy, 2012). See Table 10-1.

Table 10-1
Reports of Child Abuse in the United States

Data Type	2008	2009	2010	2011	2012
Number	2,967,024	2,978,956	2,960,292	3,019,610	2,770,403
Rate per 1,000	41	41	39	41	41

Source: Kidscount Data Center: http://datacenter.kidscount.org/data/tables/6220-children-who
-are-subject-to-an-investigated-report?loc=1&loct=2#detailed/1/any/false/868,867,133,38,35/
any/12940,12955.

Many protective services situations are handled through monitoring and referral. This means that the case worker (who very often is not a professionally trained social worker) monitors the situation and makes visits and conducts office interviews. Some cases require more intensive effort and in some cases the children are removed either temporarily or permanently. In many cases, supplemental services are provided to help support the family and prevent removal of the child.

There are a number of issues with protective services. Many of the people who are delivering services are inexperienced, undertrained, and under considerable stress (American Federation of State, County, and Municipal Employees, 1998; U.S. General Accounting Office, 2003). In some areas they carry higher than recommended caseloads. Many workers are supervised by people without professional social work training. The burnout and turnover rates can be high.

From a policy standpoint, some of this is due to a lack of adequate funding for the entire system and some is due to civil service regulations that do not require a professional social work degree. There are also difficulties in recruiting trained people for many public child welfare positions.

Another issue is that there is often no clear mandate to act in a child maltreatment situation. American society has considerable ambivalence about dealing with child welfare situations. This ambivalence is reflected in the policy framework, often giving the social worker a conflicting set of expectations. Nonetheless, current policy reflects the desire to reunify the child with family members, particularly parents.

Homemaking Services

These services are designed to help people who have trouble accomplishing daily tasks around the home (shopping, cooking, securing non-medical transportation, cleaning up the house, and doing laundry, for example) but are otherwise in good physical and mental health. Without such services, it is possible that institutionalization would be the only other option. It is often much more cost-effective to pay for a few hours of home aide assistance per week than it is to place someone in a residential setting.

Although homemaking services are frequently thought of as primarily for seniors, such assistance can be important for families where parents fall ill and children need to be cared for, or for people of any age with handicapping conditions. In order to qualify for government assistance, potential residents must generally meet low-income guidelines. Usually, a case worker makes an assessment of the individual's needs and arranges for private organizations (for-profit or nonprofit) to supply the assistance. People with sufficient means can purchase these same services through the open market.

There are many clever and creative programs that can support fragile families and prevent children from being removed unnecessarily. Homebuilders, a program in Seattle, Washington, that has been diffused to other places, is a good example. Among the supportive services that Homebuilders provides are live-in caseworkers who can provide around the clock treatment. Schorr (1997) provides a nice discussion of some of these innovative services.

Day and Respite Care

Day care often means settings for preschool aged children. Parents use day care (either in their own home or in the community) as a way to have their children safely cared for while the parent works. After-school care is important for older children who would otherwise come home to an empty house. This situation is so common as to have its own term: latchkey children. The number of latchkey children has grown considerably. One estimate is that there were six million such children in 2006 (Children's Defense Fund, 2006). This type of day care has become essential for two-career couples and single-parent families.

Day care is an important resource in supporting families and protecting children. There are a number of types of day care and a wide variety of providers. Demand for day care is often considerably above day care capacity. Special day care is available for special needs children. Related services, such as early childhood and compensatory education programs, like Head Start, are also important interventions. Although there is some public day care, most is provided by nonprofits or the private sector. Standards are set and enforced by state agencies.

The need for day and respite care frequently is felt by family members (caregivers) who take care of relatives with chronic problems, such as Alzheimer's disease (for senior citizens) or emotional issues for children and youth. Respite care is also available for foster families, kinship care providers, and adoptive parents.

Caregiver stress is a combination of physical, emotional, and psychological exhaustion caused by the unending responsibilities to be alert, prevent problems, and assure the safety of the person needing care. No matter how much love one has for the affected family member, constant stress can lead to negative impacts on the provider of care, and may lead to fatigue, anxiety attacks, or even depression. This problem, also called burnout, may, in extreme cases, lead the caregiver to harm the person being cared for.

Between 2001 and 2009, approximately 5 percent of all children and youth aged four to seventeen years in the United States were said by a parent to suffer from serious emotional or behavioral difficulties. More boys (7 percent) were labeled this way than girls (4 percent) in 2009 (Federal Interagency Forum on Child and Family Statistics, 2011a). These children may place a heavy emotional burden on their caregivers. A group of people that overlaps with children with emotional and behavioral difficulties includes people with autism spectrum disorders. The prevalence of this group is estimated by the Centers for Disease Control (CDC) to be increasing among children in the United States. In 2000, the CDC estimated that one out of every 150 children had this condition. By 2008, the estimate was up to one out of every eighty-eight children who suffered from an autism spectrum disorder (Centers for Disease Control, 2012). Because these children's primary symptoms are significant social and communication problems, as well as potentially dangerous behaviors, caregivers must be vigilant at all times, in trying circumstances. This level of stress can be relieved to some extent by day or respite care for the children.

Day or respite care is similar to homemaking services in the way it is provided. There are some government-run programs (particularly for state-run foster care, adoption, and kinship care situations) but the majority of services are provided by the private sector (nonprofit or for-profit).

Other Services

The variety of services available to help people stay in their own homes is quite large, including both social and medical services. Parent training, budgeting help, and many other possible services to help families cope with the stresses of modern life can be included here as well. One might stretch the definition of "other services" to include mortgage loan mitigation services (reducing the amount of interest someone must pay on their home loan) which help keep people in their homes. One program that is more mainstream as an example of prevention services is Adult Protective Services (APS), which is analogous to Children Protective Services but for vulnerable adults, including the elderly and persons with disabilities.

APS workers investigate allegations of abuse and neglect, as well as exploitation of people who live in the community. Once a report is received, workers have a limited amount of time (which varies by state) to begin an investigation. The ultimate purpose of APS is to end abuse, neglect, and exploitation. Services can include financial assistance, social services, medical services, and referrals to other agencies for services (governmental and private).

Substitute Care

Although the goal of the system is usually to maintain people in their homes, whether they are children, the elderly, people with disabilities, or some other category, doing so is not always possible. Thus there is a second component of the child and family services universe. It includes foster family care, group care, institution care, adoption, and emancipation.

If children or adults are removed from their family in order to prevent abuse, neglect, or exploitation, involvement of the court system is necessary. In the case of child maltreatment allegations, some parents voluntarily relinquish their children, but most are removed from the parent's custody legally by Children's Protective Services. Hearings are generally held in a juvenile or family court to determine temporary or permanent custody. The legal theory that operates in these types of proceedings is *parens patriae,* which means that the state is the ultimate parent of all of its citizens. This is also the legal theory behind mental health commitments and juvenile justice. In essence the court acts in place of the parent and renders a judgment based on what is in the "best interest" of the child. There is similar reasoning behind the state stepping in to protect vulnerable elderly people or people with disabilities by bringing to bear Adult Protective Services investigators who sometimes must determine that continuing to live with relatives puts their clients at considerable risk.

Parents have a range of parental rights under American law and these can only be interfered with for due cause. Parental rights include custody (where the child lives), consent to medical treatment, military service, marriage, and so forth. Even if custody is given to the state, the parent retains the other parental rights. Parents also have a number of duties that include support, adequate care, and so forth.

Sometimes the situation is reversed and it is the child or children who are in charge of their parent's affairs, or siblings sometimes have legal custody of a person with disabilities. If this is true, then the allegedly victimized person is protected by being removed from the abusive, neglectful, or exploitative situation.

State law normally controls how these decisions are made, what criteria are employed, and so forth. These are considered domestic relations issues and are within the constitutional jurisdiction of state government. Federal courts can and have acted in custody issues where there is a federal issue or a constitutional issue involved. Every state has different laws and different procedures. There have been efforts to standardize procedures between states and not all have met with complete success.

In general, the state provides evidence to support why the child or adult should be removed. Rules of evidence govern what can be presented. Both the parent and the child are usually represented by an attorney and the state may be represented as well. The client's lawyer is called a *guardian ad litem*. This means guardian at law.

Legal decisions concerning a child's removal from home are made at a bench trial (no jury), which is held in private. Although witnesses are called and documents examined, very few people are actually involved in the process. Proceedings are confidential and closed to outsiders. Records are also usually confidential.

The court will rule on whether a client needs to be placed in state custody or returned home, and may set conditions for either. If the state retains custody, care can be arranged with a foster family, a group home or institution, or an adoptive family, in the case of a child, or in a nursing home or other care facility for adults. In some cases the state may ask for termination of custodial rights. This means that the court will end the relationship between a child and their parent. This is a serious step and one that is usually permanent.

These proceedings put the case worker in a very difficult position. America, as a society, believes in protecting children and vulnerable adults. It also believes in keeping families together. Policies are written to reflect both of these conflicting ideals. The outcome is often a conflict between policies, which puts the worker in the middle. At the same time, decision-makers (judges, prosecutors, lawyers, etc.) feel these conflicting values as well. This means that it is often hard to get clear decisions and public support.

Foster Family Care

Foster family care is the most used method of providing alternative care for children when they cannot be left with their parents. This type of service places children with a family that will care for them until a more permanent situation can be arranged. Foster families are recruited and trained by local agencies and children are placed for a period of time (see Alpert, 2005; Hochman, Hochman, & Miller, 2004). While the child is in foster care the social worker works with the family to solve any problems that prevent the child from being returned home. This very much assumes that the worker will have the time to do this and the training and skill to make it happen.

Foster family care was a response to institutionalization and the child care institution system for orphans. Originally, foster family care was considered a short-term solution. Unfortunately, this did not prove to be true and children began to stay in the foster care system. At times, this resulted in a series of foster homes and led to what was referred to as foster care drift. This phenomenon caused attachment disorders and psychosocial difficulties. The Permanency Planning movement of the 1970s and 1980s aimed at moving children into their own homes, adoption, or long-term foster care. In the late 1970s and early 1980s permanency began to be a major issue in child welfare policy. This principle has been supported in both federal and state policy. Sadly, many children grow up in foster care in spite of efforts to the contrary.

Kinship care means placing a child with a relative. This has become a popular way to meet the needs of children who require placement. Relatives who provide care help keep family members bonded and save funding for the system.

Institutional and Group Placement

Group homes are an alternative to foster family care, particularly for older children. They are generally run by paid staff and may be in a house or other facility. Some group homes specialize in children with specific disorders or problems.

Child care institutions were once called orphanages and represented the type of care that all dependent children received. Their role has changed dramatically in recent decades. Child caring institutions are mostly for dealing with children with serious behavioral problems. Many child caring institutions have evolved into long-term psychiatric hospitals for children. Child care institutions are very costly so children with minor issues are usually treated elsewhere.

Adoption

Adoption essentially means transferring parental rights to another parent. In order for this to happen, the original parents' rights must be terminated. Sometimes this is voluntary but in other cases it is not. The adoption procedure involves placement in an adoptive home and a testing out period to determine if the placement is successful. Before a child is placed in a potential adoptee's home, a home evaluation is conducted. In uncontested adoptions (where the parent voluntarily relinquishes rights to the child), the process may not involve a social agency. When the adoption is concluded, the adoptive parent is granted full parental rights. Early in America's history, adoption was considered when the parents died. The children then became orphans and adoption was the key to finding a stable home.

Some children are difficult to adopt. Children with disabilities, older children, minority children, and children from large families require additional effort to adopt. This may include additional outreach or relaxation of criteria for adoptive homes. Policies exist to subsidize such adoptions. This may include health care and financial supports.

International adoptions are generally handled by private organizations. They largely involve parents adopting children from overseas. Many of the procedures are the same as in domestic adoptions although the legal issues are more complex. There are some considerations of fairness and oppression here as children from poorer nations are adopted by American parents who do not share their culture or heritage. Some nations are beginning to restrict this type of adoption.

Although each state has jurisdiction over people living in their own state, a system called the Interstate Compact allows transfer of children in care between states. States occasionally work together on cases. Family law is primarily a state matter, although there are federal issues.

Emancipation

Older children can be emancipated by order of the court. Emancipation means that a child is declared an adult without having to reach the age of majority. This is usually done within the context of a service plan.

The current system is underfunded and many of the workers assigned to deal with families in crisis lack any real professional training. The legal framework is complex and confusing and mandates are unclear. The mixed economy of care makes the system unnecessarily complex. In many respects, it is surprising that the system performs as well as it does.

MEASURING SUCCESS IN CHILD AND FAMILY SERVICES

What would a good society expect for its children? The National Conference of State Legislatures (2005, p. 2), following the Children's Bureau, set out three criteria: safety, permanence, and child and family well-being.

Safety generally means being free from threats to physical, mental, and social health. There are fairly good statistics on infant mortality and child death. Child injury is less well documented.

Permanence means that the child will have a stable living environment. This should be true for children in care but also true of the general population of children.

Well-being means high levels of social functioning in both the family and child. Well-being is a difficult quantity to define but might include good health, adequate income, educational opportunity, and a stable and healthy family situation.

Although these criteria seem both reasonable and clear, they represent a tall order for many state social service systems. When you take these criteria to the global level, they seem unattainable in many of the poorer societies of the world.

THE GLOBAL CONTEXT

Some nations are much more generous to their children than the United States. Others are clearly not. The U.N. Convention on the Rights of the Child released a set of standards in 1959 called the Declaration of the Rights of the Child (United Nations Children's Fund, n.d.). It sets out a comprehensive listing of principles designed to ensure minimum rights for children (see Figure 10-1). The United States has not ratified the declaration.

Although many children in underdeveloped nations suffer from poverty and hunger, there are many new evils that must be dealt with. Conflict, including civil wars and other forms of warfare, affects the lives of children. Particularly troubling is the use of children as child soldiers. Trafficking in children is another major problem. Children are sold either as laborers or as sex workers. Diasporas are another negative situation requiring children and their families to move from their homeland to other areas to escape persecution.

Figure 10-1

Selected Articles from the UN Convention on the Rights of the Child

Article   1: A child is a person below the age of 18.

Article   3: All adults should do what is best for children.

Article   4: Governments have a responsibility to take all available measures to make sure children's rights are respected, protected, and fulfilled.

Article   5: Governments have the responsibility to protect and assist families in fulfilling their essential role as nurturers of children.

Article   6: Children have the right to live.

Article   9: Children have the right to live with their parent(s), unless it is bad for them.

Article 12: Children have the right to say what they think should happen and have their opinions taken into account.

Article 14: Children have the right to think and believe what they want and to practice their religion, as long as they are not stopping other people from enjoying their rights. Parents should help guide their children in these matters.

Article 15: Children have the right to meet together and to join groups and organizations, as long as it does not stop other people from enjoying their rights

Article 16: Children have a right to privacy.

Article 17: Children have the right to get information that is important to their health and well-being.

Article 18: Both parents share responsibility for bringing up their children, and should always consider what is best for each child.

Article 19: Children have the right to be protected from being hurt and mistreated, physically or mentally.

Article 22: Children have the right to special protection and help if they are refugees (if they have been forced to leave their home and live in another country).

Article 23: Children who have any kind of disability have the right to special care and support . . . so that they can live full and independent lives.

Article 24: Children have the right to good quality health care.

Article 26: Children—either through their guardians or directly—have the right to help from the government if they are poor or in need.

Article 27: Children have the right to a standard of living that is good enough to meet their physical and mental needs.

Article 28: All children have the right to a primary education, which should be free.

Article 30: Minority or indigenous children have the right to learn about and practice their own culture, language, and religion.

Article 31: Children have the right to relax and play, and to join in a wide range of cultural, artistic, and other recreational activities.

Article 32: The government should protect children from work that is dangerous or might harm their health or their education.

Article 36: Children should be protected from any activity that takes advantage of them or could harm their welfare and development.

Article 37: No one is allowed to punish children in a cruel or harmful way.

Article 38: Governments must do everything they can to protect and care for children affected by war. Children under 15 should not be forced or recruited to take part in a war or join the armed forces.

Article 39: Children who have been neglected, abused, or exploited should receive special help to physically and psychologically recover and reintegrate into society.

Article 40: Children who are accused of breaking the law have the right to legal help and fair treatment in a justice system that respects their rights

Source: United Nations Children's Fund (UNICEF). (n.d.). A summary of the rights under the Convention on the Rights of the Child. Fact Sheet. Retrieved from http://www.unicef.org/crc/files/Rights_overview.pdf.

CONSEQUENCES

It is often said that children are our future. If that is true, it's difficult to foresee anything but the direst consequences if American society fails to take care of its children in a way that will support their growth and development. Some of the consequences of failing to provide for the care of America's children and their families are:

- Higher rates of mental illness, substance abuse, and mental disability
- Family violence (Tolan, Gorman-Smith, & Henry, 2006)
- Lower economic productivity and a stalled economy
- Wasted human potential
- Higher crime rates and rates of violent and destructive behavior
- Lower levels of educational achievement

It is clearly in the interest of American society to do what it can to have healthy families that can provide the best possible care for children.

As society changes, at least some of these impacts will accelerate. The stress of economic dislocation and change can lead to additional stress on caretakers. It can also diminish the community support networks that these parents need.

ENVIRONMENTAL ISSUES IN CHILDREN AND FAMILY SERVICES

Children are exceptionally vulnerable to the impacts of environmental depletion and destruction (see Garbarino, 1992). Developing bodies are fragile and exposure to noxious substances can often lead to lifelong issues.

Air and water pollution can lead to asthma, birth defects, cancer, and a host of other illnesses. Resource depletion leads to poverty which in turn limits possibilities and causes additional social stress. The latter can lead to family violence, neglect, and other threats to children. Children in poorer nations suffer even more from the effects of climate change and environmental destruction. These perils interact with poverty, creating profound impacts that magnify the effects of any of the factors individually.

SOCIAL JUSTICE IMPLICATIONS

Children require a healthy and nurturing environment in order to survive and develop. They also require a safe environment and continuity of relationships with caregivers. These are basic needs. The fact than many children lack these basic needs creates a problem for the realization of a just society.

This is especially true of the children from groups that have been disenfranchised, disempowered, and marginalized. Children who are mentally and physically challenged; children who are gay, lesbian, bisexual, or transgendered; and children whose parents are undocumented people are at a greater risk. No matter which population children belong to, they are a vulnerable group in society. A just society would assure their health and safety. In some cases American society does just that. In others, it does not provide that guarantee. Justice requires that every child receive the same basic guarantees.

STATISTICS

According to the Federal Interagency Forum on Child and Family Statistics (2011b), there were about 75.6 million people in the United States under the age of eighteen in 2010. Most had little to do with the child welfare or family services systems.

Abuse and Neglect

In 2012, there were an estimated 603,854 substantiated reports of children being abused or neglected out of a total of 2,770,403 reports. Thus, about 21 percent of all reported cases of maltreatment were substantiated by state child welfare workers (KidsCount, 2015). States reported that 1,537 children died as the result of abuse in 2010 (Children's Bureau, 2011, p. 58).

Foster Care and Adoption

In 2009, 397,091 children were in foster care, which represented a decrease of over 62,737 from the 459,828 in foster care in 2008 (KidsCount, 2015). Not quite half (49 percent) of the children in the child welfare system in 2009 had the goal of reunification with their families. Of the children who left the system in 2009, 51 percent were reunited with their parents. One fourth of the children had a goal of adoption, and 20 percent reached that goal in 2009 (Children's Welfare Information Gateway, 2011).

THEORIES ABOUT THE PROBLEM

Theories about the proper care of children and the support of families abound. They differ along many dimensions and reflect deeply held ideas about the role of the state and the role of families. A rigorous review of these theories goes beyond the purposes here, but some general themes are important for policy making.

Conservative Theories

Conservative theories tend to look for causes in individual and family functioning. Early psychiatrically based theories (see Besharov, 1990; Bowlby, 1969; Cicchetti & Toth, 2005; Laird & Hartman, 1985) stress these internal causality issues. Later theories stress more psychosocial causation, but the focus is still on the individual and the family. This puts the responsibility clearly on the parent and absolves the system of any responsibility. This type of approach dictates a policy that provides treatment for parents and children. Those who object to state action except in a limited frame will also object to intervention by the state in family and child relationships. This has become a more noticeable group as the so-called culture war continues, pitting conservatives who wish to use government power to uphold traditional views of families against others who have more tolerant views. Although this might seem like a new wrinkle, Platt (1969) speculates that changing children's values was one of the motivations of the "child savers."

Liberal Theories

Liberal theories tend to look at social factors that lead to family breakdown, while not ignoring psychological issues. Gil (1973) for example, looks at social stress as a causative factor in child maltreatment. Economic stress is clearly important here and some of the family violence literature establishes a relationship between stress of unemployment, economic instability, and so forth on the one hand, and violence and abuse on the other.

The ecological models of Garbarino (1995) and others also use more complex social models to explain abuse and neglect. These models look at community, neighborhood, and network contributions to child maltreatment and family breakdown.

Radical Theories

Radical theories argue that child welfare is merely a way of enforcing upper class norms and controlling the "dangerous classes." Platt (1969) argued that the juvenile court and the "child savers" were a mechanism to protect children from learning the culture of their parents. This paints child welfare as an agent of social control rather than a means of helping families in crisis. Abramovitz (1988) argues that the welfare system regulates women's choices and enforces a patriarchal society.

CURRENT POLICIES

Like other areas, the policy framework for children and family services is a complex tangle of federal, state, and local policies that vary greatly from one area to another (see Kammerman & Kahn, 2014; Maluccio & Anderson, 2000; Stein, 1998; Whittaker & Maluccio, 2002). This is one of the few areas where state policy is of primary importance. Most child and family services systems are operated either completely by the state government or in collaboration with county and municipal government. The laws they operate within are a combination of state policy and the family law that is created by the legislature (statutory law) and by the courts (adjudicatory law). Much of the latter comes from common law, which is part of the legal tradition that America inherited from England. There is also the influence of Chancellery Law and, in some cases, parts of criminal and civil law.

Federal Legislation

Most of our current child and family services policies at the federal level are in some way related to the two major child welfare sections, Title IV-B and Title IV-E of the Social Security Act (Children's Welfare Information Gateway, 2011). Also important are the block grant programs, particularly the Social Services Block Grant.

This is an area where there is a consistent stream of legislative work. Not only is there dedicated child welfare legislation, but statutes from education, health, substance abuse, and so forth have a direct and immediate impact on child and family services. Some of the most significant legislation is discussed below.

The Child Abuse Prevention and Treatment Act (CAPTA) (P.L. 93-247) was passed in 1974. This was a landmark piece of legislation because it revolutionized the child abuse and neglect function. The recognition of child abuse was long in coming and few dealt with it in academic settings or in professional leadership. CAPTA made child abuse a national priority. CAPTA also provides funding for a range of infrastructure for state social services departments. This law has been reauthorized and amended multiple times.

The Indian Child Welfare Act (P.L. 95-608) was enacted in 1978. Because Indian tribal areas are jurisdictionally different from the states, this law began to define how services could be delivered to Native American families. Several years later P.L. 96-272, the Adoption Assistance and Child Welfare Act of 1980, had a similar effect on foster care and adoption. This legislation provided support for permanency efforts for children. It supported foster care review, adoption assistance, and other ways to make children's situations permanent.

These three pieces of legislation began the framework that defined child and family services policy for more than the past three decades and the foreseeable future. Subsequent legislation offered significant improvements to the framework (Child Welfare Information Gateway, 2011).

There have been a number of pieces of legislation that modified the policies created in the 1970s and 1980s (Child Welfare Information Gateway, 2011). The Multiethnic Placement Act (P.L. 103-382) was passed in 1994 and the Adoption and Safe Families Act (P.L. 105-89) was created in 1997. The Intercountry Adoption Act (P.L. 106-279) was passed in 2000. The most recent legislation includes the Keeping Children and Families Safe Act of 2003 (P.L. 108-36), the Adoption Promotion Act of 2003 (P.L. 108-145), the Fair Access Foster Care Act of 2005 (P.L. 109-113), the Adam Walsh Child Protection and Safety Act of 2006 (P.L.109-248), the Child and Family Services Improvement Act of 2006 (P.L. 109-288), Fostering Connections to Success and Increasing Adoptions Act of 2008 (P.L. 110-351), and the Child and Family Services Improvement and Innovation Act of 2011 (112-34). Recent health legislation, such as the Patient Protection and Affordable Care Act, is also important to children. The Children's Bureau Law and Policy site (http://www.acf.hhs.gov/programs/cb/laws_policies/index.htm) provides excellent resources for examining the current path of legislation.

Public policy for children, like most of the American policy enterprise, is in constant flux. Major changes will be needed in the near future. It remains to be seen if America's political system is up to the task.

CHANGING REALITIES AND CHILD AND FAMILY SERVICES

The children and family services system was created to protect children and promote stable and healthy families in a time of industrialization. Families were strained by the forces of social, political, and economic change. The family form changed from the extended family that characterized agrarian times to the nuclear family that was needed for industrial organization. The scheme that developed was guided by an understanding of that new system and what was expected of families in the new industrial order. The system developed with a strong dose of psychiatry and an overlay of mental health ideology.

Families today are encountering new realities and are experiencing stresses that this system is not designed to address. The level of uncertainty that families feel in the new economy promises to set in motion a process that will easily overwhelm the slim resources of the children and family services. For many of the past few years, unemployment rates have been historically high, leading to financial stress on individuals and families. Economic dislocations since the beginning of the transition to an information economy have created major problems for workers, their families, and their communities. These dislocations have created immediate child welfare crisis situations and long-term erosion of resources.

The fabric that supports families and their children has been frayed. Economic, technological, and social forces have made these support networks inadequate to the task of supporting families, especially troubled families. This is a situation that also existed at the beginning of the industrial revolution. Societal transitions affect individuals, families, and communities. Children ultimately pay the price for these dislocations.

In the long run, society will evolve new support systems. These systems will again support families and communities. In the meantime, the social services system will have to address these dislocations in proactive and creative ways. Solutions for this issue will involve rebuilding communities around family concerns. This will require community-building and the development of stronger social networks. Most of the important work being done in this area is part of community development efforts. Individual approaches will be ineffective without a long-term support system that the troubled family can be grafted into. You might want to consider this like the medical treatment of wounds. If there is enough surrounding healthy tissue, the treatment is straightforward. If not, highly sophisticated efforts are needed.

Technology, particularly social media, provides excellent tools for building networks and relationships. These tools can be helpful in regrowing community. Children are also growing up differently. The influence of media, technology, and other forms of communication has almost certainly altered the coming generation's view of the world. They are more diverse and accepting of diversity, more global in their outlook, and more team-oriented than previous generations (Howe & Strauss, 2000; Zukin, et al., 2006). On balance, new issues such

as cyberbullying and online predators make technology a potentially dangerous place for children.

Rebuilding communities and creating additional support networks
are problems to be addressed. Another problem is revising the system of children and family social services to incorporate more evidence-based practices
(Gambrill, 1999). This is a system under pressure. Caseloads could skyrocket and
easily outstrip not only the capacity of the public sector but the potential capacity of both the nonprofit and commercial sectors. Trying to address the situation
that faces families and communities today with individual interventions is not
going to work. More comprehensive approaches are needed. An individualistic approach cannot address the changes in the economy and the workplace
and will not solve any of the underlying issues, including environmental degradation that is occurring in many places. Because America lacks a comprehensive
family policy, agencies cannot even deal holistically with families, much less
communities.

Previous chapters have shown that the fit between the policy framework
that was created during the industrial period and the current realities of an
emerging information economy is far from perfect. This is equally evident in
the area of services to children and families. A system that can respond to current and future changes is clearly needed.

ADVOCATING FOR CHILDREN

The child advocacy movement in the United States has a long and distinguished
history of advocating for children's issues (DeVita & Mosher-Williams, 2001).
These advocates have included national organizations, such as the Children's
Defense Fund, the Children's Partnership, and the Child Welfare League of America, supported by national foundations like the Annie E. Casey Foundation
(Annie E. Casey Foundation, 2012). Though most children's policy is made at
the state level, there are national networks of state-level child advocates such
as the Kids Count network, sponsored by the Annie E. Casey Foundation. These
organizations use lobbying, community organization, research, and other advocacy techniques to keep children's issues visible among a forest of other needs.

REVISITING CHILDREN AND FAMILY SERVICES

Creating a system that makes sense will depend on the creation of a comprehensive policy network to support individuals and families in the new economy. Developing comprehensive income support and national health care

policies will go a long way toward ensuring the well-being of children and their families.

Although children and family services have moved away from the psychiatry-based model of early child welfare, they still have a pointedly individualistic orientation and rarely look at communities. This obsessively individualistic vision is certainly not consistent with current views, but the model needs to move further. This is a needed shift of perspective and paradigm. Healthy families do not grow in unhealthy communities. Healthy communities do not thrive on an ecosystem that is destroyed, depleted, and damaged. Trying to solve the problems of unhealthy families within an unhealthy context with one-to-one interventions is unlikely to work.

This is a case where social services need to develop a more developmental view. Building sustainable communities that children and families can thrive in is the goal of this type of approach. This will require rethinking the social work practice and policy framework (Price, 2005).

CONCLUSION

Children are vitally important to the future of society, and the state of their care provides a bellwether to the way social policy is working. There is a long way to go in developing and refining some aspects of social policy.

Children face the considerable issues of negotiating both childhood and adolescence. In addition, societal transition combined with environmental destruction and the political winds of change create an increasingly threatening situation for children in the United States and throughout the world. America needs the political will to make this situation right. It will take creativity, commitment, and a substantial investment of public funds. Rebuilding the system will be a massive task and one that will take years to accomplish. It has to be done.

Questions for Discussion

1. What aspects of the children and family services system seem to work the best? Which sections are the most challenged? What explains the differences?

2. How would a comprehensive family policy help children and family services?

3. If you could redesign the children and family services system, how would you do it?

4. What forces will be most likely to promote change in child welfare? Which groups will be most likely to resist change?

5. Assume that nothing is done to reinvent children and family services. What would be the worst case situation that would develop? What about the best case outcome?

Exercise

1. Design the ideal community to support children's health and development. How will you handle the economy, the government, housing, and other community systems? After you have designed this ideal community, compare it with the community that you live in. How are they different?

Websites

Child Welfare League of America: http://www.cwla.org/

Children's Defense Fund: http://www.childrensdefense.org/

Federal Interagency Forum on Child and Family Statistics: http://www.childstats.gov

UNICEF: http://www.unicef.org/index.php

Further Reading

Bogenschneider, K. (2002). *Family policy matters: How policymaking affects families and what professionals can do.* Mahwah, NJ: Erlbaum.

Bok, D. (2011). *The politics of happiness: What government can learn from the new research on well-being.* Princeton, NJ: Princeton University Press.

Downs, S., Moore, E., McFadden, E., & Costin. L. (2008). *Child welfare and family services: Policies and practice* (8th ed.). New York, NY: Pearson.

Garbarino, J. (1992). *Toward a sustainable society.* Chicago, IL: Noble.

Platt, A. (1969). *The child savers: The invention of delinquency.* Chicago, IL: University of Chicago Press.

Schorr, L. B. (1997). *Common purpose: Strengthening families and neighborhoods to rebuild America.* New York, NY: Anchor.

Chapter 11

Crime and Violence in an Information Society

Crime and violence are serious issues in any advanced society. They speak to a breakdown of social control, order, and social relationships. Historically, crime and corrections have been one of the major interests of social welfare since the Industrial Revolution (Gumz, 2004). As society evolves, crime changes in important ways. These new challenges require a new policy response from the criminal justice system. This chapter looks at the structure and dynamics of the criminal justice system, examines its policy environment, and considers the changes made necessary by the shift to an information society.

Every society needs social control because the social order depends upon it. Although there are other means of enforcing social expectations, the criminal justice system is often considered the method of last resort. The overall responsibilities of the criminal justice system are broader than that. In areas where other services are unavailable or ineffective, the criminal justice system comes in to solve the problem. It has a broad mandate that encompasses almost any situation that can occur. Still, one should acknowledge that the criminal justice system is better at some things than others and that no system can address all the needs of society.

This chapter will discuss crime, corrections, and violence from a policy perspective. It will examine the system as a whole and the policies that guide and govern these arenas.

WHAT IS CRIME?

A crime is usually defined as a violation of the criminal code. This makes the criminal code one of the most important policy statements available to the criminal justice system. Without a criminal law, there is no crime. Societies can agree that something is wrong from a moral standpoint but still not involve criminal behavior because there is not a law against it.

Legal scholars usually divide crime into *mal in se* crimes (those that are bad in and of themselves) and *mal in prohibita* crimes (those that are bad because they are prohibited). Most people would agree that murder is a bad act and so are theft, assault, and kidnapping. On balance, not everyone agrees that certain banned drugs ought to be illegal.

Many of the *mal in se* crimes are part of the common law, which America inherited from England. Common law was created by judges who rendered opinions on the cases that came before them. Judges still do this today. Law that is created by judges is called adjudicatory law. Although pundits occasionally charge that unelected judges have no authority to "make their own laws," the process of adjudicatory law is many hundreds of years old and was well known to the drafters of the constitution. All of the *mal in prohibita* crimes and many of the *mal in se* crimes are created by legislatures. These are called statutory law. America's law, both civil and criminal, is created by the combination of statutory and adjudicatory law.

Civil law and criminal law are different systems of justice. In the civil system, wrongs are called torts and the system pits a plaintiff against a defendant. In the criminal system, wrongs are crimes and the defendant is charged by the state. You can attract the attention of both systems with a single act. If I hit you I have committed a crime and can be arrested. You can also sue me for damages because the act of hitting you is also a tort.

Juvenile justice is different in many ways. It has elements of both civil and criminal systems. Instead of being arrested, you are detained. The emphasis in the juvenile system is on rehabilitation rather than punishment. Juveniles have special courts (either juvenile or family courts) and the proceedings are confidential. There is usually a limit to how long a juvenile can be incarcerated.

Some crimes are clearly more serious than others. Different levels of severity are generally defined by the penalty imposed. The highest level crimes are felonies. These are serious crimes that involve a sentence of over a year and usually involve some loss of other civil rights. Capital crimes, those that can involve the death penalty, are felonies and are usually homicides with special circumstances. Of lesser weight are misdemeanors, which can still involve jail time but only a year or less. The lowest level crimes are violations, which usually involve a fine.

The criminal code provides the basic policy framework for the criminal justice system. Other policies are also influential in how the work of criminal justice is conducted.

THE CRIMINAL JUSTICE SYSTEM

The criminal justice system is generally thought to have three parts: law enforcement, the court system, and corrections. These are, of course, interconnected activities and, in practice, it is often difficult to see the divisions. They also involve a number of jurisdictions and layers of government. There are relationships with the schools, mental health, and other systems. Unlike some nations, the United States has a highly complex system. This becomes more complex as additional governments are involved.

Law Enforcement

The law enforcement subsystem consists of different levels of law enforcement and the prosecuting attorney. They are charged with investigating crime, apprehending offenders, collecting evidence, and charging the defendant. They also decide who is charged and what charges are to be brought. Police agencies have jurisdiction over geographic areas. In some cases, more than one organization has jurisdiction. Specialized law enforcement deals with issues like drugs, terrorism, immigration violations, and counterfeiting. When the police learn about criminal activity, it is recorded and assigned to be investigated. In some cases the most likely suspect is obvious and some turn themselves in to police. A great many crimes are never solved. Law enforcement agencies have limited staffs and a limited amount of resources so they tend to concentrate on crimes where there is a possibility of solution.

When the investigation leads to a suspect, evidence is gathered and if there is sufficient evidence, an arrest is made. The prosecutor makes the decision whether or not to charge the suspect. In some cases, the defendant is diverted from prosecution by either the police or prosecutor. This might be for treatment or for deferred prosecution. Deferred prosecution means that the case is suspended for a period of time with a condition. The condition might be good behavior or some type of treatment. If the condition is met the case is dismissed and there is no conviction on the person's record. If the condition is not met the prosecutor is usually free to pursue the original prosecution.

Law enforcement personnel, especially at the local level, must cultivate a relationship with the communities they serve and protect. In recent history, this has proved to be problematic in some communities. Events in Ferguson, Missouri, and New York City have created friction between police agencies and members of minority groups. This is in no one's interest. Building and nurturing positive relationships is critical to effective law enforcement and community safety.

The Court System

The court system determines guilt or innocence of the defendant. There are several levels of courts that deal with different types of criminal activity. If the case is a misdemeanor or a violation, a lower court will hear the case. This will usually be a bench trial with only a judge. In some cases, it can be a jury trial. Felonies are heard in upper court but must first be heard by the grand jury. The grand jury determines if there is enough evidence for a trial. If not, jury members issue a "no bill." If yes, they issue a "true bill" and the defendant is indicted. Sometimes prosecutors take the case to the grand jury before the defendant is arrested. In cases like this the arrest is made on the basis of the indictment.

An arraignment is held to inform the defendant of the charges and obtain a plea. There may be separate hearings for bail and other matters. There are also discovery motions and hearings to determine the available evidence. In all but the highest profile cases, significant efforts are made to settle the case with a negotiated plea or plea bargain. A trial is held if a negotiated plea is not possible. In some cases these are jury trials; in others there are bench trials, which are heard only by a judge. In the case of a jury trial, a jury is selected from a jury pool called by the court. The process for selecting a jury is called a *voir dire*. Each lawyer is able to challenge a certain number of potential jurors. Jury selection, especially in high profile cases, has become a highly sophisticated undertaking that often involves social science consultants who study how potential jurors might vote.

The trial is held when all the preliminary issues are disposed with. Some trials take a day or even an hour. Others go on for many weeks. There are rules of evidence that determine what kind of information can be used and rules of procedure that determine how arguments and evidence can be presented. The judge arbitrates between the parties and enforces the rules. In the end, it is the jury that makes the decision based on the idea of proof beyond a reasonable doubt. This means that the state (which has the burden of proof) has to prove something to the point that reasonable doubt is eliminated. Proof beyond a reasonable doubt is the highest standard in America's court system. Other standards, such as clear and convincing evidence (used in many child welfare hearings) and preponderance of evidence (used in civil hearing), require less proof. Juries can find someone guilty or not guilty. In some cases, a jury cannot make a decision and the judge is forced to declare a mistrial.

If the defendant is convicted and does not plan to appeal, the correctional system begins to come into play. A probation officer typically conducts a presentencing investigation and makes recommendations to the judge. Probation is a suspended sentence based on conditions. In general, conditions include good behavior, compliance with supervision, no additional arrests, and so forth.

The sentencing phase of the trial is when punishment is imposed. Judges have a wide variety of potential sentences. In recent years, sentencing guidelines and mandatory sentencing laws have reduced the discretion that judges have, but sentencing is far from completely prescribed. The judge will take note of the presentencing investigation, the victim impact report, and any witnesses or documents the defendant might offer to support mitigation. In many courts, victims have the right to speak. The judge usually determines sentencing, but in a few instances (as in death penalty cases), the jury determines the punishment. Juries occasionally recommend sentences as well.

Corrections System

After being tried and sentenced, the offender becomes a client of the correctional system (Clear, Cole, & Reisig, 2008). Correctional systems pursue a number of goals (Fox, 1972). Deterrence (the prevention of future crime) is one goal. There are two types of deterrence: specific deterrence and general deterrence. Specific deterrence means deterring the offender from committing the crime again. General deterrence means deterring others from committing the crime. Another goal is incapacitation, which means preventing the offender from doing it again. A third goal is rehabilitation, which means improving the offender so that he or she will no longer see crime as acceptable. Restitution means making the victim whole again. Punishment is certainly another goal. A more controversial goal is revenge. Some feel that it is appropriate for society to seek revenge against those who have done wrong.

The major correctional programs are probation, incarceration, community-based corrections (including parole), and aftercare. The dividing line between these interventions is often thin, but there are specific rationales for each type of programming intervention.

Probation is one possibility for many non-violent crimes (Abadinsky, 2014b; Gibbons & Rosecrance, 2005; McCafferty & Travis, 2014). Probation is a suspended sentence based on good behavior. This means that the sentence is rendered but isn't imposed and if the offender successfully completes the time on probation then the jail time is unnecessary. On the other hand, if the conditions of probation are violated then the time on probation doesn't count. The probationer is usually supervised by a probation officer who enforces the conditions of probation. Probation supervision varies widely in scope and intervention.

Some offenders are sentenced to residential facilities and programs such as work release, restitution, and so forth. Sometimes the options are combined. Incarceration in a county jail is another possibility for certain offenders.

Incarceration and Institutional Corrections

If the case is a felony the offender can be committed to the Department of Corrections. This can mean prison or one of the other alternatives created by the agency. The decisions are generally made by the correctional administration and they involve classification and placement of the offender. Classification is the process of evaluating offenders and determining how they can be treated in the correctional system. Offenders normally go to a diagnostic and reception unit and, after classification, are sent to a facility consistent with their diag-

Cell block from Philadelphia's Eastern Penitentiary. This was the first true reformatory when it was built by the Quakers in the early 1800s. It was closed in 1971 and is now a museum.

nosis. The size of the correctional system often determines how many options are available, but the options generally include the following:

- Maximum Security: This is the highest level of custody and security. These are usually walled prisons and are reserved for dangerous and violent offenders. There is extensive supervision of offenders. These prisons often have constant surveillance of every aspect of an inmate's life. A special type of maximum security prison is designed for very dangerous offenders and is referred to as a supermax prison.

- Medium Security: This level represents middle security and custody and is generally reserved for nonviolent offenders. These are usually prisons with a wall or fence and lighter security than maximum security institutions. Most medium security programs are more committed to inmate programming than maximum security institutions.

- Minimum Security: These are prisons for nonviolent offenders who require little in the way of security and custody and who have low potential for escape. Many of these inmates are white collar criminals and others who present little threat to the public. Some of these facilities look more like college campuses than prisons and may have work and study release programs for inmates. Although they are frequently disparaged as country clubs for prisoners, they are actual prisons and living conditions can be harsh.

There are also specialized prisons for certain kinds of offenders, such as women (see Harm, 1992), youthful offenders, and offenders with psychiatric or medical problems. Some prisoners are allowed to do their time in county or regional jails. Jails are intended to be for holding defendants and recently sentenced offenders. Most have some facilities for correctional treatment, but that is often limited. Prison overcrowding and mandatory jail sentences for some misdemeanors have placed considerable stress on jails as facilities.

The majority of prisons are run by state or federal governments. Jails are run by local governments in most states. Some of the smaller states contract with larger states for some of their correctional needs. A newer wrinkle is private correctional care (see Shapiro, 2011; Wright, 2010). What this means is that private organizations take over the operation of correctional institutions and programming. This is, in many ways, a return to earlier days when corrections was managed as a "for-profit" enterprise. At one time in American history, auctions were held for the care of prisoners.

Inmates can be released from prison in several ways. They can complete their sentence. This is often called maximum expiration and it is rare for most inmates to reach that point. Many receive a shorter sentence because of incentive "good time" plans.

Community-based Corrections

Community-based corrections refers to "a non-incarcerative sanction in which offenders serve all or a portion of their sentence in the community" (Leone, McCarthy, & McCarthy, Jr., 2007, p. 3). They have a goal of repairing the damage caused by the criminal action and offer a milder way of having the offender "pay back to society" for the harm done. Different means of community-based corrections exist, including residential programs in halfway houses, economic sanctions (such as fines), and nonresidential approaches (including probation, parole, house arrest, and electronic monitoring (Leone, McCarthy, & McCarthy, Jr., 2007).

Parole is the most common form of community-based corrections. Parole means serving time in the community and is typically granted by a parole board based on the inmate's progress in prison. Unlike probation, time on parole actually counts as part of the inmate's sentence (Abadinsky, 2014a, 2014b). Time on probation is lost if the inmate does not complete probation. The same office may handle both probation and parole but the underlying legal dynamics are far from the same. There are different systems for conditional release including work and study release, furloughs, and leaves.

Aftercare

Even after people are released from supervision, their convictions will haunt them in many ways. In most states, you lose your right to vote, your right to carry a handgun, your ability to receive a professional license (sometimes a driver's license as well), and other rights as a consequence of conviction. For some types of crimes, there are other restrictions and reporting requirements, such as those for sex offenders. Some of these rights can be returned but others cannot. These are collectively called the disabilities of a conviction.

Most correctional systems offer inmates job training and placement, counseling, and other services as part of aftercare programs. These are often difficult to distinguish from other programming and are designed to work with probation, parole, and conditional release. The reentry population (as ex-prisoners are sometimes known) is at high risk for reoffending and other social problems, such as poverty, health issues (including contracting HIV/AIDS), and substance abuse.

Many programs designed to treat these problems are created by nonprofits, such as the John Howard Society (a Canadian organization that seeks to provide ex-prisoners with needed assistance). There are also many faith-based organizations in this group. The faith community has always had an interest in criminal justice.

Although there is certainly at least some coordination at the case level, the criminal justice system is far from an organized whole. Given the large number of public and private entities involved, this is hardly a surprise. Attempts have been made to promote system-wide coordination, but the issue of getting units to work together still continues.

THE JUVENILE SYSTEM

The juvenile system is different from the adult justice system in many important ways (Siegel & Welch, 2010). The principal goal is rehabilitation, not punishment. The system is separate from regular criminal processing and deliberations are done in private with records that are difficult (although not impossible) to examine. The juvenile system operates on the principle of *parens patriae*, which means that the country is the ultimate parent to all children and serves to protect them when parents do not. This is also the legal theory behind mental health commitments and other actions. The courts are juvenile or family courts, not criminal courts. The juvenile system evolved in the late 1800s (first in Chicago) and social workers were part of its founding (Abrams & Curran, 2000). Originally, the system operated in the same fashion for both adults and children. Children were jailed and even executed. Social reformers objected to this situation and eventually new procedures were developed.

In a juvenile system, terminology is different. Juvenile offenders are detained, not arrested, and are adjudicated, not tried. Some categories of juvenile offenders are called status offenders. A status offense is one that can be committed only by a child (like truancy or running away). Juvenile sentences generally expire when the offender turns twenty-one. This limits the severity of the sentence and offenders usually serve their sentences in a training school or other facility rather than a prison or jail. There is often a fine line between juvenile justice and child welfare in dealing with status offenders.

In the case of very serious crimes the state can attempt to try the juvenile as an adult. In many cases this is called certification. A hearing is held and the state argues that the crime is such that the status of juvenile offender is not appropriate. If the judge agrees, the case is transferred to adult court. The juvenile loses the advantages of a juvenile court trial.

The juvenile trial is generally more informal than a criminal court trial. The rules of evidence are followed and children have an attorney to represent them. If a trial is held and the offender is adjudicated, the judge has a wide range of possible dispositions. These include probation, group home or foster care placement, or institutional care. The juvenile system is less formal than the adult justice system and, in the past, was much less formal. In the 1960s and 1970s the Supreme Court asserted a larger set of rights for juvenile defendants beginning with *in re: Galt*, 387 U.S. 1 (1967). Procedures became more formalized and the system began to resemble a criminal trial.

In many ways, the juvenile justice system reflects the same questions that plague the adult system. These questions will become ever more haunting as the information age progresses.

MEASURING THE CRIMINAL JUSTICE SYSTEM

The criminal justice system seeks to control crime and the fear of crime. The most popular measure of criminal activity is "crime known to the police." This is reported crime and may or may not reflect the actual amount of criminal activity. Some crimes, like murder, are almost always reported while others, like rape, are less often reported. These statistics are generally reported as Part I Crimes (which are more serious) and Part II Crimes (which are less serious).

The Justice Department also conducts victimization studies, which help gauge how accurate the crime rate statistics are. For much of the criminal justice system, caseload statistics are important. How many people are processed by each part of the system and what were the outcomes for them?

Box 11-1

Part I Offenses

Criminal homicide
Forcible rape
Robbery
Aggravated assault
Burglary (breaking or entering)
Larceny-theft (except motor vehicle theft)
Motor vehicle theft
Arson

Source: Federal Bureau of Investigation 2004, https://www2.fbi.gov/ucr/cius_04/appendices/appendix_02.html.

One statistic that has been very troubling is the incarceration rate. This is the portion of the population that is imprisoned (prisoners per 100,000 in population). The United States rate is the highest in the world, and is over four times the world average. The United States also imprisons the most women in the world (National Council on Crime and Delinquency, 2006).

The U.S. rate is substantially higher than all developed nations and raises significant social justice questions. It also raises questions about resource use and the costs of incarceration. When people are incarcerated, they produce little or nothing, and the cost to the state is substantial. This situation also has long-term implications for families and for the life chances of offenders. The incarceration rate is higher for African Americans.

Recidivism is another commonly used measurement. Recidivism means rearrest and conviction after an initial conviction. This is a controversial measure of criminal justice system performance but it is frequently used by many stakeholders. Law enforcement authorities often look at previous offenders first when a new crime is committed. Although this is certainly understandable, it puts prior offenders at greater risk.

For other parts of the criminal justice system there are other metrics. Prosecutors often tout their conviction rates. Conviction rates are convictions as a portion of defendants tried. Although some might argue that this is an incentive to excessive plea bargaining, it is seen as a useful measure of prosecutor performance.

"Crimes cleared by arrest" is a measurement of police performance. This is the number of crimes where someone is arrested as opposed to the number of total crimes reported to the police.

These measures leave a lot to be desired as overall evaluations of evidence-based policy in criminal justice. In the past few decades, policy makers have been adding victimization and fear of crime studies to the mix (see Lauritsen, 2010). Because crime is a very political issue in advanced societies, the creation of agreed upon measures is frequently difficult.

Consequences

Crime and violence have a number of serious consequences. There are the physical costs of crime in terms of injury and death. These can be substantial at the societal level and devastating at the individual level. A recent editorial in the *New York Times* noted that the average cost of a single murder was $17.5 million (Blow, 2010).

There are the psychological costs of trauma and victimization. A criminal act can scar the victim for a lifetime, and the person may never feel whole again. The fear of crime is also an important dimension here. Fear of crime limits people's lives and their options. There are also the economic costs of crime, which include health care costs from violent crime, increased insurance costs, and costs from theft, vandalism, and other crime. The cost of lost productivity as well as the material costs of crime add to the total price tag of crime. In addition to the costs of crime, there are the costs of law enforcement, the legal system, and corrections. These are also substantial in terms of economic costs. Then there are the costs to society in terms of what people have to do to comply with the criminal justice system. The development of a surveillance regime always raises issues of personal liberties and rights. Technology has evolved to the point where that is a substantial concern (Lohr, 2011). The opportunity costs (opportunity costs consider the alternative use of resources) for criminal justice activities are another consequence. Much of the cost of criminal justice is borne by state and local governments that must make tough choices between criminal justice expenditures and those for education, health care, and child welfare. The cost for offenders can also be substantial. Stigma can survive long after offenders have served their time. The costs of being criminal offenders also accrue to their families and their communities. Crime is a serious problem in American society and one that affects most subgroups. The consequences are often substantial.

Relationship to Environmental Issues

The environment seems like an unlikely participant in crime, until you dig deeper. Certainly, there is environmental crime. This is usually a civil and regulatory matter but criminal litigation is possible as well. Some environmental offenses involve white collar crime, and some involve global institutions and multinational corporations (see White, 2010).

The tie between poverty and environmental destruction and between poverty and crime is hard to ignore. As environmental destruction increases the economic pressure for criminal activity also increases. This can lead to criminal activity.

Another horrific dimension is the potential relationship between chemical pollution and criminality. Can chemical pollutants cause brain dysfunction leading to crime? It is entirely possible and chemical combinations may lead to unknown behavioral and biochemical reactions.

Social Justice Implications

The criminal justice system is almost a perfect mirror of the social justice problems of American society. If you are poor or a member of an oppressed group you are more likely to be both a victim of crime and a person arrested for a crime. You are also more likely to be incarcerated and less likely to be granted a community sentence. You are also much more likely to receive the death penalty. Your life chances upon release from prison are also substantially less (Wakefield & Uggen, 2010). This means that the system is far less fair for you.

STATISTICS

The statistics on American crime tell two stories. The first is that criminal acts (violent and nonviolent) occur in large numbers. The second, however, is that the crime rate is falling and the raw number of crimes has decreased in the last decade (see Table 11-1).

According to the Federal Bureau of Investigation (2014), in 2013 there were 1,163,146 violent crimes reported in the United States, for a reported crime rate (per 100,000) of 367.9. This total number of reported violent crimes is made up of 14,827 murders and nonnegligent manslaughters, 79,770 forcible rapes, 345,031 robberies, and 724,149 aggravated assaults (Federal Bureau of Investigation, 2014). It should be remembered that the number of crimes reported

Table 11-1

Reported Violent and Nonviolent Crime, 2001–2010

Year	Violent Crime Cases	Violent Crime Rate	Property Crime Cases	Property Crime Rate
2001	1,439,480	504.5	10,437,189	3,658.1
2002	1,423,677	494.4	10,455,277	3,630.6
2003	1,383,676	475.8	10,442,862	3,591.2
2004	1,360,088	463.2	10,319,386	3,514.1
2005	1,390,745	469.0	10,174,754	3,431.5
2006	1,418,043	473.6	9,983,568	3,334.5
2007	1,408,337	466.9	9,843,481	3,263.5
2008	1,392,629	457.5	9,775,149	3,211.5
2009	1,325,896	431.9	9,337,060	3,041.3
2010	1,246,248	403.6	9,082,887	2,941.9

Source: FBI Uniform Crime Reports

can differ greatly from the number of crimes actually committed. Although murders tend to be accurately reported, the figures on rapes (for example) are not as accurate because many rapes go unreported.

More property crimes are reported than violent crimes, and rates are higher. In 2013, a total of 8,632,512 property crimes were reported. This includes 1,928,465 burglaries, 6,004,453 larceny-theft cases, and 699,594 motor vehicle thefts (Federal Bureau of Investigation, 2014).

Although these are large numbers of both violent and property crimes, and each exacts a toll on the victims, crime rates have declined greatly in the first part of the twenty-first century. The violent crime rate in 2001, for example, was 504.5 per 100,000 people. This had declined to 469.0 in 2005, and continued to decrease to 403.6 in 2010. A decrease of 100 violent crimes per 100,000 population is significant improvement. These results are not due to population growth as the actual number of crimes reported declined, even as population in the United States continued to grow. Similar declines exist in other nations ("The Curious Case," 2013).

A similar story can be told regarding property crimes. In 2001, 10,437,189 property crimes were reported, for a rate of 3,658.1 per 100,000 people. Property crime reports reduced to 10,174,754, with a 3,431.5 rate in 2005. By 2010, reported property crimes fell to 9,082,887, with a rate of 2,941.9 per 100,000 people in the country.

No definitive reasons for this decline have been proven and some accounts indicate that declines in major crimes over the decade were "baffling" ("The Curious Case," 2013; Oppel, 2011; Von Drehle, 2010). Police chiefs credit better police work. Demographers say it reflects an aging population, less likely or able to commit crime. One economist speculates that an increased rate of abortions plays a part in lowering crime rates. An increasing number of people in prison has also been mentioned as a possible reason (Von Drehle, 2010). Although a definitive conclusion may not be fully available, there are theories about what causes the problem, just as there are in other social policy arenas.

THEORIES ABOUT THE PROBLEM

Why do people commit crimes? The discipline that studies crime causation is called criminology (Siegel, 2008). There are many theories about why people commit crime and each leads to a different type of conclusion about what policy is likely to be effective.

Conservative Theories

Conservative theories tend to stress individual responsibility, deterrence, and retribution as themes. Crime is seen as the product of greed and character flaws. Classical criminology stressed the idea of cost and benefits. Utility theory led to the Principle of Less Eligibility, which argued that prisons will deter criminals only if the prison conditions are harsher than the lot of the worst off free person. Also within this group are people who believe that there are born criminals. Early theorists like Caesar Lombroso felt that there were born criminals who could be identified by their physical characteristics. This approach evolved into somatotype (body type) theory and finally to genetic approaches that seek to establish a genetic marker for criminality. Many psychiatric theories of criminality also fit here because they stress individual causation. Conservative theories tend to favor deterrence, punishment, and individual change solutions.

Liberal Theories

Liberal theories look at environmental causation in addition to individual characteristics. Shaw and McKay (1969) argued that social disorganization and the breakdown of norms lead to crime. Cloward and Ohlin (1960) explained delinquency as a response to blocked pathways to legitimate achievement. There are legitimate avenues to the good things of society. When those are blocked by poverty, discrimination, and other means, people will take illegitimate avenues. Labeling theory (Shur, 1973) is another approach that emphasizes environmental causation, as does Cohen's (1955) subculture theory. In this approach, people are labeled by the system and they adapt their behavior to live up to the label. They become criminals because others label them that way. Liberal theories lend themselves to environmental change programs.

Radical Theories

There are two major themes in radical theories about crime. One theme looks at the criminal justice system as a way to oppress the poor and groups of people that society wants to exclude. There is ample evidence of the use of police to deal with political radicals and even legitimate political leaders. Some of the scholarship in this area looks at how activities like drug use, abortion, and other matters are criminalized. The social reality of crime and law fit here (Quinney, 1970). The other major theme is that crime is actually a revolutionary activity that strikes a blow for humanity. This set of theories leads to community/social action strategies and policy change strategies.

As noted in other areas earlier in this book, current theories are heavily invested in the industrial economy and the assumptions of industrial society. It remains to be seen what post-industrial theories of crime and crime control look like.

CRIME IN AN INFORMATION SOCIETY

Changing social systems alter the criminal justice arena as well as the nature of crime. A good deal of criminal activity won't change. Human nature is resilient in both its positive and negative aspects. There will still be street crime, interpersonal violence, and organized corruption. Those existed in other eras and it is unlikely that they will go away. Increased levels of stress and insecurity are likely to make these problems worse. On balance, the information society creates new opportunities for crime (Wall, 2007).

Identity theft and similar crimes have certainly expanded with the digital age. Access to information technology makes people tempting targets for technology savvy thieves. These crimes have always existed and there are actually better tools to combat them today than ever before (Von Drehle, 2010). Hacking of databases and websites for criminal or political reasons is still a threat to individuals, companies, organizations, and nations, as much sensitive information is now stored on computer servers.

The combination of technology and globalization has created the opportunity for new and serious criminal threats. These include international criminal organizations, terrorism, trafficking, and cyberattacks (see Deibert, 2013). Although some of these are not new, the growth of technology makes them a growing concern.

There have always been international criminal organizations. The growth of technology has made the barriers to entry for potential new criminal organizations far lower. Although law enforcement and intelligence organizations have gotten much more sophisticated in dealing with these issues, there are still new and continuing threats. Similar issues exist with regard to terrorism, which is both a national security and law enforcement issue. Organizations like Al Qaeda make significant use of technology to plan and organize their operations. Domestic terrorists also use the Internet to organize and plan activities and recruit new members.

International crime is increasingly becoming a problem that our justice system must deal with on a daily basis. There are some garden variety crimes that have developed international dimensions and there are others that have emerged recently. One of the more serious issues is trafficking, particularly in women and children (Lehti & Aromaa, 2007; Logan, Walker, & Hunt, 2009; Weitzer, 2014). Although slavery is certainly not new, the growth of technology, globalization, and other forces has made this age-old scourge an even more serious problem. A concurrent problem, the international trafficking in human organs, is also a serious issue. There is a worldwide effort to deal with trafficking, but the work is complex and success represents the expenditure of substantial time and resources.

CURRENT POLICIES

Unlike other areas of social welfare policy, the criminal justice system is responsible for a wide range of laws. Criminal law is a huge amalgamation of federal, state, and local laws, as well as a set of treaties and regulations on the statutory side. On the adjudicatory side, it is even more complex, reflecting a host of court decisions. In addition to the criminal law and criminal procedure, a wide variety of policies affect how programs are funded and managed.

Criminal justice is influenced by jurisdiction so it is for the most part a state and local matter. Federal agencies enforce federal criminal law and consult with state and local agencies. There are also federal officers who deal with international issues. There are, of course, times that all levels of government have concurrent jurisdiction. This is an important issue in the legalization of marijuana because, irrespective of state laws, possession of the drug is a violation of the federal Controlled Substances Act.

State and local courts have original jurisdiction over most criminal issues. Federal courts intervene if there is a federal issue or disparity of jurisdictions. Federal courts have original jurisdiction over federal law.

Correctional policy is generally made by the state correctional agencies, the Federal Bureau of Prisons, and, in the case of local corrections, local government. Much of what the federal system does at the local and state level is to provide financial support and expertise. Federal agencies provide statistical and planning support, training, and other types of consultation.

One of the major issues in understanding criminal justice is the problem of interpretation. Although it may seem easy to decide the outcomes of most cases, much research exists that shows that there are sentencing disparities, particularly that African Americans and members of other minority groups receive longer sentences than whites for the same crime. This disparity has been exacerbated by changes in sentencing law and policy, according to the Sentencing Project (n.d.-b). Racial and ethnic minority members make up more than 60 percent of the people in prison. The war on drugs has disproportionally caused imprisonment for people of color (Sentencing Project, n.d.-a).

Once banned in the United States (prior to *Gregg v. Georgia, 428 U.S. 153)*, capital punishment is allowed in thirty-four states (as of January, 2015), and 1,414 people were executed in the United States between 1976 and 2013 (Death Penalty Information Center, 2015). There are a number of studies that show that the death penalty is much more likely to be applied when the murder victim is white rather than black (Death Penalty Information Center, 2012). The federal system also allows executions for certain offenses.

Gaps in Current Policies

In many ways, the American legal system is not an industrial legal system—it is an agrarian legal system. The American legal system that exists today owes much to the United Kingdom's *Magna Carta*. Today's society is a global one, yet America's legal system is by design fragmented and local. This means that it is hard for the system to respond to global threats and issues. International terrorism, trafficking in human beings, international drug smuggling, and a plethora of other crimes with a global dimension exist today. America's system will need some serious work to respond to those challenges.

The United States incarcerates a larger proportion of its population than any other nation of the world. This is a fantastically expensive process and one that cannot be easily justified by any realistic measure. This includes not only the cost of incarceration but frequently also the costs of caring for the inmate's family during the incarceration. Aside from the financial costs there is a substantial expense in human potential. People go to prison for nonviolent offenses. This does little to protect members of society and has many costs. Most prisons have insufficient funding for rehabilitation and the stigma of having served time excludes many ex-prisoners from the primary labor market. There are certainly people from whom society wants to be protected because they are predatory criminals. Incarceration is appropriate for this group. Unfortunately, an over-crowded correction system may have a hard time dealing with these serious offenders. Properly funded community-based corrections is a much better strategy for other offenders.

Capital punishment (execution), which cannot rehabilitate and has little or no deterrence potential, has its own high costs and provides little in return.

California, for example, spent over $4 billion on death penalty cases from 1978 to 2011. Estimates for capital offense cases resulting in the death penalty in Maryland are that it costs the state $3 million per case (Death Penalty Information Center, 2012). Capital punishment, too, is applied disproportionately to people of color, resulting in irreversible social injustices. Poor defendants often lack the resources to defend themselves.

Prevention programs have not received the attention that they deserve. Treating people after they have committed a crime is not the best strategy. In this regard, poverty, violence, and anger sow the seeds of crime. Intervening at that level will most likely have the best possibility for change. It is often difficult for criminal law and criminal justice organizations to keep pace with developments in technology and change in society. This is a serious issue and one that promises to continue.

The nexus between terrorism and criminal justice has created a range of policies that have changed the funding of criminal justice and altered how certain criminal cases are managed. The USA PATRIOT Act (P.L. 57-106) was passed in 2001 after the September 11 attacks on the United States. It changed laws related to surveillance and apprehension of suspected terrorists and altered aspects of federal procedure.

FUTURE POLICIES

In an information society, human potential is one of the principal stores of knowledge. This makes the development of human intelligence and human ideas of primary importance. The criminal justice system deals with a multitude of social problems in a direct way, but not always the best way for the good of society. In some cases, it is the court of last resort for the issues that our social welfare system cannot manage. It might be considered the ultimate residual social system. The system is underfunded, understaffed, and must deal with a withering array of conflicting expectations.

In addition to its traditional issues, the rise of the information society has created an entirely new set of issues for the system to contend with. New crimes, such as identity theft, intellectual property theft, malicious hacking, and a variety of new crimes against personal privacy, are featured on the news on a regular basis. The growth of cybercrime is a serious issue and is probably just beginning. In addition to these newer forms of criminal activity, technology has facilitated the conduct of organized crime and such activities as human trafficking, drug trafficking, money laundering, and other malicious acts. These are not new activities, but technology can make them easier to conduct and more efficient. Digital currencies like bitcoin can make law enforcement's job more difficult. Child predators can take advantage of social media to prey on children. America's legal system has a difficult time dealing with these new threats.

America's laws, written for a simpler time, are often not adequate to deal with these new threats. New policies are needed and that will require advocacy and lobbying.

On balance, a large number of new technology tools are available to assist law enforcement. Better surveillance technologies are available to track criminal behavior. Cameras, license plate readers, drones, and other devices allow law enforcement to extend its reach. Although there are certainly civil rights issues in the use of these technologies, they can assist in the discovery and prevention of crime.

New technologies can aid in the discovery of technology-based crime. Law enforcement often teams with other agencies and private security firms in the prevention of technology-based crime. The growth of huge databases and sophisticated data mining techniques makes predictive policing a possibility. This allows law enforcement to identify areas of risk and deploy resources to prevent crime. Finally, technology can be used to improve community relations (Brainard & McNutt, 2010).

Evidence-based policy and practice can add to the effectiveness of correctional interventions. Research can help create a range of interventions based on a more nuanced appreciation of different offender situations.

If American society is to flourish as an information society, it must let fewer and fewer matters fall to the criminal justice system. If America invests in its people and its communities, far less criminal justice system intervention will be needed. If the system is to operate in a more beneficial way, it will have to change and grow. Part of that change will be narrowing the jurisdiction of the criminal code to things that are actually harmful, not merely controversial. Incarceration should be saved for the most serious offenders who endanger everyone. Community treatment is more useful for others. The criminal justice system should not be used as a dumping group for difficult cases by the mental health and child welfare systems.

It would also be beneficial to reorganize the system to attack crime in a coordinated way over a global arena. This will mean renegotiating jurisdictional issues but will ultimately result in a more effective and less costly response to crime. Criminal activity often hides behind national borders.

Criminal justice frequently intervenes when other systems fail. Many mental health and child welfare issues fall first to police and may be dealt with by the courts and corrections when other dispositions are more appropriate. Tragedies like the Newtown/Sandy Hook shootings required a police response because a serious mental health problem went unchecked.

Issues of diversity and social justice are particularly poignant in criminal justice. Frequent encounters between police and oppressed communities are often problematic. The 2014 deaths in Ferguson and Staten Island are cases in point. The outcomes of the courts and corrections often favor the rich and privileged and penalize the poor and members of minority groups. The poor have less access to representation and often have a difficult time enforcing their rights. This is a situation that cries out for redress. Robert Kennedy (1964) said, "The poor man looks upon the law as an enemy, not as a friend. For him the law is always taking something away." This speech was given over fifty years ago and still rings true today. The ability of both the criminal law and criminal justice organizations to respond to change in a thoughtful way is more complex than ever. Increasing the research and analysis capacity of the system is certainly important. On balance, the system must often act quickly in difficult situations. This does not lend itself to cool deliberation. Crime will always be an important issue. Dealing with it effectively in the new millennium will involve moving focus from the agrarian past to the information economy future.

Questions for Discussion

1. Laws can be made in two ways: by court decision and by statute. Why are both methods needed?
2. Compare the type of criminal justice response suggested by radical, liberal, and conservative theories.
3. What are the implications of America's incarceration rate for social justice?
4. How can better social welfare services lead to lower crime?
5. What are the implications of globalization for crime and punishment in America?
6. What new crimes has the growth of the information society created?
7. Can new tools help deal with emerging criminal justice problems?

Exercise

1. Imagine that you have been convicted of a crime. How will this change your life? List the changes in your life that you would expect. How would you overcome those changes?

Websites

Chicago's Million Dollar Blocks: http://chicagomilliondollarblocks.com

Cornell Law Library: http://www.law.cornell.edu/uscode/

Human Trafficking: http://www.humantrafficking.org

NCJRS: http://www.ncjrs.gov/

Office on Violence against Women: http://www.ovw.usdoj.gov/

United Nations Crime and Justice Information Network: http://www.uncjin.org/

United States Court System: http://www.uscourts.gov/Home.aspx

United States Department of Justice: http://www.justice.gov/

Visual Media

The Hurricane (1999). Directed by Norman Jewison. The story of Rubin "Hurricane" Carter, a championship boxer unjustly convicted of murder, and his fight for vindication.

Further Reading

Abadinsky, H. (2014). *Probation and parole: Theory and practice* (12th ed.). Englewood Cliffs, NJ: Prentice Hall.

Clear, T. R., Cole, G. F., & Reisig, M. D. (2008). *American corrections* (7th ed.). Belmont, CA: Wadsworth.

Quinney, R. (1970). *The social reality of crime*. Boston, MA: Little Brown.

Shapiro, D. (2011). *Banking on bondage: Private prisons and mass incarceration*. Washington, DC: American Civil Liberties Union.

Chapter 12

Housing and Community Development

Community is an important part of American society and an equally important part of America's national self-image (Putnam, 2000). America values what a community can add to people's lives and society. Although this view of communities might seem idealized, America puts considerable stock in what its communities can do and why they are important. Communities are where the social welfare system interacts with people and where social workers work with their clients.

Communities today are affected by globalization, the challenge to keep their workforce employed, energy and ecological crises, crime and violence, chronic poverty, and declining social capital. Even providing sufficient amounts of safe water is a challenge in some places. Many of these forces threaten to tear communities apart. Although the pace might have picked up in recent years, this is not a new situation. Concern about the destruction of community by outside forces has a long history in both popular thought and the social sciences. Communitarian thought (McNutt, 1997) and social capital theory both put substantial emphasis on the importance of community and the conflict between policy and community (Putnam, 2000).

Social policy efforts to strengthen communities make use of all areas of social welfare, but housing is the one area most associated with community-level macro social work. Many of the programs that relate to community development are connected with housing. Exceptions include rural development and adult education, but even in those areas there is overlap.

This chapter considers housing and community development as two interrelated problems for social policy. The chapter will also examine the ongoing housing crisis and what that means for social policy and for efforts in other policy areas.

THE COMMUNITY IN AMERICA

Community is sacred to the American psyche. It is a long-held view evident in the writings of Thomas Jefferson and other founders that small communities bring out the best in Americans. Home ownership is considered vital to putting

Houses in the Lower 9th Ward of New Orleans nearly five years after the Katrina hurricane disaster left the area flooded. This demonstrates that natural disasters can have an impact on less affluent communities for many years. The poor have fewer resources to rebuild. Some of the markings on one of the houses were used by emergency workers as they searched for survivors.

down roots and providing the glue that helps hold communities together (Santiago & Galster, 2004). The past seventy or so years have not been particularly kind to America's communities. Global economic forces, population shifts, and other national priorities have created a variety of problems for the nation's cities and towns.

The industrial economy, with its emphasis on capital mobility, has destroyed the economic base of many communities. In some cases this happened because a natural resource (such as coal or oil) ran out, and in other cases it happened because a major industry moved elsewhere. These were the communities left behind that characterized life in Appalachia, the Ozarks, and large swaths of the South and Midwest. The industrial heartland of states such as Pennsylvania, Indiana, and Michigan have been renamed "the rust belt" as once-mighty factories, providing economic life for tens of thousands of people, were shuttered and left to decay. This process continues as American society continues to evolve.

Local residents in the Lower 9th Ward of New Orleans express their feelings about the Federal Emergency Management Agency.

Many regional planning approaches, like the growth pole model used by the Appalachian Regional Commission in the 1960s and other places around the United States and the world, encouraged people to migrate to urban areas. Because cities had an already built infrastructure, they were the "poles" around which economic growth could occur, diffusing jobs and housing to the surrounding non-urban areas. The task of community developers and regional planners in this model is to decide where and how to invest resources in order to maximize the ability of the pole urban centers to provide adequate diffusion. Experience over the last half century showed that in many cases the diffusion did not occur in a way that was sustainable, or did not occur at all. Instead of diffusing jobs, for example, urban centers became saturated, drawing in large numbers of migrants who overwhelmed the service provision capabilities of the cities. This left depopulated rural areas without a sustainable number of working age adults to maintain community structures and economies.

Sometimes, however, the major positive attributes of urban areas actually left the center, rather than diffusing. Industry often relocated to surrounding areas, leaving the central city tax base devastated and potential jobs too far away for urban residents to be hired (Bluestone & Rose, 1997). Suburbanization (also known as "urban sprawl") followed the path of major highways built in the United States during the 1960s and onward. With new homes, better schools, more green space, and other amenities unavailable in central cities, people left behind urban centers. At first, due to housing discrimination, only whites were able to escape the city. By the late 1970s and 1980s, African Americans who were better off financially took advantage of Fair Housing laws to move to the suburbs. They increasingly abandoned run-down and dangerous urban areas (Wilson, 1990). When the middle class African-American community left the cities, along with the industrial jobs that once employed large numbers of people, their stabilizing influence also left, leaving behind people who were "truly disadvantaged" in many ways, and contributing to the downward spiral of American urban areas. Drugs (especially crack cocaine), crime, and violence added to the misery.

It is certainly possible that a move toward an information economy could ameliorate issues of lack of employment. It could reintroduce an economic base in some areas. As transaction costs for moving information around the world have decreased (due to innovations like easy access to high-speed broadband Internet, more powerful personal computers, and cloud computing where access to data depends only on connection to the Internet), rural areas can compete economically for information age jobs. Telecommuting can break the formerly necessary linkage between one's location and employment, if one has the correct sort of work. This was one of the ideas behind the National Information Infrastructure policy development in the 1990s. Rural areas, however, still struggle with the difficulty of building a sufficient critical mass for community-level improvements.

Urban areas can also benefit from information age economic realities. Some cities are trying to meld their assets, such as population density and information-technology infrastructure, with increased educational opportunities in technology-related fields, using magnet high schools and community colleges as two approaches to expanding opportunities for areas that otherwise have little hope. Training in infrastructure maintenance and low-start-up-cost entrepreneurial activities on the Internet can provide incomes in previously unavailable ways. The growth of smart cities and civic technology promises to usher in a new era in government effectiveness and civic participation.

Although this is a very complex issue, one thing is clear: The strong tie between location and employment is a serious barrier for many workers in both rural and urban settings. Educational opportunities also play a role in qualifying people for jobs that are specific to the information age economy. Not every job can be done via telecommuting. Services such as tending to the ill or young are face-to-face jobs. Making or repairing material goods must be done in person. Low-skill jobs that can be found in restaurants or in the construction industry can only be completed by showing up. William Julius Wilson (1996) explored the issues concerning location that confront the poor in their efforts to seek employment. Many inner city workers are effectively barred from jobs in the suburbs by a combination of long distances and poor public transportation.

Although transportation policy goes beyond the scope of this book, there is no question that a great number of the policy issues that America confronts are a consequence of decisions that it, as a nation, has made in terms of transportation. Cars are the base of the transportation system. A system of roads and highways supports this choice, and communities have developed around the patterns of transportation. This has led to a suburban model of development that has both social and ecological consequences. In other nations there is more emphasis on walking, bicycling, and mass transportation as ways of getting around. This leads to different patterns of development and affects communities in different ways. The most obvious effect of the decision to be a car-based transportation society is America's dependence on a quickly dwindling resource—fossil fuels. Burning gasoline and oil adds to urban air pollution and has serious consequences for other areas of American life. High rates of obesity are related not only to what Americans eat but also to the relatively sedentary lifestyle they adopt as they move around from place to place in the seat of a motor vehicle.

National policy for American communities has been fragmented and insufficient. Although Americans talk about community in glowing terms, they do little to protect community from the forces that can tear it apart. More attention to the needs of America's communities is clearly warranted. The place where many of the community development efforts tend to be represented is housing policy.

HOUSING IN AMERICA

Owning one's home is part of the American consciousness in a way that few other things are. Home ownership is central to the American dream (Turner, 2010). Americans feel that everyone should have the right to safe and adequate housing. Unfortunately, reality does not live up to this ideal. Many people live in homes that are unsafe, dilapidated, and inadequate. Others live in housing that they cannot afford. Still more lack any permanent housing at all.

The underlying premise of housing policy in the United States is that housing is considered a commercial matter. Although there are small federal and state programs to build homes, they pale in comparison with the commercial housing market. Housing is not only considered a commercial product, it is considered an investment.

For many years, people assumed that the price of housing and real estate in general would appreciate. This led to a situation called the housing bubble where more and more wealth was concentrated in the real estate sector. Home prices continued to rise and the mortgages that supported these rising prices got larger and larger. Deregulation and the creation of new financial instruments led to instability in the mortgage market. Mortgages were often larger then borrowers could afford and some lenders created opportunities for people without sufficient collateral to borrow.

In the latter part of the past decade the housing bubble burst. Coupled with rising unemployment and other economic issues (part of a worldwide recession), the mortgage market suffered reversals. This had a significant impact on the financial sector (banks, brokerage houses, and so forth). Many financial institutions faced a crisis and the federal government intervened to stabilize the economy. The American Recovery and Reinvestment Act of 2009 (ARRA) (P.L. 111-5) was passed to stabilize the economy, and the Dodd-Frank Wall Street Reform and Consumer Protection Act (P.L. 111-203) was intended to reregulate the financial sector.

The problems of the financial sector, rising unemployment, energy issues, and so forth came together in the Great Recession. This was a worldwide recession and the collapse of housing markets occurred in a number of nations. Housing prices fell and many owners found themselves unemployed and overextended.

Even today, many Americans now own a house that is worth less (sometimes substantially less) than the mortgage that they owe. This condition (frequently referred to as being "under water" or "upside down") would have been unthinkable just a few years ago.

The housing system in the United States is still in crisis. The current situation reflects a number of major issues in the American economy, as well as some that are specific to the housing sector. It should be remembered that the housing crisis is not a new crisis. Unacceptably high numbers of Americans have lacked safe and affordable housing for decades. Because housing is intimately connected with other aspects of economic development, the housing crisis is a major issue for the financial and social health of communities.

As noted earlier, housing is considered a commodity in American society. This means it is a market-based product, much like furniture or cars, not a fundamental human right. Many people grew up thinking that buying a house to live in was a no-lose financial decision, given historic price appreciation patterns and tax policy that reduced the costs of ownership. This combination of history and policy caused people to buy "more home" than needed and caused some people to become "house poor." This means they were spending so much on their home they had little disposable income left for other items. People justified this decision by believing that they would receive raises at work and that, over time, the high mortgage payments would become a less significant aspect of their monthly cash flow. In addition, believing that home prices would only increase, people thought they could always sell their home for more than they paid for it should the need arise to cut back expenses.

Just a few decades ago, unemployment levels were low, wages were rising, and optimism about the future was high. With a booming stock market, people felt wealthier than they should have and the rate of savings in the United States fell to less than zero—in other words, average Americans spent more than they saved. People in very hot housing markets could buy a home at one price, live in it for a while, and sell it for more than they had paid for it, using the inflated price to purchase another, usually larger and more expensive home. This did not occur in every community, but it was very much in the news.

Banks and financial institutions were involved in this arrangement. Deregulation and the increased use of creative financial instruments flourished. These practices were new because regulations on the banking industry had been made more lax, allowing questionable practices to be used that had not been allowed before. Some of these methods led to the issues that the economy continues to deal with. Thus, after years and years of rising home prices, house prices in the United States began a long period of decline. This followed a decline in other nations, such as Japan. This meant that home owners were in the position of owning homes that were worth less than they paid for them.

Mortgages have been traditionally created on the assurance that borrowers could pay the mortgage back. This was assessed on the basis of credit ratings, income, collateral, and other measures. In addition, regulation of banks kept loan rules tight.

Banks began to feel pressure to make additional profits when regulations were loosened. Between the push of politics and the pull of profit making, banks began to make loans to some borrowers who did not meet strict criteria for a mortgage. These types of loans were sub-prime mortgages. Sub-prime mortgages were touted as a way to extend the benefits of home ownership to people who normally would not be able to receive a bank loan because their credit worthiness was considered less than ideal (thus the term "sub-prime").

One of the ways that financial institutions contributed to the housing bubble was through the bundling and sale of sub-prime mortgages to investors. Although the process is complicated, the essence is that a large number of risky home loans were put together into one investment package and sold to raise money to use to make additional loans. Investors believed that the bundle of mortgages was secure, even though each individual loan was risky. These bundles thus seemed like a good risk and many financial institutions (including firms making decisions about how to invest retirement accounts) around the world bought them as an investment.

Then unemployment began to rise, housing prices slid, the economy cooled, and the credit market tightened. Suddenly people who were marginal prospects in better times were pushed beyond their means. When you cannot pay your loan the bank begins foreclosure procedures and seizes your home. Your home is sold and the bank gets the proceeds. Even after foreclosure you still owe the total amount of the loan, less what the bank was able to obtain from the sale.

In cases like this, the financial institution must find some way to deal with the loss from the foreclosure sale. They loaned you the money and, even after selling your house, they fall short of recovering their money. Although you still owe the money, they may not be able to collect it all from you. This means that they have losses on their balance sheet. A few losses are expected but having many losses will be a serious issue for both regulators and the banking industry. Many of those losses were in loans that were sold by the banks through the stock market. Most of this is a failure of business judgment and a far too limited federal regulation. The Troubled Asset Relief Program (TARP) was created by the Emergency Economic Stabilization Act of 2008 (Division A of P.L. 110-343) in an attempt to deal with the impact of all of these "toxic assets" on the health of America's financial community.

The financing of real estate transactions is a complex system of institutions and markets. Three federally related organizations (the Federal National Mortgage Association, the Government National Mortgage Association, and the Federal Home Loan Mortgage Corporation), along with the Federal Housing Administration influence how much financing is available and what the requirements for borrowing are. Federal action to take control of two of these organizations was a significant indication of crisis. Ultimately, it seems that banking industry officials were able to offload their bad choices to the public, which wound up compensating investors for their losses. Bank executives were able to keep the lavish bonuses that they were paid during the height of the housing bubble.

AFFORDABLE HOUSING

Affordable housing is a related part of this issue (Goering & Feins, 2008; Mueller & Tighe, 2007; Tighe, 2010). Many working Americans are in serious straits because their mortgage or rental costs consume an unacceptably high portion of their income. Although this varies, the general rule of thumb is that no more than a third of your income should be spent on housing. If you have to spend more, you become "house poor" and other aspects of your life suffer.

The production of relatively low-cost housing in the United States has fallen seriously behind the production of more expensive houses. In addition, the stock of low-cost housing is being destroyed through gentrification and other means. Gentrification is the conversion of low-income housing to mid- to upper-income housing. Houses in poorer neighborhoods are redeveloped and offered to more affluent people at much higher prices. This pushes the less affluent previous residents out of the housing. The former residents generally move to other places but can become homeless. Some people who cannot find housing that they can afford move in with others. Some low-income housing stock is being destroyed for other types of land use such as parking lots, shopping centers, and other commercial uses.

Housing is usually divided between rental housing and home ownership. America, as a nation, prefers home ownership. Home ownership is in decline. In 2014, home ownership fell to its lowest level since 1995 (64.8 percent) (Gopal, 2014). There is a complex range of reasons for this, but it follows a trend that ranges back for a number of years to the middle of the past decade.

Housing is related to and in some ways controlled by availability and cost of land. In some cases, the high cost of land makes building affordable housing impossible if normal levels of profit are expected. Because of natural terrain features, some communities have little or no additional land available for housing, which pushes people with lower incomes to other locations. Other cities have plenty of land surrounding them that can be purchased for later development purposes. This practice continues to create sprawling communities that grow along the routes of major highways and roads.

Housing is connected in profound ways to economic development. If your workforce cannot afford the local housing stock, then it may not be possible to expand or even maintain the local economic base. Many cities that have high living costs (of which housing is a major part) find themselves passed over in the competition for industry or large corporate headquarter relocations, regardless of other positive features. Low wage job holders (such as many social workers or nonprofit employees) can find themselves priced out of living in desirable locales due to a lack of affordable housing options. This is also happening in relatively rural areas with small economic bases. Some of these areas are popular with retirees who have incomes and assets far in excess of what most local people have. Their greater purchasing power drives up housing and land values and makes it difficult for local people to compete.

HOMELESSNESS

Perhaps the most serious aspect of the affordable housing crisis is people without homes. Homelessness is not a problem that is going away and many of the ideas that people have about why people are homeless don't stand up to scrutiny. The definition of homelessness sometimes varies according to the intent of the user. People who want to minimize the problem use figures that are strictly defined and are smaller. People who want to play up the seriousness of the issue use a broader definition, which increases the number of people who fall into the category.

Because of confusion regarding how homelessness should be defined, the Department of Housing and Urban Development produced a final rule on December 5, 2011, pursuant to the Homeless Emergency Assistance and Rapid Transition to Housing Act of 2009 (HEARTH Act), which sets forth a single definition of homelessness. It divides the population of the homeless into three categories:

- Literally homeless: an individual who lacks a fixed, regular, and adequate nighttime residence
- Unstably housed: an individual who has not had a lease, ownership interest, or occupancy agreement in permanent housing during the sixty days prior to a homeless assistance application, has experienced persistent housing instability as measured by two moves or more during the preceding sixty days, and can be expected to continue in such status for an extended period of time

- Fleeing domestic violence: any individual who is fleeing, or is attempting to flee, domestic violence, has no other residence, and lacks the resources or support networks to obtain other permanent housing (United States Department of Housing and Urban Development, 2011)

The National Alliance to End Homelessness (2012) discusses different populations of the homeless as well. It divides the homeless population into different categories, such as:

- Chronically homeless: About 124,000 people suffer from chronic homelessness, usually combined with a disability, including a mental illness or substance abuse problem
- Families: About 250,000 people are included in this group; they are very similar to other families living in poverty
- Veterans: The Department of Veterans Affairs and the United States Department of Housing and Urban Development (HUD) estimated that 76,000 veterans are homeless on any given night
- Youth: Although exact figures are unknown, the National Alliance to End Homelessness estimates that 50,000 youth are homeless for six months or more each year, with about 20 percent of homeless youth being lesbian, gay, bisexual, transsexual, or questioning (LGBTQ)
- Rural: Rural homelessness rates are about half of urban rates (14 per 10,000 compared to 29 per 10,000) but vary considerably from one area to another, with a lack of available services making the problem worse for those individuals and families who are homeless
- Domestic violence: According to research, one of the primary causes of homelessness for women and families is domestic violence
- Mental/physical health: About half of all the homeless have mental and physical health issues
- Reentry population: One-fifth of those leaving prison or jail become homeless soon afterwards, as there are often not enough supports for this population to find stable housing upon release

The foreclosure crisis has added significant numbers of newly homeless people to the ranks of the homeless. Homelessness has significant impacts on a person's life and life chances (Varney & van Vliet, 2008). These include issues related to health, mental health, crime, and safety. This is especially problematic for children and young people.

Although there are programs aimed at dealing with homelessness in the United States, it is unlikely that they would be large enough to deal with the large number of homeless individuals and families. National efforts to both prevent homelessness and care for its victims are needed (National Alliance to End Homelessness, 2012).

The impact of natural disasters is another aspect of homelessness. In 2005, Hurricanes Katrina, Wilma, and Rita hit the Gulf States in the United States. These storms devastated several major cities including New Orleans, Mobile, and Biloxi and made many residents of the area homeless. Other disasters, such as floods, tornadoes, and fires, have created additional local housing emergencies. The policy response to these issues is often less than needed.

Social scientists have learned a great deal about domestic homelessness (Lee, Tyler, & Wright, 2010) in the past two decades. The National Alliance to End Homelessness (2012) advocates for evidence-based solutions to the varying problems faced by the different types of homeless people. Many of these ideas have yet to be reflected in policy making, but it is important to remember that there is no one-size-fits-all solution to the problems of homelessness. Each subpopulation has different reasons for being homeless and thus requires different approaches to creating a solution.

GLOBAL HOUSING ISSUES

There are also important global dimensions to housing. In most developed market economies, housing is considered a right. Many European nations have extensive housing efforts and comprehensive policy networks. But the situation is very different in the third world where a lack of adequate housing is widespread. Squatter communities surround third world cities. Many of these slums lack clean water or disease control.

Amnesty International (2011), which considers housing a human right, presents alarming numbers about what it calls the global housing crisis:

- Estimates indicate that there are currently more than a billion people living in slums around the world.
- The United Nations predicts that this number will double to two billion by 2030.

- Forcible eviction of people due to invasion and armed conflict is a large problem in some countries, with specific mentions of problems in Nigeria, Zimbabwe, and Cambodia.
- Kissick, Leibson, Kogul, Bachmann, Anderson, and Eckert (2006) found that a large percentage of urban housing units in sub-Saharan Africa (70 percent), South Asia (50 percent), and Latin American/the Caribbean (25 percent) is poorly constructed and violates local rules.

Amnesty International (2011) also states that there is only one country among the top eight industrialized lands (the G8) that has not ratified the International Covenant on Economic, Social and Cultural Rights, which guarantees the right to housing. That country is the United States.

MEASURING HOUSING

The United States has a relatively good statistical system for following housing issues (McNutt & Robinson, 2008). It is fairly easy to tell how many building permits are issued, how many housing starts are created, how much land and how many buildings are bought and sold, and for how much. All of these data are collected by local governments and disseminated to a number of state, federal, and commercial organizations. Statistics are also available on average home prices, foreclosure rates, vacancy rates, and other statistics about the housing market. Home ownership statistics and household statistics are also essential. The Department of Housing and Urban Development is probably the best source (www.hud.gov) but the Census Bureau (www.census.gov) has a great deal of information. Also useful are commercial sources such as the National Association of Realtors. It is important to remember that, unlike anything else in social policy, housing is first and foremost a commercial activity and many of the statistics and measurements that are relevant are economic statistics.

The United Nations has an office dedicated to housing issues. Created in 2002, it is called the United Nations Housing Rights Programme and examines issues related to housing, land use, and collecting information about these topics (United Nations Habitat, n.d.).

CONSEQUENCES

Housing is a serious problem in American society and around the world. It has major effects on the economies of every country on earth. It creates major issues for the environment and for social justice. Housing decisions have massive consequences for individuals and families, communities, and the economy. Housing can mean the difference between a bleak existence and a comfortable life. Inadequate housing also has serious implications for health, mental health, poverty, economic development, and survival.

RELATIONSHIP TO ENVIRONMENTAL ISSUES

Housing issues and community issues are intertwined with ecological issues (Hoff & McNutt, 1994, 2008; Edwards, 2005). The way people develop their settlements is an important factor in the degree to which they can have a sustainable society. Housing issues have created a race for land in many nations, including the United States. This has led to housing construction pushing out other land uses (such as farming) and housing being constructed in areas that are at-risk environmentally (such as flood plains). Poorly planned development of ocean-front property has also destroyed areas that took the brunt of tropical storms in the past, leading to greater devastation now and in the future.

A United States Government Global Climate Change report written in 2009 predicts these effects from global environmental change:

> Likely future changes for the United States and surrounding coastal waters include more intense hurricanes with related increases in wind, rain, and storm surges (but not necessarily an increase in the number of these storms that make landfall), as well as drier conditions in the Southwest and Caribbean. These changes will affect human health, water supply, agriculture, coastal areas, and many other aspects of society and the natural environment (Karl, Melillo, & Peterson, 2009).

There is still time to respond to the predicted changes in climate. Housing and community development are critical areas in people's response to the environmental and energy crisis. How people change the way that they live their lives will determine if they can respond effectively to these critical issues. Redesigning housing and reinventing communities can make extensive contributions to reducing energy use and preserving the environment (Brown, 2006).

SOCIAL JUSTICE IMPLICATIONS

Housing is a basic human need. Although not recognized by the United States government, it is also a human right, as reflected by the United Nations (United

Nations Habitat, n.d.). The fact that there are homeless people and people living in substandard housing, while others have multiple houses or housing that far exceeds what they need, offends social justice. In a just society, everyone would have sufficient housing. From a social justice perspective, it is very difficult to defend the current way of allocating housing.

The problem is even more pronounced in the global arena. In many nations, particularly those in the third world, housing is unavailable for large numbers of poor people. Squatter settlements or *favellas* surround many cities (Davis, 2006). The one billion people who live in these conditions usually lack clean water and sanitation. Sometimes shelter is an equipment box or a shanty made of scrap wood or metal. Latrines are nothing but open ditches shared by all. Violence is common. Such conditions create breeding grounds for disease while quashing hope for their residents.

THEORIES ABOUT THE PROBLEM

The commercial nature of housing in a capitalist society means that theories about the problem tend to reflect theories about the economy. They also take into account perspectives regarding the role of government.

Conservative Theories

Housing is a consumer good. It is bought and sold in the marketplace and government intervention will harm the operation of the market. Some conservatives would be in favor of small subsidies for those who are poor or disabled. There might also be some support for incentives for developers to create new affordable housing. People who believe in the conservative agenda prefer a "hands off" approach with incentives provided. Minimal regulation is desired but few conservatives would argue for no regulation.

Liberal Theories

As with conservative approaches, liberal theories also hold that housing is a commercial good and most housing needs are taken care of by commercial builders, developers, and realtors. This is the expected way that housing is provided but there is recognition that all of the population's issues will not be resolved by the market. Meeting some needs requires government planning. This is the community development/urban planning dimension at the local level and national housing planning at the level of economic planning. This group prefers strategies that involve planning, regulation, private enterprise, and subsidy programs.

Radical Theories

Radical theorists see housing as a basic human need and therefore a right. They also tend to advocate for planning to meet housing needs. Although approaches vary from society to society, one common advocacy method is to use state power to break up concentrated land ownership. Radical theorists tend to favor government action without involvement of the private sector.

CURRENT POLICIES

The current policy framework uses a combination of vouchers, tax incentives, subsidies, and a limited range of community development activities. These responsibilities are spread over several federal agencies and a host of state and local agencies.

Much of what can be called our housing policy is incorporated in the Federal Tax Code (the Internal Revenue Code of 1986)—most of which is found in Title 26 USC and which provides incentives for home buyers and governs the tax treatment of various activities. The Internal Revenue Service is responsible for administration of these policies. The most well-known of these is the credit for mortgage interest. If you buy a home and borrow the money through a mortgage, you can deduct the interest you pay on your loan from the personal income tax you owe. This is a tax expenditure that promotes home ownership. In very few areas of tax law are interest payments deductible.

The agency that is most identified with housing is the United States Department of Housing and Urban Development (HUD). Created in 1965 by the Department of Housing and Urban Development Act (P.L. 89-174), this department is responsible for many of the federal government's housing and community development activities. Many people associate affordable housing with public housing projects. This was true at one time but it has been nearly thirty years since public housing was constructed by HUD.

HUD does continue to work on public housing issues (the Home Ownership and Opportunity for People Everywhere [HOPE] program, for example). Most of the activities that HUD engages in revolve around regulation and enforcement (such as Fair Housing and the Community Reinvestment Act), housing vouchers, and a very few community planning projects. HUD is also involved in group housing programs.

The Federal Housing Authority (FHA), a part of HUD, is engaged in the mortgage market. Also involved in home ownership assistance are the HOPE program and the HOME Investment Partnerships Block Grant Program. HUD also administers the Community Development Block Grant Program, Stewart B. McKinney Homeless Assistance Act of 1987 (P.L. 100-77), the Renewal Communities and Urban Empowerment Zones program (part of which is administered by the Department of Health and Human Services and the Department of Agriculture [see P.L. 103-66]), and construction and rehabilitation projects. Some policies address the banking and mortgage sectors. The Community Reinvestment Act of 1977 (12 USC 2901) helps to assure that fair credit is available to all segments of the community. It provides oversight to lending institutions.

Many other federal agencies have programs that deal with community development and housing. The Environmental Protection Agency has programs that deal with brownfields and other environmentally despoiled areas. The Department of Agriculture has extensive programming in rural communities. The Department of Commerce works with communities on community economic development projects.

Federal civil rights laws provide protection from discrimination in housing, including insurance and lending practices. Regulators inspect banks, insurance companies, realtors, and others for evidence of discrimination. One practice that is illegal but nonetheless occurs is called "red-lining" because lenders figuratively draw a red line around certain neighborhoods and do not provide any funds for projects within that area. This allows some parts of a city to become run-down and dilapidated, decreasing in value until the land can be bought very cheaply by slum lords or speculative developers. If enough property can be purchased inexpensively, the new owner can gentrify or otherwise redevelop the neighborhood, possibly making large profits.

State and local governments also have policies that promote home ownership and regulate the housing market. At the local level, zoning and planning regulations can help to insure community needs are met in the face of development. The planning and zoning practices at the local level are not inherently exciting, however, and so pro-development forces often are able to do whatever they wish, due to a lack of countervailing efforts by citizens negatively affected by decisions made by private sector actors. There are also state and local laws protecting home buyers and renters from discrimination.

Gaps in Current Policies

In very few areas of social welfare are the efforts of government so diminutive when compared to those of the private sector. This leaves the housing of the American people at the mercy of market forces. Although there is a relatively complex regulatory environment, the ability of regulators to protect the general good has been called into question in the past few years (Trumbull, 2007).

Currently, decision-making is vested in the hands of developers who may not be concerned about community stability. Some developers are clearly interested in their communities, although others are not. There is little incentive for those who are not interested to do the kinds of things that promote community such as adding green space between buildings, including safe and convenient places for residents to interact (such as playgrounds and community rooms) in planning, and investing in activities that bring cohesion to the fore.

The current system does little to encourage the growth of ecologically sustainable communities (Brown, 2006). Although it is quite possible to develop communities that can save energy and conserve scarce resources, current policy doesn't do enough to make this happen. Examples of low-cost things that can be done to improve energy conservation are myriad. The Smart Communities Network (n.d.) offers these points:

- If one-tenth of the homes in the United States used solar water heaters, there would be 8.4 million metric tons fewer of carbon emissions annually.
- Siting homes along an east-west axis can allow the south-facing wall to include passive solar features that reduce the need for heating in the winter and cooling in the summer.
- Using already-available products in place of the usual wood-frame house prevalent in many areas of the country would save tons of waste material for every house built, keeping landfills open for many additional years and lowering costs.
- Adding more insulation during construction adds long-term value as operating costs are considerably lower both in winter and summer.

Finally, although the concept of a smart or IT-enabled community is a recent idea, current policy does not advance that thought. The integration of technology could augment both quality of life and productivity. Without an understanding of what technology can be used for, however, and how to apply it appropriately, computers and Internet access do nothing to improve anyone's life.

America's housing policies can be seen against the backdrop of its urban policy and transportation policy. Its car-based transportation system and cheap oil encouraged suburbanization and sizable commuting burdens. Because the time of peak oil may already have passed (Brown, 2006), this type of development is problematic.

On balance, most of America's community development was planned within the assumptions of agrarian and industrial society. As Garvin and Cox (1987) argue, urbanization was a byproduct of the factory system. Many original settlements developed along trading routes and rivers, which were the transportation routes of their day. City planning was a more recent development within the industrial economy, including first railroads and then motor vehicles as major methods of moving goods from one place to another.

Post-industrial society is changing this dynamic by moving people farther afield. Many of the things that supported industrialization are no longer needed. The economic forces that compete with community needs are clearly changing, becoming global in nature rather than local or regional and being information-based, rather than raw materials based.

HOUSING POLICY IN A CHANGING SOCIETY

Housing policy in the future will encounter no less than five important challenges. These include:

1. The need to provide all Americans with safe, adequate, and affordable housing
2. The ability to promote community development and planning toward sustainable communities that are ecologically friendly and energy efficient
3. The ability to engage within a radically changed economic system
4. The ability to promote a learning and information-rich environment within communities
5. The ability to deal with homelessness in the face of a changing economy and an escalating pattern of natural disasters precipitated by climate change

America's current system cannot address any of these challenges. Although America's housing system will eventually recover some of its economic value from the meltdown it experienced in 2008, the system itself is much less relevant because the world has changed and continues to change its shape.

The future could bring the possibility of adequate, affordable housing for all. This will, however, take a major rethinking of the way that housing is planned, financed, and maintained. The most serious issue that must be tackled is financing. Although reregulation of the housing financing sector is inevitable, serious safeguards must be developed to assure that the problems do not reoccur.

The supply of land is finite. Unless people move to other planets, they will have to be satisfied with what they currently have. Given global warming and the potential for rising sea levels, there may be much less land available. The United States Environmental Protection Agency states that it is possible that as much as 5,000 to 10,000 square miles of American coast could be lost due to rising sea levels (United States Environmental Protection Agency, 1989). Small nations in the Pacific are facing the probability that their islands will be completely covered by sea water in the next few decades, as noted at the Threatened Island Nation Conference held at Columbia University (Voice of America, 2011).

The world population is growing and the available supplies of energy and many renewable resources necessary for common methods of house construction are failing to keep pace. Expanding the housing stock using the methods of the past will not be possible. Instead, the solution is to make better use of what exists. Besides being smarter about building methods, this means developing new modes of organizing communities. Community land trusts are one way of guaranteeing the land that is needed for residential purposes won't be used for other functions or bought speculatively for investment. Zoning and creating planned communities can also increase sustainable practices.

The movement toward sustainable communities has been given a boost by the energy crisis, public concern about global warming, and the political situation in the Middle East. Building sustainable communities requires community-wide planning and the involvement of many stakeholder groups. It also requires integration with energy and transportation policy. Yet making changes to the accustomed ways of doing things will not be easy.

Community planning is often a difficult matter given the economic power of developers. In some areas, restrictive zoning is nearly impossible because people with entrenched economic interests almost always prevail. These people hold on to their property rights tightly, unwilling to let go of their ability to influence their neighbors' rights negatively. If planners are to make intelligent choices, however, stronger centralized community development is needed.

Local building codes can also be a barrier to affordable housing. Some of these codes were created many years ago when current technology was not available. Outdated codes create unnecessary costs that make affordable housing difficult. New ideas are slow to be allowed by regulators and then adopted at the individual builder and owner level.

Changes in the nature of work have implications for housing. One of the reasons for housing shortages is the concentration of workers in a geographic area. The trend toward interventions like telecommuting will ease, but not solve, part of the housing shortage. If people prefer, they can select their area of residence based on their costs rather than living close to the physical location of an office, store, or factory. Changing work hours to a compressed work week is another method of altering the nature of work to make a positive change in environmental practices; this, too, will have an impact on housing decisions.

A relevant system will promote community development and meaningful community dialogue. The creation of a long-term housing plan, combined with efforts in other arenas, such as transportation and employment, will be a good step. The development of a sustainable community that works with the natural environment and has a lower impact on resources and the environment is critical. This will require newer building methods and organizing the community to develop human scale planning methods.

The integration of the information economy is another important task. Building a smart community that makes good use of technology is needed. Sustainable practices within construction are necessary. Technology and a changing economic order can undo urban over-concentration, eliminate long commutes, and increase worker options. People might be able to work from or closer to their homes, interacting with co-workers via text, email, telephone, and/or video conferencing at a moment's notice. A typical day could include using public transportation, walking, or bicycling to work, school, shopping, or entertainment.

This discussion of housing reveals another fact that is often lost in discussions of social welfare policy. No one can understand the policies that govern social welfare without at least some appreciation of public policy and economic policy. Transportation policy has a huge impact on communities and the economic condition of the poor. Banking policy is a major predictor of housing efforts. Sadly, these policies tend to be ignored in discussions of social welfare policy. Social workers typically do not attempt to intervene in these arenas, much to the detriment of society and clients.

In many ways communities are the places that social policy is experienced by the public. Communities also provide many of the mediating structures (Berger & Neuhaus, 1996) that intervene between people and the megastructures of the economy and government. Communities can be (but aren't always) nurturing environments for individuals and families.

The new policies that are necessary will protect, encourage, and reward activities and development that support communities. The changing nature of the overall system due to globalization, the spread of information technology, and the recognition of the vital importance of environmental sustainability will reward appropriate community development in the future. Policy need only create the initial push in order for it to work.

Communities are important for people. Policies can and must be created to insure that communities are well supported and healthy. The intimate relationship between human well-being and housing must be respected in order to develop a system that promotes the positive goals that the United States has as a society.

Questions for Discussion

1. How is current housing policy a product of industrialization? What is likely to change in the future?
2. What are some ways that a community can be more eco-friendly?
3. How can the information economy change the need for housing?
4. What effect will the crisis in housing have for the economy as a whole?

Exercises

1. Consider the situation in your town. What is needed in order to develop a sustainable community that will have a minimal impact on the environment? Research some ideas that push your town firmly in that direction within a few years.
2. What is the housing situation like in your state? Gather the appropriate statistics and compare them with at least one nearby state.

Websites

Federal National Mortgage Association (Fannie Mae): http://fanniemae.com

Federal National Mortgage Association (Freddie Mac):
http://www.freddiemac.com

Government National Mortgage Association (Ginnie Mae):
http://www.ginniemae.gov

National Alliance to End Homelessness: http://www.endhomelessness.org/

United Nations Habitat: http://www.unhabitat.org/categories.asp?catid=282

Visual Media

Inside Job (2010). Directed by Charles Ferguson. Set during the 2007 financial crisis.

Further Reading

Amnesty International (2011, October 6). *11 numbers you need to know about the global housing crisis*. Retrieved from http://blog.amnestyusa.org/us/human-right-to-housing-11-numbers-you-need-to-know/.

Edwards, A. R. (2005). *The sustainability revolution*. Garbolla Island, BC: New Society.

Chapter 13

Aging and Social Policy

Aging does not seem to be a problem, in one sense. If you're like most people, you probably believe that growing older is better than the alternative. In addition to other changes that are occurring in the technology and environmental arenas, the United States is also on the brink of a longevity revolution. By 2030, the proportion of the U.S. population aged sixty-five and older will more than double (compared to 2000) to about 72.1 million older adults, or about one in every five Americans (19 percent) (Administration on Aging, 2011). This is a global phenomenon, as the United Nations predicts that, by 2050, the proportion of the world's population that is over sixty years of age will equal that of children younger than fifteen years for the first time in recorded history (United Nations, 2002, p. 15).

At the same time, for millions of Americans who have reached the age of sixty-five, insecurity is higher and quality of life is lower than it might be if a different set of policies were in place. This chapter defines aging, examines how aging is measured, relates the policy area of aging to the environment, and shows how social justice is not being achieved in many ways for the elderly. It also discusses political theories around service provision to the elderly and describes current policy in the area. Finally, the chapter identifies gaps in current policies and how aging policy might look in the future.

WHAT IS AGING?

What does life offer for this increasingly large group of Americans? As Bette Davis is quoted as saying, "Old age is no place for sissies." Aging is a biological process that occurs to all living organisms and is defined as "a progressive deterioration of physiological function, an intrinsic age-related process of loss of viability and increase in vulnerability" (Magalhaes, 2012). Although it is universal, it is also "a largely mysterious process" (Magalhaes, 2012). Whether aging is largely the result of accumulated damage at the cellular level or the outcome

274

of genetically programmed processes is unknown (Magalhaes, 2012), but some of the effects of the aging process in humans are:

- Graying or loss of hair
- Wrinkling of skin
- Diminution of senses (sight, smell, taste, hearing, touch)
- Decreases in heart, lung, and kidney capacity
- Loss of brain weight and muscle strength

These natural aspects of the aging process are inevitable. In addition, about 80 percent of older Americans are living with at least one chronic condition (Centers for Disease Control, 2007), many of which are preventable if addressed earlier in life and may still be treatable in the elderly. These include conditions such as high blood pressure, high cholesterol, and some types of diabetes. Other chronic conditions are less preventable but nonetheless take a heavy toll on individuals and the health care system.

Aging is not just about physical changes, however—it is also about changing roles and places in society. Perhaps the most common expectation is that the elderly will stop working for pay. Before the baby boomer generation, old age was often seen as a time to slow down, let go of work and other possibly stressful situations (retire), and live out one's "golden years" by fishing, baking cookies, or sitting on the porch in a rocking chair, watching the world go by. Reality rarely matched this view of retirement, however. First, pensions did not adequately address income needs. In 1959, the poverty rate among the elderly was over one in three (35 percent), more than any other group. By 2007, it had fallen dramatically to just 10 percent (Federal Interagency Forum on Aging-related Statistics, 2010, p. 12). The Great Recession destroyed many life savings as the stock market lost value. Second, health often deteriorated, leaving the older person unable to pursue previous pastimes or start new ones. Finally, life expectancies were lower than now, and so people frequently did not live much longer than their retirement age. In 1960, the life expectancy at birth for all Americans as a whole was 69.7 years of age. In 2007, the live expectancy had increased to 77.9 years. Assuming a retirement age of sixty-five years, in 1960 one would expect to live for less than five more years at retirement. A quarter of a century later, one would expect to live nearly thirteen more years, close to three times as long (Centers for Disease Control, 2011). That is a long time to be sitting in a rocking chair or baking cookies.

Baby boomers (who were born between 1946 and 1965) have redefined every life stage and they may redefine aging, as well (Randall, 2012). Boomers want to stay active, live in their community, be healthy, and contribute meaningfully to society. Randall's optimistic view is that advances in medical treatments, higher levels of education, and continued buying power may allow the boomers to live longer, with a higher quality of life, than any other generation before it (Randall, 2012). Thus, the societal definition of aging is changing, even if the biological definition is not.

HOW IS AGING MEASURED?

The most common way that aging is measured is the passing of time, a person's chronological age. Chronological age is how you mark milestones in your life. It is how the government knows that you are eligible to receive certain program benefits, such as Medicare and Social Security retirement payments. Interestingly, there is not one set chronological age that makes you eligible for all things related to being a senior citizen. You can join the American Association of Retired Persons (AARP), a private organization, at age fifty; McDonald's gives you a senior citizen discount at age fifty-five; you become eligible for Medicare at age sixty-five. The age you may begin to draw Social Security retirement checks depends on a number of factors. First, you must have worked for forty quarters, contributing to the Social Security retirement fund. Once that threshold is met, your eligibility age varies, depending on when you were born and your own choices. For example, if you were born in 1960 or later, you must wait until you are sixty-seven to draw full retirement benefits. However, you may choose to draw reduced benefits earlier, at age sixty-two. Alternatively, you may delay beginning your payout, receiving an additional 8 percent for each year you delay.

This objective way of measuring age is important for the delivery of services, just as an objective way of measuring poverty is important to determine who receives government financial assistance. Yet there are other ways of measuring aging. As the popular phrase puts it, "You're only as old as you feel." The subjective sense of aging is important to understand as baby boomers seek to redefine what "old age" is by maintaining a vigorous lifestyle as long as possible (Randall, 2012). Cognitive functioning, which can now be judged more accurately using short-term memory measures, is seen as a way to assess "functional aging," leading to a more accurate measure of possible impairment than just chronological age (Nauert, 2011).

AGING AND ENVIRONMENTAL ISSUES

Of course, a general degradation of the quality of air, water, and soil have effects on those over age sixty-five, just as there are negative impacts of these conditions on people of all ages. But the elderly share a special vulnerability, along with the young, to air, water, and soil pollution. Their immune systems are sometimes more easily compromised by exposure to environmental problems, and they suffer more health and even emotional problems as a result.

Problems with the aged population and a degraded environment begin long before people become elderly. Some researchers studying the aging process posit that damage at the molecular or sub-cellular level causes (or at least contributes to) the degenerative aging process. Although such scholars accept the role of genetics in the overall aging equation, they believe that environmental factors, such as exposure to harmful chemicals, affect the aging process in individuals. Damage is concentrated in certain organs that may fail after years of being stressed. Such damage can begin while a baby is in the womb. As an example, water pollution in the Great Lakes has led to warnings not to eat any of certain types of fish (carp and catfish) from those bodies of water and to restrict consumption of many other types, due to dangerous levels of mercury, PCBs, and dioxin that can be ingested and induce harm, including negatively affecting fetal development (Michigan Department of Community Health, 2011). When the environment contains poisons, the cumulative effects at the physical and cognitive levels may have an impact later in life.

Environmental deterioration thus certainly affects the elderly, who may have chronic conditions that are caused by past environmental issues. Current problems such as air pollution and excessive levels of ozone can exacerbate breathing difficulties, such as emphysema, and circulatory problems, such as heart disease. People who are already frail are most at risk for additional complications.

SOCIAL JUSTICE ISSUES

Just as social justice is not fully present in other areas of social policy, it is lacking among those over the age of sixty-five as well. American society has many fault lines around racial and ethnic diversity as well as gender, so it is no surprise that the aged also show disparities along these lines, including problems around disparities in income, health and health care, and other areas. One bright spot is that poverty among the aged is remarkably lower now than half a century ago. Then, over one-third of the elderly were poor. In 2010, the figure was 9 percent (Administration on Aging, 2011).

Despite the good news regarding decreased levels of poverty among the aged, the gains have not resulted in equality across America's elderly of different races. Table 13-1 shows the poverty rate of the elderly for selected years between 1992 and 2009, by race. Whites show the lowest rate of poverty (lower than the "all" level) for all years, with Asian elderly being somewhat more likely to be poor. Black and Hispanic elderly are considerably more likely to be poor. In fact, a person who is elderly and black is about two-and-a-half times more likely to be poor than is an elderly white person. Elderly Hispanics are about as likely as elderly blacks to be poor. The reasons for this include lower incomes by blacks and Hispanics over their work life compared to whites. This leads to lower benefits from any pensions a person might have as well as lower savings and smaller checks from Social Security. Jobs that fall outside of the Social Security system also tend to be jobs that people of color have, such as farm work, day labor, house cleaning, child care, and other types of jobs with informal work arrangements. Minorities in the United States also tend to have worse health, and this can drain resources, too.

Another problem area is the income distribution between men and women. According to the Administration on Aging (2011), elderly women are considerably more likely to be poor (10.7 percent) than are elderly men (6.7 percent). This is due to many reasons. Chief among them are:

Table 13-1
Poverty Rates of the Aged, by Race and Ethnicity, 1992–2009

Year	Black	Hispanic	Asian	White	All
1992	33.5	22.1	10.8	10.5	12.9
1997	26.0	23.8	12.3	8.1	10.5
2002	23.8	21.4	8.4	8.3	10.4
2007	23.2	17.1	11.3	7.4	9.7
2009	19.5	18.3	15.8	7.5	8.9

Sources: For 2009, United States Census Bureau, Statistical Abstract of the United States, 2012, Table 713. Retrieved from http://www.census.gov/compendia/statab/2012/tables/12s0713.pdf. For other years, United States Census Bureau, Current Population Survey, 2009, Table 3. Retrieved from http://www.census.gov/hhes/www/poverty/histpov/perindex.html.

- Women have lower lifetime earnings than men
- Women spend fewer years in the workforce than men
- Women live longer than men
- Women are less likely to receive pension income
- Women have lower financial net worth (Anzick & Weaver, 2001)

LIFE EXPECTANCY BY RACE

One important statistic is which groups live long enough to become the aged (life expectancy). Table 13-2 is instructive, showing that at any given age, whites are expected to live longer than blacks. According to this information, for babies born in 2007, at the time of birth, white males will live, on average, to be almost seventy-six years old, while white females will live to be almost eighty-one years of age. Black males, on the other hand, will live, on average, to only seventy years of age, and black females will live to about seventy-seven years of age (Centers for Disease Control, 2011).

The disparity between whites and blacks decreases the longer people live. For example, at the age of seventy-five, the difference in expected life left between white males and black males is only 0.7 years compared to the 5.9 years' difference at birth. The gap between white women and black women disappears by age seventy-five, having started out being almost seven years longer for white women. Females of both races have a life expectancy that is longer than men of either race, although white women tend to live longer than black women (Centers for Disease Control, 2011).

The good news is that a great many people are living longer and fuller lives. The bad news is that they are not all sharing in the fruits of progress equally. It is important to work to ensure that all the aged receive equal benefits from government policy and that all people have equal life chances no matter what their race, ethnicity, or gender is.

Table 13-2
Life Expectancy, by Race and Gender (2007)

At Age	White Males	White Females	Black Males	Black Females
0	75.9	80.8	70.0	76.8
65	17.3	19.9	15.2	18.7
75	10.6	12.4	9.9	12.4

Source: Centers for Disease Control and Prevention (2011). *Health, United States: With special feature on death and dying.* Table 22. Washington, DC: National Center for Health Statistics.

STATISTICS

The Census Bureau estimated that, in 2010, more than 40 million Americans were sixty-five years of age or older, with about 18.5 million of them being seventy-five years of age or older (see Table 13-3). This represents a 15.1 percent increase in number for the sixty-five and over population, and an increase of nearly 12 percent for the seventy-five and over age group, compared to the numbers in 2000. Breaking these numbers down by gender reveals that, in 2010, there were almost 23 million women sixty-five or more years of age, with a total of over 11 million women seventy-five years or older. These are increases of over 11 percent and 7 percent, respectively, compared to 2000. Women tend to live longer than men, so the number of males in these two age ranges is lower than females (about 17.3 million males sixty-five and over and 7.3 million males who are seventy-five and older). But the rate of increase among men is even higher than for women: over 20 percent for the sixty-five-plus group of males and a 19 percent increase for males aged seventy-five or more years compared to 2000 (United States Census Bureau, 2011).

Those over the age of sixty-five continue to increase in number and percentage of the overall population. This is true for at least two reasons. First, life expectancy has increased a great deal. Just over 100 years ago, in 1900, life expectancy at birth for the entire population was a bit over forty-seven years. More recently, in 2010, projected life expectancy at birth for the total population lengthened to 78.3 years. The predicted age of death is 75.7 for men and 80.8 for women; women are thus expected to live over five years longer than are men (United States Census Bureau, 2012a). Because life expectancy is increasing, more people are living into their post-retirement years and living well into their seventies and eighties. And, if you live to be seventy-five years of age, you

Table 13-3
Population Estimates, by Age and Gender, 2000 and 2010 (in 000s)

	2000	2010	Percent Increase
All: 65 and older	34,992	40,268	15.1%
All: 75 and older	16,601	18,555	11.8%
Females: 65 and older	20,582	22,905	11.3%
Females: 75 and older	10,496	11,288	7.5%
Males: 65 and older	14,410	17,363	20.5%
Males: 75 and older	6,106	7,266	19.0%

Source: United States Census (2011). Table 7: Resident Population by Sex and Age: 1980–2010. Retrieved from http://www.census.gov/compendia/statab/2012/tables/12s0007.pdf. Percentage change is from calculations by the author.

have, on average, another twelve years of life ahead of you. The elderly are thus becoming a larger percentage of the American population as well as greater in number than ever before. This is also generally true around the world, especially in industrialized countries (Centers for Disease Control, 2007).

THEORIES ABOUT AGING

Other social policy arenas have theories that can be considered conservative, liberal, or radical. That is not so true when it comes to aging. Everyone agrees that aging exists, regardless of political persuasion, and generally everyone agrees that it is something that happens at an individual level. Even the disagreements as to what causes aging are usually couched in terms of the relative weight of damaging environmental factors compared to genetic factors, not whether the environment plays a role at all. Debates occur concerning society's and government's roles in addressing the negative effects and aspects of aging, including leaving the workforce, increased illness rates with higher health care costs, and possible need for assistance in taking care of an elderly person's problems.

Conservative

Conservatives believe that families should work together to take care of the needs of the elderly persons in their lives. The first line of defense against problems is that people themselves take responsibility for having adequate amounts of resources through hard work and thrift all through life. Taking care of one's health through individual activities of exercise, eating well, regular health care, avoiding smoking, and so on are important aspects of being a healthy older person. A second line of defense, argue conservatives, is that younger members (such as the older person's children) provide assistance, as needed. When elderly people find it hard to take care of their needs adequately, children should make them welcome in their home or provide practical and financial help to find another living situation, such as in an assisted living facility. Community organizations, particularly faith-based ones, can provide socialization and quality of life programs without the need for government support.

Liberal

Liberals view the world differently, noting how often adult children (if any) live far away from their parents and how few organizations provide time off for their employees to take care of the needs of aging family members. Many of the ideas coming from a liberal perspective are designed to work around the restrictions of the capitalist system without changing them. Thus, working adults may ask for family leave time to take care of elderly relatives but employers are not required to pay the employee during the leave. Liberals prefer to provide government intervention in an institutional model of policy making, where it is anticipated that almost everyone will need assistance in some way at some points in their life. Yet current American policy initiatives in this area are more concerned with saving money than in expanding programs to assist additional people to a greater extent.

Liberals resisted the call to privatize Social Security, which was an important policy proposal set forth by conservatives when the stock market was climbing to new highs almost every day. But there are not many new ideas on how to improve economic security for the elderly coming from the liberals at this time. Individuals are supposed to be looking to improve their human capital on their own, with few resources being devoted to helping the elderly keep their jobs when the economy is weak.

Radical

Radicals see the problems of the aged as stemming from a flawed economic system that pushes aside the old in favor of the young. Maggie Kuhn, founder of the Gray Panthers, states: "Men and women approaching retirement age should be recycled for public service work, and their companies should foot the bill. We can no longer afford to scrap-pile people" (Gray Panthers Affiliation of California Networks, n.d.). Radicals link the profit motive and thus capitalism to many of the problems the aged face in terms of employment discrimination, finding affordable and safe housing, environmental destruction and pollution, health care, and other concerns. A basic restructuring of the economy is needed, radicals say, in order to protect not only the elderly but also everyone else, because everyone is vulnerable to these threats.

CURRENT POLICY AREAS

This section examines some of the policy areas of most concern with the aged population, including retirement, income security, physical and mental health, substance abuse, and other services.

Retirement

Retirement can be thought of as the period after a worker leaves the labor market. Retirement can be voluntary or involuntary. Involuntary retirement can be caused by not being able to find work, or can be due to disability or other factor inhibiting the ability to work. The question, of course, is where the money will come from to pay for housing, food, medical care, and so on. Two primary sources exist for the aged who are not poor: private retirement plans and Social Security, or, as it is formally known, the Old Age, Survivors, and Disability Insurance (OASDI) fund.

With retirement also comes uncertainty for most Americans. Sources of income after you leave the labor market are not necessarily either sufficient or guaranteed. Some of the elderly decide to reenter the labor market, or come out of retirement, in order to make ends meet. In recognition of this, statistics show fewer Americans are retiring by age sixty-five. In 1967, 43 percent of Americans of the age range sixty-five to sixty-nine were in the labor force. This decreased to only 24 percent in 1985. Since then, the labor participation rate among the elderly has increased and was at 36 percent in 2008 (Federal Interagency Forum on Aging-related Statistics, 2010, p. 18).

By 2015, it is expected that one out of every ten workers will be women over the age of sixty-five, mostly due to increased need for income (United States Census Bureau, 2009). Others, who are unable to work, may find themselves in difficult economic situations.

Private Retirement Plans

Private retirement plans can be classified as either defined benefit plans or defined contributions plans. The more traditional approach is defined benefits plans. With this type of pension, a worker contributes to a company or union retirement plan a certain amount every pay period and, in return, during retirement years, receives a certain amount of income (a defined benefit) every month. The risk is on the company or union, which must manage the retirement funds in such a way as to meet its obligations to former workers. In some cases, retirement funds go bankrupt, and the pensions are then funded by a federal retirement insurance fund, known as the Pension Benefit Guaranty Corporation (PBGC), which currently protects the pensions of nearly forty-four million American workers and retirees (see Pension Benefit Guaranty Corporation, 2012).

The other type of private pension is called a defined contribution plan. Defined contribution plans, such as 401(k) plans, take a certain amount of funds each month out of your paycheck and allow you to invest it in a variety of ways. The amount you have at retirement is dependent on how well your investments do over time. Although allowing for more profit than traditional defined benefit plans, defined contribution plans also have tremendous downsides when the stock market declines. Retirees who happen to be caught in the stock market during bear markets (when stock prices fall) can see much of their asset base disappear just when it is needed most. A recent study (Pfeffer, Danziger, & Schoeni, 2013) suggested that many Americans lost much of their assets during the Great Recession.

Social Security (OASDI)

Social Security, also known as Old Age, Survivors, and Disability Insurance, is the federal government's primary income maintenance program for the elderly. Social Security is set up on a "pay-as-you-go" system, where current retirees are paid from contributions of current workers. The funds that are taken from your earnings are *not* set aside in a special account that only you have access to. The pay-as-you-go feature is leading to a problem for future retirees: Social Security funds are projected to be gone in a few decades, even though there is currently a surplus. According to the Social Security Administration, Social Security trust funds will be exhausted in 2033. After that, current taxes will be adequate to fund payments at only about 75 percent of what it is currently scheduled to pay through 2086 (Social Security Administration, 2012b).

The Social Security program clearly is a major part of the retirement system in the United States at the current time, and is of vital importance to the senior population. The decrease in poverty among the aged is generally attributed to Social Security benefits becoming larger and being indexed automatically to inflation, so that as prices rise, so do pension payments (Engelhardt & Gruber, 2004). This research provides strong evidence that, properly envisioned and run, governmental programs can have a positive effect on decreasing income inequality and problems of income insecurity.

The Social Security system was never intended to be the only source of income for retirees. In fact, in 2008, elderly Americans reported a variety of sources of income. The largest percent said they received Social Security retirement benefits (87 percent), followed by income from assets (54 percent), private pensions (28 percent), earnings (25 percent), and government employee pensions (14 percent) (Administration on Aging, 2010).

Despite the existence of private pensions and Social Security benefits for retirees, income security is not assured for the aged. Because of the low savings rates of Americans, many of the elderly in the United States do not have enough assets to provide income security after retirement. This is a growing problem because of the large numbers of people reaching the age of sixty-five each day for the next two decades. Even people who saved for their retirement (and many have not done a good job of this) have seen their nest eggs decrease in value if the money was invested in the stock market or tied up in the value of their home. Although these assets may rebound in value, the fact that their worth fluctuates can cause a sense of insecurity.

HEALTH AND THE AGED

With age comes greater likelihood of health problems and disability. Health problems that increase dramatically with age include heart disease, hypertension, stroke, emphysema, asthma, cancer, diabetes, arthritis, and the like. One research team explains the situation in this way:"... [A]s age increased the percentage of adults with excellent health or very good health decreased, and the percentage of adults with fair or poor health increased" (Pleis & Lethbridge-Çejku, 2007, p. 10). The elderly use a great deal of all medical care dollars spent by government programs and individuals alike, costing three to five times more than those under the age of sixty-five (Centers for Disease Control, 2007).

Fortunately, due to government programs, almost all elderly persons have health insurance. According to the United States Census Bureau (2012b), in 2009, only 1.8 percent of the elderly were without health insurance. For those over age sixty-five with private health insurance, 44 percent felt they had excellent health, 37 percent had good health, and 20 percent had fair or poor health. For the aged with Medicare, the figures are 39 percent, 33 percent, and 28 percent, respectively (Pleis & Lethbridge-Çejku, 2007, p. 58).

Health Programs: Medicare

The main health care program for the aged is Medicare, which is designed for people sixty-five years and older, people under age sixty-five with certain disabilities, and everyone with end stage renal disease. Part A helps cover hospital, skilled nursing, hospice, and home health care. Part B helps cover doctors' services, outpatient care, and some preventative health care. Part C (Medicare Advantage plans) are approved by the federal government and act like a Health Maintenance Organization or Preferred Provider Organization. These are chosen *instead* of Medicare Parts A and B and may offer different benefits at different costs than Medicare or other Part C programs. Part D is the relatively new prescription drug benefit that helps cover the cost of medicine. To cover costs not paid for by Parts A and B, "Medigap" private insurance is available (Centers for Medicare and Medicaid Services, 2012).

Health Programs: Medicaid

Medicaid is a joint federal and state government program for people (of all ages) with limited income and resources. The Medicaid program was created under the 1965 amendments to the Social Security Act. It is means-tested, with benefits that differ from state to state. Some states, for example, have pharmacy assistance programs to help with the costs of medicines. According to Barusch (2011), although the elderly and disabled are only a minority of Medicaid recipients, they account for more than half of all Medicaid costs. Medicaid covers around half of all nursing home costs, making it an important element of health care for the aged. Because Medicaid is jointly funded by state and federal government, decisions to cut budgets by state-level legislatures have immediate and far-reaching effects on low-income elderly persons covered by this program. With many states facing large budget deficits in recent years, Medicaid program funding is being cut across the country. The future effects of these cuts will in all probability increase the level of inequality in terms of health care access for seniors.

Health Programs: Supplemental Security Income

The Supplemental Security Income program was begun in 1974 as a way to combine many state-run programs at the national level as a federal-state partnership. Supplemental Security Income (SSI) is a monthly amount paid by Social Security to people with limited income and resources who are disabled, blind, or age sixty-five or older. SSI benefits provide cash to meet basic needs for food, clothing, and shelter. Unfortunately, the program's promise to help the elderly and other needy Americans is compromised by payments that are so low that they do not lift recipients out of poverty and by low levels of participation by people eligible for the program but not enrolled.

There are special programs in Puerto Rico, the Virgin Islands, Guam, the Northern Mariana Islands, and American Samoa to help people with limited income and resources pay their Medicare costs because these people are generally not eligible for SSI.

Health Programs: Long-term Care and Nursing Homes

As a result of declining health or increasing motor problems, seniors sometimes have problems living in their own homes. One option is to provide assistance such as home nursing care or other long-term care services so that the aged can stay in their homes. According to the National Clearinghouse for Long-term Care Information (n.d.), "Long-term care services include personal care services like bathing, doing household chores, and other activities, to help you stay independent in your community. Long-term care also includes community services, such as meals, adult day care, and transportation services." Having a person come in to help three times a week can cost more than $19,000 a year (as of 2010) (National Clearinghouse for Long-term Care Information, n.d.).

Another option is to move in with a relative or friend. The aged may also move to a nursing home or long-term care facility. These are state-licensed facilities of varying quality and cost. Because most nursing homes and other long-term care facilities in the United States are privately owned, for-profit businesses, concerns are rampant as to whether residents receive care as needed, or as the owner deems profitable. A comprehensive meta-analysis of eighty-two research articles shows that care in nonprofit nursing homes is better than is care in for-profit nursing homes (Comondore, Devereaux, Zhou, Stone, Busse, et al., 2009).

Almost 70 percent of people over the age of sixty-five will require living in a nursing home at some point (National Clearinghouse for Long-term Care Information, n.d.). Long-term care facilities can range, however, from very low quality to extremely high quality. Naturally, the higher quality residences tend to be much more expensive. The national median cost in 2012 for a single room, single occupancy, assisted living facility was $3,300 per month ($39,600 per year); living in a nursing home in a semi-private room had a national median cost of $200 per day ($73,000 per year), while living in a private room in a nursing home cost a median of $222 per day ($81,030 per year) (Genworth Financial, 2012).

MENTAL HEALTH AND THE AGED

The elderly are as prone to mental health problems as anyone, and with normal life changes (decreasing mobility, deaths of family members and friends, move from own home to institution) some mental health problems such as depression can occur. One approach to combating mental illness is through greater awareness and education. This technique is being used by the Geriatric Mental Health Foundation (n.d.-b).

Facts about Mental Health and the Aged

According to the Women's Health Center (n.d.) website, dementia/Alzheimer's disease and depression are of special concern when working with the aged. Elderly patients (especially women) are more sensitive to medications used to treat mental health issues and are more prone to experience negative side effects. Because women have a longer life expectancy than do men, the health

The Advice Shop in Edinburg, Scotland, UK, offers services to low income residents. Attractive, nonstigmatizing facilities are more inviting ways to deliver services.

care system will spend more years treating women for depression and the side effects of such medication.

Alzheimer's disease is the most common form of dementia among Americans sixty-five years of age and older. Nearly 10 percent of all people over age sixty-five and up to half of those over age eighty-five are thought to have Alzheimer's disease or another dementia. As the population of older Americans increases, so will the number of people with Alzheimer's disease (Geriatric Mental Health Foundation, n.d.-b).

Sometimes medications are used to treat symptoms that are secondary to dementia, such as sleep disruption, depression, and aggressive behaviors. These medications are only treating the symptoms that arise out of the underlying dementia, and do not treat the dementia itself. Currently, there is no treatment that can stop or cure Alzheimer's disease. Some medications may help slow the disease and control behavioral symptoms, such as insomnia, irritability, anxiety, and depression.

Depression among the elderly is common, particularly among elderly women, according to the Women's Health Center (n.d.). It is commonly misdiagnosed or missed altogether. Personal issues, such as loss of mobility; decreased independence; death of spouse, family members, and/or friends; and increased health problems can lead to depression, especially when these occur close together in time. Certain medications that are more commonly prescribed to the elderly are known to be linked to depression as well. Women are two to three times more likely to experience depression at some time in their lives than are men.

Substance Abuse and the Aged

A large number of older adults misuse alcohol, prescription drugs, or other substances, and this number is growing bigger. Almost one in every five older Americans drinks alcohol or uses medications unsafely (Geriatric Mental Health Foundation, n.d.-a). Substance misuse can occur and cause mental health problems if someone accidently uses alcohol or other drugs in combination with prescribed medicines. Older women may be especially at risk for alcohol problems because they are more likely than men to outlive their spouses and face other losses that may lead to loneliness and depression. Physiologically, women are also at greater risk for alcohol–related health problems as they age (Blow & Barry, 2003).

OTHER SERVICES FOR THE AGED

General

One set of laws, called the Older Americans Act, was passed in 1965, with the aim of improving the quality of life for seniors. This law offers social services such as senior citizen centers; nutrition services such as congregate food services (usually lunches) and "Meals on Wheels" for seniors who cannot leave their homes; and, perhaps most important, Area Agencies on Aging (AAAs), which were created to coordinate services to older people. AAAs provide transportation, needs assessment, information and referral, and advocacy for seniors. Some adult day care centers exist to provide a safe location for seniors when other people cannot be with them.

Adult Protective Services (APS)

The National Center on Elder Abuse (2010) indicates that more than one in ten of the elderly are victims of some type of elder abuse. State laws vary, but usually include protections against physical, emotional, and sexual abuse, as well as financial exploitation, neglect, and abandonment. Adult Protective Services (APS) are established to protect the elderly (and others who are dependent adults) from abuse. Interventions provided by Adult Protective Services include, but are not limited to, receiving reports of adult abuse, exploitation, or neglect; investigating these reports; and case planning, monitoring, and evaluation. In addition to casework services, Adult Protective Services may provide or arrange for the provision of medical, social, economic, legal, housing, law enforcement, or other protective, emergency, or supportive services (National Center on Elder Abuse, 2011).

The Patient Protection and Affordable Care Act and the Elderly

In 2010, Congress passed the Patient Protection and Affordable Care Act (P.L. 111-148). The provisions of this law will affect senior citizens in many ways (Berenson & Holahan, 2010). Although the details are many, the bottom line is that, as passed, services for the elderly will likely be more comprehensive in some aspects, although costs will also be higher, particularly for high-income aged persons. Payments to medical providers might also be lower, leading to possibly greater inequality between government-pay patients and private-pay patients. Because of increasing numbers of Americans eligible for medical services, competition for the attention of medical personnel may increase, leaving the elderly facing longer wait times and more trouble receiving medical attention.

AGING POLICY IN A CHANGING SOCIETY

The current policy framework for the aged population builds on the original Social Security Act of 1935 and its amendments. There are a variety of other programs that also are relevant, which were discussed earlier in this chapter. The underlying nature of these programs is that the elderly are a special class of individuals who are "deserving" of program benefits. This status may be helped by most people's hope that they will one day be among the ranks of the aged, and thus be eligible for benefits from these programs themselves. The status may also be strengthened because those over the age of sixty-five are among the most politically active, voting at high rates, and may belong to one of the strongest interest groups in Washington, the American Association of Retired Persons (AARP).

In addition to this status of being "deserving," programs for the elderly are generally based on an industrialized view of the world. Seniors are supposed to retire at age sixty-five (or so) from their paying jobs, though early retirement is allowed at age sixty-two, with reduced payments. In the 1930s when the Social Security Act was passed, retirement for many people meant happily leaving a job of heavy labor. Some who made payments into the Social Security fund never received benefits because their occupations and living conditions contributed to premature death. As office, or white collar, work became more common in the 1950s and 1960s, the program did not change its essential nature. Those above the retirement age were expected to leave the workforce and allow their job positions to be filled by younger workers. This idea was accepted by both the older worker and the younger ones coming along. Retirement was seen as a short-lived part of life, the golden years, to be enjoyed before death ensued.

The nature of work has largely shifted from heavy and sometimes dangerous labor which broke people's backs and crippled their bodies. Manufacturing, construction, and farming jobs now constitute a small percentage of work opportunities, and those that are left are typically safer than half a century ago due to government regulations and, sometimes, union contracts. Most jobs are now in retail, service, government, and education, which have low demands for physical strength and typically have extremely low mortality and injury rates. Workers now begin retirement with better health and a longer life expectancy than their parents did. They are thus living longer and with a higher quality of life than just a generation ago. But policy has been slow to catch up.

Another pillar of policy towards the elderly is that of individualism. A Social Security retirement benefit was never considered to be sufficient to meet all the financial needs that a person or couple would have. Retirees were expected to have saved additional amounts on their own to supplement the governmental pension payment. Medicare, the medical program for the aged, also is premised on the idea that the doctor and hospital insurance it provides is not sufficient. "Medigap" insurance plans have been created to cover the areas where Medicare falls short. These insurance plans, although useful, or even essential, are an added expense to people who may be living on a fixed income.

Although services funded by the Older Americans Act are important and valuable to recipients, they do not challenge the typical assumptions of the industrial model of work and life underlying current policy for the elderly. Finally, much of the policy for seniors is consistent with maintaining a for-profit approach to services. Many services, such as medical or nursing care, homemaking services, nursing homes, and other services or programs run to benefit the aged, are designed to make money. The status quo is definitely not challenged by current policy.

Gaps between Current Policy Framework and Current Reality

Work no longer has to end at age sixty-five for most employed Americans. With the rise of information work, physical strength is not very important. In partial recognition of this, the age of retiring with full Social Security benefits is gradually rising. With the increases in life expectancy of the baby boom generation, the largest cohort of Americans ever, the Social Security and Medicare trust funds are projected to be exhausted in the future if changes in the law are not made. Policy gridlock has set in, however. Republicans and Democrats agree that something must be done but agreement is elusive on what that something is.

One important aspect of the reliance on individuals largely funding their own retirements from savings and investments is that many senior citizens who are close to retirement or have already retired lost a great deal of their retirement assets in the massive stock market decline of 2008 and 2009. When coupled with the profit motive of venders of investment vehicles and insurance, additional millions of the elderly have lost savings that they will never be able to gain back, even if (when) the stock market recovers. They may have been sold investments that were too risky for their situation, or taken out variable-rate home-equity loans at rates that have escalated. Although there is some responsibility on the part of the seniors who may have invested and borrowed unwisely, there is considerable evidence that the profit motive put the interests of the sellers of these products at odds with the interests of the seniors involved.

Because the current system is built around the idea of work relevant to the industrial age, and the assumption that employees will leave the workforce at a certain age, existing policies frequently seem outmoded. Globalization, with greater mobility of individuals and employment opportunities, means there is greater competition for existing jobs. Many jobs requiring technological training are now outsourced to countries with lower pay scales, such as India and China. People who are older may not have the skills to compete for this work, or they perhaps expect a salary that is far higher than the norm outside the United States. Losing a job in one's fifties can decimate chances for a substantial retirement fund, as it can be very difficult to obtain a new job at a similar salary at that age.

Although it is true that information technology changes quickly, and younger workers may be more able to pick up new approaches to using technology, there is no doubt that the life experiences that seniors have had in applying new ideas and technologies can assist any organization facing a decision about using new ideas. As the baby boomer generation reaches retirement age over the next two decades, a massive "brain drain" of important non-technical knowledge may ensue. The costs of lost experience and information to the economy may be staggering.

As noted earlier, however, the pace of retirement may be slowing for those reaching the age where it is possible to begin receiving a Social Security pension. People who believed that they were financially ready to leave the workforce have reconsidered their situation in the light of large losses to their retirement savings. Others, without much savings to start with, may just continue working in their current position, or, if among the many who have suffered job loss, may find a new position in order to bring in some income.

One of the aspects of life today that makes retirement years increasingly difficult to navigate is the industrial age social change of young workers moving away from where their parents live. This results in older parents without a family social network to provide care and support as they age. In addition, the unpaid labor of women who used to provide a great deal of care to aging family members has been sharply curtailed as more women work in paying jobs. Because information jobs can be done from almost anywhere, and at any time, it is more possible that children can live in the places their parents do and also that children of the elderly (both sons and daughters) may be able to provide at least some of the caregiving associated with earlier times.

To bring in another theme of this book, that environmental changes affect all members of society, consider the impact of the increasing number of carcinogenic chemicals in the air, soil, and water. Rachel Carson, in her classic 1962 book *Silent Spring*, warned us of the danger of DDT and other chemicals that were having a serious impact on the environment and all living organisms. Jenkins (2011) provides updates on this topic, calling the past 100 years the "synthetic century." He indicates that there are nearly 80,000 synthetic chemicals in use today (up from about 62,000 in the mid-1970s), 99 percent of which have never had their effects on human health evaluated. Fewer than 3 percent have been tested for being carcinogenic (Jenkins, 2011). Jenkins argues that it is not possible to escape from the huge amounts of known toxic synthetic compounds used as herbicides and flame retardants, much less other chemicals that are of unknown toxicity. Still, there is a cost to be paid in terms of health, particularly in the number and variety of cancer cases that have become epidemic in America. Naturally, those who have lived the longest have had the most exposure. Currently, one out of every three American women dies of cancer. One out of every two American men dies of cancer (Jenkins, 2011). Although technology has created new treatments that may cure individual cases of illness, it seems that technological innovation has also created many of the health risks that American society faces. Without a change at the social level, the burdens are left for individuals, especially the aged, to deal with on their own.

FUTURE POLICIES

Of all the policy arenas where policy change is discussed seriously, the aging arena is one of the most active. The effects of demographic change (greater longevity, the changing nature of work, the increase in the number of people of color, for example) on the Social Security system have been the topic of much research and debate. Possible solutions have ranged from eliminating all Social Security taxes and benefits to increasing Social Security taxes by raising the amount of income that can be taxed and/or increasing the tax rate from the current 6.2 percent. Decreasing the level of benefits, or making Social Security a means-tested program, has also been suggested. Reforms have already increased the age to receive full benefits from sixty-five to a sliding retirement age depending on the year a person was born.

An issue that is unprecedented in scope concerns the numbers of baby boomers who are approaching retirement and who are currently single. The rate of being single between the ages of forty-five to sixty-three increased by 50 percent between 1980 and 2009, from 20 percent to 33 percent. This statistic is important because being single and elderly is associated with higher risk factors for a low quality of life. Examples include higher rates of poverty, more likelihood of disability, and lower probabilities of having health insurance (Sobolewski, 2012). The most worrisome type of single baby boomer is that of "never married," as these individuals are unlikely to have children who can help monitor and care for their health and social needs. Compared to never-married boomers, for example, divorced boomers tend to have more assets and a larger network of family members, especially children, which can improve their quality of life after retirement. The one-third of the boomers who may enter old age without a spouse or children will probably put the greatest burden on the care system, and yet no provision is being made to address this problem (Sobolewski, 2012). In the current economic and government budget-cutting climate, existing social services are having a difficult time surviving, much less expanding. Future policy efforts must support the needs of elderly persons with no caregiver supports.

Medicare reform is another perennial hot topic because it is difficult to deal with this one aspect of the health system without addressing all the other parts of the complex public-private, interrelated system. Almost everyone acknowledges that the system is broken, but there is no agreement on how to fix it. Some say it has built in inefficiencies that must be improved with more government oversight and intervention, while others argue that government initiatives lead to more inefficiency and lack of patient choice. The insurance, pharmaceutical, and health care industries vie for their interests, while interest groups for doctors, the aged, and nearly every other group affected by health care (including social workers) struggle to get their viewpoints heard and adopted by decision-makers. It is quite possible that many policy changes will have become law between the time this is being written and when you read this chapter. It is an exciting and challenging time to be active in the aging policy arena.

The country's medical system is not adequately preparing for the increasing number of elderly people. A report from the Institute of Medicine (2008) argues that the United States faces a massive health care shortage that threatens to leave millions of seniors without proper health care within the next three decades. The report goes on to say, "By 2030 the United States will need an additional 3.5 million formal health care providers—a 35 percent increase from current levels—just to maintain the current ratio of providers to the total population" (p. 5).

According to the Bureau of Labor Statistics, "Employment of healthcare social workers is expected to grow by 34 percent, much faster than the average for all occupations. As baby boomers age, they and their families will require help from social workers to find care, which will increase demand for healthcare social workers" (Bureau of Labor Statistics, 2012). Policies, such as tuition reduction and educational loan forgiveness for health care and social workers, would be steps in the right direction of improving the lives of senior citizens.

Current debates among policy makers seem to suggest that the most important health care program for older Americans, Medicare, will be reduced in scope and budget to assist in balancing the national government's budgetary woes. The passage of the Patient Protection and Affordable Care Act will make more preventive care available to senior citizens and to the American public in general. This should have an impact in future years as the elderly, who have had more routine access to medical care when they were younger, should arrive at their retirement years stronger and in better health than the current group of elderly people.

Better medical care throughout their lives should also reduce differences between demographic groups. The gaps in critical medical outcomes between the elderly of different races and genders will be reduced as millions of people receive better and more consistent health care.

The ability of elderly people to remain a part of the community is highly dependent upon their environment. Although only about 5 percent of the elderly have a health problem so severe that mobility is limited (Ambrosino, Heffernan, Shuttlesworth, & Ambrosino, 2011), their ease of movement is drastically affected by the micro-environment. Difficulties in getting out of a chair, for example, due to lack of upper body strength, can be eliminated if a special type of chair is available. The macro-environment is also an issue. People using a walker can be stranded at a street crossing if the curb is too high and there are no curb cuts, and crossing a street can be hazardous if traffic lights are not timed properly to allow slower-moving pedestrians enough time to cross. Although changes in such streetscapes may seem unnecessary to some, they are vital to the ability of others to be mobile and active citizens of their localities. Attention needs to be paid to these local ordinances and policies as well as to the larger-scale policies.

CONCLUSION

What the facts presented in this chapter mean for social work and social workers can be debated. Almost everyone sees these facts as leading to the conclusion that social workers should move into the field of gerontology because the need for workers with an understanding of the aging population will continue to increase. This interpretation leads also to a conclusion that social work programs must ramp up their level of knowledge by faculty members and students in order to be positioned to serve the elderly population. The Geriatric Social Work Initiative is one approach to increasing the number of social workers who are aware of and able to work with the geriatric population. This initiative works with "social work programs, organizations and other funders around the country" to accomplish this goal (Geriatric Social Work Initiative, 2012).

As social workers, it is important to take into account that the elderly are individuals, just as people of all ages are. They have their own life histories, their own desires, and their own needs. The question is not just, "What are the problems of the elderly?" but also, "What are the strengths of older adults?" From these questions arise better social policies. Social workers can, and should, work at both the micro level up to the largest levels of national and international policy.

As with all areas of policy, however, it is necessary to look beyond the individuals affected to understand how larger-scale changes—globalization of the world economy, changes in living patterns, and increasing damage to the environment—affect their situations. Working at higher levels of policy making as advocates can make some of the problems individuals face less daunting and more manageable.

Questions for Discussion

1. In what ways is the aging of America likely to affect the profession of social work and your own career?

2. Should the aging process be looked upon as natural and beneficial to the individual and society, or is it a process to be resisted?

3. What type of retirement do you feel should be available to most Americans? Should it be the individual's responsibility to bring that about, or should a certain level be guaranteed by governmental policy?

Exercises

1. Check the websites of several nursing homes in your area. If you can, visit a few of them. Try to find at least one that has higher costs and one that has lower costs. What differences are there in the seeming quality of care? How would you feel about placing a relative of yours in one that costs just what Medicaid reimburses?

2. Spend an hour or two teaching a non-retired "older adult" about some aspect of technology that you are familiar with. Describe what happened. How does this experience affect your ideas about the employability of this person?

3. Ask your classmates and colleagues about the plans they have for their own retirement. How confident are they that they will be able to maintain a similar or better lifestyle than they currently have? What steps have they taken to make their hopes a reality?

Websites

Administration on Aging: www.aoa.gov

Alliance for Retired Americans: http://www.retiredamericans.org/

Alzheimer's Association: http://www.alz.org/index.asp

American Association for Geriatric Psychiatry: http://www.aagpgpa.org/

American Association of Retired Persons: www.aarp.org

American Geriatrics Society: http://www.americangeriatrics.org/about/

American Society on Aging: http://www.asaging.org/index.cfm

Centers for Disease Control and Prevention, Healthy Aging: http://www.cdc.gov/aging/saha.htm

Family Caregivers Online: www.familycaregiversonline.net

Fighting Fraud: www.stopmedicarefraud.gov

Medicare: www.medicare.gov

National Institute on Alcohol Abuse and Alcoholism: www.niaaa.nih.gov

Substance Abuse and Mental Health Services Administration: www.samhsa.gov

U.S. Department of Health and Human Services: www.hhs.gov

Visual Media

"Aging in America—Stuck in the Middle": http://www.cbsnews.com/news/aging-in-america-stuck-in-the-middle/

Further Reading

Cox, C. (2015). *Social policy for an aging society: A human rights perspective.* New York, NY: Springer.

Irving, P. (2014). *The upside of aging: How long life is changing the world of health, work, innovation, policy and purpose.* Hoboken, NJ: Wiley.

Coda

Coda (music): a more or less independent passage, at the end of a composition, introduced to bring it to a satisfactory close.

The purpose of a coda is neither to be a summary nor to recapitulate all of the important aspects of the preceding work. It is, instead, a way to draw to a close a longer piece of work in a pleasing way. The hope is that these concluding thoughts will help you bring to a close your course in social policy in a way that you can feel that you have spent your time well.

Some may wonder if the world really needed another social welfare policy text. The answer is yes, because incredibly important changes are happening in technology, the environment, and the economy that are likely to last for generations, changes that should be profoundly interesting to students and scholars of social policy. Yet these changes weren't reflected in the textbooks that were being written.

The lack of information being presented on these trends can be likened to being on the scene of the early years of the Industrial Revolution and not noticing that people were crowding into urban centers and factories, that the air was being fouled by new inventions that created clouds of sooty smoke, and that trains and steamships were overtaking wagons and sailing ships as means of mass transportation of goods and people. To be silent in the face of change of this magnitude serves no one. This book was needed in order to highlight the tremendous disconnect between the social policy assumptions of the Industrial Age and the social policy needs of the information age.

Another way that this book is different is that the information in this book is intended to be not only thought-provoking, but action-inducing. That is why the book includes tools for describing the politics and ideology behind policy decisions, a method to analyze policy, and techniques to create new policy through the use of advocacy. This allows readers to use their understanding and expanded view of social policy to make positive change happen.

Now that you have finished reading the book, you have been exposed to information of great importance to the United States and to the globe. The very interconnected essence of the way America and the world move forward is

A portion of the Berlin Wall at the Imperial War Museum in London. The Berlin Wall was erected by the Warsaw Pact during the cold war to prevent people from leaving the Eastern European countries. The removal of the Berlin Wall was considered a major victory for human freedom.

encapsulated in understanding the impact of the globalization of the economy, the changes to the environment, and the way that technological advances can be used to solve problems as well as create them. Social policy that does not take these trends into account is bound to be less than effective.

Of course, this book hasn't included everything that you *could* know. But it has included enough information and ideas that you are much further along in your understanding of these matters than before you read this book. Understanding the three key themes is more important than knowing all the details of current policies. The details are important as you practice social work—indeed, they are vital and will have a large impact on you, your work, and your clients. But the details of social policy will almost certainly change between the time this manuscript is written and the book is published. You may not even read it for some time after its publication, in which case the details will have changed more. Thus, a text that is focused on overarching themes that you apply for yourself in the future is of greater value than one that tries to explain all the details of current policy. There is nothing like the power of the Internet to provide up-to-the-moment information on current policy details. A more permanent entity such as a book needs to stress information that has a longer shelf life.

Your time is the most valuable asset you have. Grappling with concepts such as those in this book is one way to use your time productively. Some ideas you may agree with wholly, some partially, and some not at all. As long as you understand the book's viewpoint and have good reasons for your reactions, that is what counts. You are *living* the changes in technology, economy, and environment described here. Feel free to take the ideas that make sense to you and adopt or adapt them.

In the final analysis, this book is for you. The ideas about policy, politics, and advocacy are ones that you will abandon or you will use. Some students want to sell back their books and so treat them very carefully, leaving the book in excellent condition for the next user. But other students, the ones who get the most out of class, highlight and mark up the book on just about every page, writing in the margins, and finding blank spaces for impromptu diagrams, doodles, and disagreements. They mark the book to create a unique reflection of their ideas, their questions, and their thoughts. In this way, such students make it *their* book. They not only read the book but they complete the exercises at the end of the chapters, think deeply about them, and talk about the ideas both in and out of class.

It would bring us great satisfaction if you have been challenged by and interested in the ideas presented in this book enough to make the book your own. We would be interested in hearing from you about the ways you have done so. Use the Internet to find our current email addresses, and drop us a line. By doing so, you will be finalizing your understanding of the present—the way you understand social policy currently. But you will be doing much more than that—you will be helping us improve our ideas for future readers. You will become a co-author of a social policy text, one that is needed for the world to create a better fit between the type of policy we need and the type of policy we have.

With that as the final incentive, we offer one final wish. We hope that, using the information from this book and all the others that you will use in your professional social work education, you are able to do what social work students throughout the years have universally wanted—to make a difference for the better in this world. We believe you can, and we know that the world needs your input to improve.

References

Abadinsky, H. (2014a). *Law, courts, and justice in America*. Long Grove, IL: Waveland.

Abadinsky, H. (2014b). *Probation and parole: Theory and practice* (12th ed.). Englewood Cliffs, NJ: Prentice Hall.

Abramovitz, M. (1988). *Regulating the lives of women: Social welfare policy from colonial times to the present*. Boston, MA: South End.

Abrams, L., & Curran, L. (2000).Wayward girls and virtuous women: Social workers and female juvenile delinquency in the Progressive Era. *Affilia, 15*, 49–64.

Adler, N. E., & Rehkopf, D. H. (2008). U.S. disparities in health: Descriptions, causes and mechanisms. *Annual Review of Public Health, 29*, 235–252.

Administration for Children and Families (2012a). *Fact sheet*. Retrieved from http://www.acf.hhs.gov/programs/ocs/ssbg/about/factsheets.htm.

Administration for Children and Families (2012b). *FY 2012 SSBG allocations*. Retrieved from http://www.acf.hhs.gov/programs/ocs/ssbg/docs/esalloc12.html.

Administration on Aging (2010). *A profile of older Americans: 2010*. Retrieved from http://www.aoa.gov/aoaroot/aging_statistics/Profile/2010/docs/2010profile.pdf.

Administration on Aging (2011). *Aging statistics*. Retrieved from http://www.aoa.gov/aoaroot/aging_statistics/index.aspx.

Almond, G., & Verba, S. (1965). *The civic culture: Political attitudes and democracy in five nations*. Boston, MA: Little, Brown.

Alpert, L. T. (2005). Research review: Parents' service experience—A missing element in research on foster care case outcomes. *Child and Family Social Work, 10*(4), 361–366.

Ambrosino, R., Heffernan, J., Shuttlesworth, G., & Ambrosino, R. (2011). *Social work and social welfare: An introduction* (7th ed.). Belmont, CA: Brooks/Cole.

American Federation of State, County, and Municipal Employees (1998). *Double jeopardy: Caseworkers at risk helping at-risk kids: A report on working conditions facing child welfare workers.* Washington, DC: Author.

Amnesty International (2011, October 6). *11 numbers you need to know about the global housing crisis.* Retrieved from http://blog.amnestyusa.org/us/human-right-to-housing-11-numbers-you-need-to-know/.

Annie E. Casey Foundation (2012). *About us.* Retrieved from www.aecf.org.

Anzick, M. A., & Weaver, D. A. (2001). *Reducing poverty among elderly women* (ORES Working Paper Series No. 87). Washington, DC: Social Security Administration.

Avlon, J. (2005). *Independent nation: How centrism can change American politics.* New York, NY: Three Rivers.

Bachrach, P., & Baratz, M. (1962). The second face of power. *American Political Science Review, 56,* 947–952.

Baradat, L. (2011). *Political ideologies: Their origins and impact* (11th ed.). Englewood Cliffs, NJ: Prentice Hall.

Bardach, E. (2011*). A practical guide for policy analysis: The eightfold path to more effective problem solving* (4th ed.). Washington, DC: CQ Press.

Barth, R. P., Lee, C. K., Wildfire, J., & Guo, S. (2006). A comparison of the governmental costs of long-term foster care and adoption. *Social Service Review, 80*(1), 127–158.

Barusch, A. (2011). *Foundations of social policy: Social justice in human perspective* (4th ed.). Belmont, CA: Brooks/Cole.

Baxandall, P., & Wohlschlegel, K. (2010). *Following the money.* Washington, DC: U.S. PIRG Education Fund. Retrieved from http://cdn.publicinterestnetwork.org/assets/b3ba157e28d82952ee5b7a3f84e88499/Following-the-Money-USPIRG.pdf.

Becker, H. (1964). *Human capital: A theoretical and empirical analysis, with special reference to education.* Chicago, IL: University of Chicago Press.

Bedell, G. (2000). *Three steps to yes: The gentle art of getting your way.* New York, NY: Crown Business.

Bell, D. (1973). *The coming of the post-industrial society.* New York, NY: Basic.

Beniger, J. (1986). *The control revolution: Technological and economic origins of the information society.* Cambridge, MA: Harvard University Press.

Beniger, J. (1988). Information society and global science. *Annals of the American Association of Political and Social Science, 495*, 14–29.

Benkler, Y. (2006). *The wealth of networks.* New Haven, CT: Yale University Press.

Bennis, W., Benne, K., & Chin, R. (1985). *The planning of change.* New York, NY: International Thompson.

Berenson, R., & Holahan, J. (2010). *How will the Patient Protection and Affordable Care Act affect seniors?* Washington, DC: Health Policy Center, Urban Institute. Retrieved from http://www.urban.org/uploadedpdf/412131-ppaca-seniors.pdf.

Berger, P., & Neuhaus, R. (1996). *To empower people: From state to civil society* (2nd ed.). Washington, DC: American Enterprise Institute for Public Policy Research.

Berry, J. M., & Arons, D. (2002). *A voice for nonprofits.* Washington, DC: Brookings.

Besharov, D. J. (1990). *Recognizing child abuse.* New York, NY: Free Press.

Betcher, G. (n.d.). *Medieval guilds.* Retrieved from http://www.public.iastate.edu/~gbetcher/373/guilds.htm.

Blow, C. M. (2010, October 8). High cost of crime. *New York Times.* Retrieved from http://www.nytimes.com/2010/10/09/opinion/09blow.html.

Blow, F., & Barry, K. (2003). *Use and misuse of alcohol among older women.* Retrieved from http://pubs.niaaa.nih.gov/publications/arh26-4/308-315.htm.

Bloy, M. (2002a). Implementation of the Poor Law. *The Victorian Web.* Retrieved from http://www.victorianweb.org/history/poorlaw/implemen.html.

Bloy, M. (2002b). Southwell workhouse. *The Victorian Web.* Retrieved from http://www.victorianweb.org/history/poorlaw/southwh.html.

Bloy, M. (2002c). The Speenlamhand system. *The Victorian Web.* Retrieved from http://www.victorianweb.org/history/poorlaw/speen.html.

Bluestone, B., & Harrison, B. (1982). *Deindustrialization in America.* New York, NY: Basic.

Bluestone, B., & Rose, S. (1997). Overworked and underemployed. *The American Prospect, 31*, 58–69.

Booth-Butterfield, S. (2010). *Dual process persuasion.* Retrieved from http://healthyinfluence.com/wordpress/steves-primer-of-practical-persuasion-3-0/.

Bowlby, J. (1969). *Attachment and loss.* New York, NY: Basic.

Brainard, L. A., & McNutt, J. G. (2010). Virtual government-citizen relations: Informational, transactional, or collaborative? *Administration and Society, 42*(7), 836–858.

Bridges, W. (1994). The end of the job. *Fortune, 129,* 62–74.

Brilliant, E. L. (1990). *The United Way: Dilemmas of organized charity.* New York, NY: Columbia University Press.

Brown, L. (1981). *Building a sustainable society.* New York, NY: Norton.

Brown, L. (2005). *Outgrowing the Earth: The food security challenge in an age of falling water tables and rising temperatures.* New York, NY: Norton.

Brown, L. (2006). *Plan B 2.0: Rescuing a planet under stress and a civilization in trouble.* New York, NY: Norton.

Brown, L. (2009). *Plan B 4.0: Mobilizing to save civilization.* New York, NY: Norton.

Brown, L. (2011). *World on the edge.* New York, NY: Norton.

Brown, V. A., Grootjans, J., Ritchie, J., Townsend, M., & Verrinder, G. (2014). *Sustainability and health: Supporting global ecological integrity in public health.* London, England: Routledge.

Brulle, R. J., & Pellow, D. N. (2006). Environmental justice: Human health and environmental inequalities. *Annual Review of Public Health, 27*(3), 1–22.

Bullard, R. (2005). *The quest for environmental justice: Human rights and the politics of pollution.* San Francisco, CA: Sierra Club.

Bureau of Labor Statistics (2012). *Occupational outlook handbook: Social workers: Job outlook.* Retrieved from http://www.bls.gov/ooh/Community -and-Social-Service/Social-workers.htm#tab-6.

Burris, B. H. (1998). Computerization of the workplace. *Annual Review of Sociology, 24,* 141–158.

Carson, R. (1962). *Silent spring.* New York, NY: Houghton Mifflin.

Castells, M. (2009). *The rise of the network society* (2nd ed.). Oxford and Malden, MA: Blackwell.

Cellini, S. R. (2008). The dynamics of poverty in the United States: A review of data, methods and findings. *Journal of Policy Analysis and Management, 27*(3), 577–605.

Centerpartiet (Center Party of Sweden) (2014). *Our positions.* https://www .centerpartiet.se/languages/english/.

Centers for Disease Control (CDC) (2007). *The state of aging and health in America, 2007 report.* Whitehouse Station, NJ: Merck Company Foundation.

Centers for Disease Control (CDC) (2011, September 2). Mental illness surveillance among adults in the United States. *Morbidity and Mortality Weekly Report, 60*(3). Retrieved from http://www.cdc.gov/mmwr/preview/mmwrhtml/su6003a1.htm?s_cid=su6003a1_w.

Centers for Disease Control (CDC) (2012). *Autism spectrum disorders: Data and statistics.* Retrieved from http://www.cdc.gov/ncbddd/autism/data.html.

Centers for Medicare and Medicaid Services (2011). *CHIP ever enrolled year graph.* Retrieved from http://www.cms.gov/NationalCHIPPolicy/downloads/CHIPEverEnrolledYearGraph.pdf.

Centers for Medicare and Medicaid Services (2012). *Medicare and you, 2012.* Washington, DC: Department of Health and Human Services. Retrieved from http://www.medicare.gov/publications/pubs/pdf/10050.pdf.

Central Intelligence Agency (2012). *The world fact book.* Washington, DC: USGPO.

Chambers, D., & Wedel, K. (2008). *Social policy and social programs* (5th ed.). Boston, MA: Allyn and Bacon.

Child, C. D., & Gronbjerg, K. A. (2007). Nonprofit advocacy organizations: Their characteristics and activities. *Social Science Quarterly, 88*(1), 259–281.

Children's Bureau (2011). *Child maltreatment 2010.* Washington, DC: Author. Retrieved from http://www.acf.hhs.gov/programs/cb/pubs/cm10/cm10.pdf.

Children's Defense Fund (2006). *The state of America's children.* Washington, DC: Author.

Children's Welfare Information Gateway (2011, May). *Foster care statistics, 2009.* Washington, DC: Author. Retrieved from http://www.acf.hhs.gov/programs/cb/pubs/cm10/cm10.pdf.

Cialdini, R. (2000). *Influence: Science and practice* (4th ed.). Boston, MA: Pearson.

Cicchetti, D., & Toth, S. (2005). Child maltreatment. *Annual Review of Clinical Psychology, 1,* 413.

Clear, T. R., Cole, G. F., & Reisig, M. D. (2008). *American corrections* (7th ed.). Belmont, CA: Wadsworth.

Cleveland, H. (1985). The twilight of hierarchy: Speculations on the global information society. *Public Administration Review, 45,* 185–195.

Cloward, R., & Ohlin, L. (1960). *Delinquency and opportunity*. New York, NY: Free Press.

CNN (2013, December 26). *Poll: This is a do-nothing Congress*. Retrieved from http://politicalticker.blogs.cnn.com/2013/12/26/poll-this-is-a-do-nothing -congress/.

Cohen, A. (1955). *Delinquent boys*. New York, NY: Free Press.

Collins-Camargo, C., McBeath, B., & Ensign, K. (2011). Privatization and performance-based contracting in child welfare: Recent trends and implications for social service administrators. *Administration in Social Work, 35*(5), 494–516.

Comondore, V., Devereaux, P., Zhou, Q., Stone, S., Busse, J., et al. (2009). Quality of care in for-profit and not-for-profit nursing homes: Systematic review and meta-analysis. *British Medical Journal*. Retrieved from http://pnhp.org/nursing_home/nursing-homes.pdf.

Conservative Party of Canada (2015). *Jobs growth and long term prosperity*. Retrieved from http://www.conservative.ca/where-we-stand/jobs-growth -and-long-term-prosperity/.

Conservative Party of the United Kingdom (2015). *Manifesto*. Retrieved from https://s3-eu-west-1.amazonaws.com/manifesto2015/Conservative Manifesto2015.pdf.

Coven, M. (2005). *An introduction to TANF*. Washington, DC: Center for Budget and Policy Priorities. Retrieved from http://www.cbpp.org/1-22-02tanf2.htm.

Crenson, M. (1998). *The invisible orphanage: A prehistory of the American welfare system*. Cambridge, MA: Harvard University Press.

The curious case of the fall in crime. *Economist* (2013, July 20). Retrieved from http://www.economist.com/news/leaders/21582004-crime-plunging-rich -world-keep-it-down-governments-should-focus-prevention-not

Daly, H., & Cobb, J. B. (1989). *For the common good: Redirecting the economy toward community, the environment and a sustainable future*. Boston, MA: Beacon.

Davis, K., Schoen, C., & Stremkis, K. (2010). *Mirror, mirror on the wall: How the performance of the U.S. health care system compares internationally*. Washington, DC: Commonwealth Fund. Available at www.commonwealthfund.org.

Davis, M. (2006). *Planet of slums*. London, England: Verso.

Death Penalty Information Center (2012). *Fact sheet*. Retrieved from http://www.deathpenaltyinfo.org/documents/FactSheet.pdf.

Death Penalty Information Center (2015). *Fact sheet*. Retrieved from http://www.deathpenaltyinfo.org/documents/FactSheet.pdf.

Deibert, R. J. (2013). *Black code: Inside the battle for cyberspace*. New York, NY: Random.

Democratic National Committee (2015a). *About our party*. Retrieved from www.democrats.org.

Democratic National Committee (2015b). *Civil rights*. Retrieved from www.democrats.org.

Democratic National Committee (2015c). *Health care*. Retrieved from www.democrats.org.

Democratic National Committee (2015d). *Retirement security*. Retrieved from www.democrats.org.

DeNavas-Walt, C., Proctor, B. D., & Smith, J. C. (2014). *Income and poverty in the United States: 2013*. Washington, DC: United States Census Bureau.

DeVita, C. J., & Mosher-Williams, R. (Eds.) (2001). *Who speaks for America's children?* Washington, DC: Urban Institute.

Dewitt, L. (2001). *Research note #17: The Townsend Plan's pension scheme*. Retrieved from http://www.ssa.gov/history/townsendproblems.html.

Dillman, D. (1985). The social impacts of information technologies in rural North America. *Rural Sociology, 50*(1), 1–26.

Dillman, D. (1991). Information society. In E. Borgetta & R. Borgetta (Eds.), *The encyclopedia of sociology*. New York, NY: Macmillan.

DiNitto, D. (2010). *Social welfare politics and public policy* (7th ed.). Boston, MA: Allyn and Bacon.

Dobrow, M., Goel, V., & Upshur, R. E. G. (2004). Evidence-based health policy: Context and utilization. *Social Science and Medicine, 58*, 207–217.

Doe Network (2011). *About us*. Retrieved from http://www.doenetwork.org/.

Dolgoff, R., & Feldstein, D. (1980). *Understanding social welfare*. New York, NY: Harper and Row.

Dolgoff, R., & Feldstein, D. (2007). *Understanding social welfare: A search for social justice* (7th ed.). Boston, MA: Allyn and Bacon.

Dublin, T. (n.d.). *Women and the early Industrial Revolution in the United States*. New York, NY: The Gilder Lehrman Institute of American History. Retrieved from http://www.gilderlehrman.org/history-by-era/jackson-lincoln/essays/women-and-early-industrial-revolution-united-states.

Dunn, W. H. (2011). *Public policy analysis: An introduction* (5th ed.). Englewood Cliffs, NJ: Prentice Hall.

Ebo, B. (Ed.) (1998*). The cyberghetto or cybertopia: Race, class, gender and marginalization in cyberspace*. New York, NY: Praeger.

Edwards, A. R. (2005). *The sustainability revolution*. Garbolla Island, BC: New Society.

Eherenreich, P. (1985). *Altruistic imagination: A history of social work and social policy in the United States*. Ithaca, NY: Cornell University Press.

Elazar, D. (1972). *American Federalism: A view from the states* (2nd ed.). New York, NY: Thomas Y. Crowell.

Engelhardt, G., & Gruber, J. (2004). *Social Security and the evolution of elderly poverty: NBER working paper 10466*. Retrieved from http://www.nber.org/papers/w10466.

Erickson, R., McIver, J., & Wright, G. (1987). State political culture and public opinion. *American Political Science Review, 81*(3), 797–813.

Ezell, M. (1993). The political activity of social workers: A post-Reagan update. *Journal of Sociology and Social Welfare, 20*(4), 81–97.

Fang, X., Brown, D., Florence, C., & Mercy, J. (2012). The economic burden of child maltreatment in the United States and implications for prevention. *Child Abuse & Neglect, 36*(2), 156–165. Retrieved from http://www.science direct.com/science/article/pii/S0145213411003140.

Federal Bureau of Investigation (2014*). Crime in the United States 2013*. Washington, DC: Author.

Federal Interagency Forum on Aging-related Statistics (2010). *Older Americans 2010: Key indicators of well-being*. Retrieved from http://www.agingstats.gov/agingstatsdotnet/Main_Site/Data/2010_Documents/Docs/OA_2010.pdf.

Federal Interagency Forum on Child and Family Statistics (2011a). *America's children: Key national indicators of well-being: 2011*. Retrieved from http://www.childstats.gov/americaschildren/health3.asp.

Federal Interagency Forum on Child and Family Statistics (2011b). *Child population*. Retrieved from http://www.childstats.gov/americaschildren/tables/pop1.asp?popup=true.

Finn, J. (1999). An exploration of helping processes in an online self-help group focusing on issues of disability. *Health and Social Work, 24*(3), 220–231.

Fisher, P., & Pratt, T. (2006). Political culture and the death penalty. *Criminal Justice Policy Review, 17*(1), 48–60.

Flynn, J. (1992). *Social agency policy: Analysis and presentation for community practice* (2nd ed.). Belmont, CA: Brooks/Cole.

Fountain, J. (2001). *Building the digital state*. Washington, DC: Brookings.

Fox, V. (1972). *Introduction to corrections*. Englewood Cliffs, NJ: Prentice Hall.

Friedman, J. (1973). *Retracking America: A theory of transactive planning*. New York, NY: Anchor.

Friedman, T. (2005*). The world is flat: A brief history of the twenty first century*. New York, NY: Farrar, Strauss and Giroux.

Friedman, T. (2007a, March 16). Marching with a mouse. *New York Times.* Retrieved from http://www.edf.org/article.cfm?contentID=6088.

Friedman, T. (2007b). *The world is flat* (Release 3.0). New York, NY: Picador.

Galbraith, J. (2008, September 28). How much will it cost and will it come soon enough? *American Prospect*. Retrieved from http://www.prospect.org/cs/ articles?article=how_much_will_it_cost_and_will_it_come_soon_enough.

Galper, J. (1977). *The politics of the social services*. Englewood Cliffs, NJ: Prentice Hall.

Gambrill, E. (1999). Evidence-based practice: An alternative to authority-based practice. *Families in Society: The Journal of Contemporary Human Services, 80*(4), 341–350.

Garbarino, J. (1992). *Toward a sustainable society*. Chicago, IL: Noble.

Garbarino, J. (1995). *Raising children in a socially toxic environment*. San Francisco, CA: Jossey-Bass.

Garvin, C., & Cox, F. (1987). A history of community organization since the Civil War with special reference to oppressed communities. In F. Cox et al. (Eds.), *Strategies of community organization* (4th ed.). Itasca, MN: Peacock.

General Accounting Office (2014). *Medicaid program integrity: Increased oversight needed to ensure integrity of growing managed care expenditures* (GAO report 14-341). Washington, DC: GAO. Retrieved from http://www.gao.gov/ assets/670/663306.pdf.

Genworth Financial (2012). *Executive summary: Genworth 2012 Cost of Care Survey*. Retrieved from http://www.genworth.com/content/etc/medialib/ genworth_v2/pdf/ltc_cost_of_care.Par.85518.File.dat/Executive%20 Summary_gnw.pdf.

Geriatric Mental Health Foundation (n.d.-a). *Substance abuse and misuse among older adults*. Retrieved from http://www.gmhfonline.org/gmhf/ consumer/factsheets/substnabuse_factsheet.html.

Geriatric Mental Health Foundation (n.d.-b). *Understanding the most common dementing disorder*. Retrieved from http://www.gmhfonline.org/gmhf/consumer/factsheets/alzheimer_disease.html.

Geriatric Social Work Initiative (2012). *Get involved*. Retrieved from http://www.gswi.org/.

Gibbons, S., & Rosecrance, J. (2005). *Probation, parole, and community corrections*. Boston, MA: Pearson.

Gil, D. (1973). *Violence against children*. Cambridge, MA: Harvard University Press.

Gilbert, N., & Specht, H. (1974). *Dimensions of social welfare policy*. Englewood Cliffs, NJ: Prentice Hall.

Gilbert, N., & Terrell, P. (2009). *Dimensions of social welfare policy* (7th ed.). Boston, MA: Allyn and Bacon.

Gladwell, M. (2002). *The tipping point*. New York, NY: Back Bay.

Global Greens (2001). *Charter of the Global Greens*. Retrieved from http://www.globalgreens.info/globalcharter.html#Ecological.

Goering, J., & Feins, J. (2008). Social science, housing policy, and the harmful effects of poverty. *Journal of Urban Affairs, 30*(2), 139–148.

Gopal, P. (2014, April 29). *U.S. homeownership rate falls to the lowest since 1995*. New York, NY: Bloomberg. Retrieved from http://www.bloomberg.com/news/2014-04-29/u-s-homeownership-rate-falls-to-the-lowest-since-1995.html.

Gray Panthers Affiliation of California Networks (n.d.). *Homepage*. Retrieved from http://graypanthers.org/index.php?option=com_content&task=view&id=44&Itemid=10.

Green Party of the United States (2012a). *10 key values*. Retrieved from http://www.gp.org/10-key-values.

Green Party of the United States (2012b). *Platform—social justice*. Retrieved from http://www.gp.org/platform-social-justice.

Gumz, E. (2004). American social work, corrections and restorative justice: An appraisal. *International Journal of Offender Therapy and Comparative Criminology, 48*, 449–460.

Hale, K., & McNeal, R. (2010). Election administration reform and state choice: Voter identification requirements and HAVA. *Policy Studies Journal, 38*(2), 281–302.

Halstead, T., & Lind, M. (2001). *The radical center: The future of American politics.* New York, NY: Doubleday.

Harm, N. J. (1992). Social policy on women prisoners: A historical analysis. *Affilia, 7*(1), 90–108.

Hartford Institute for Religious Research (2012). *Megachurch definition.* Retrieved from http://hirr.hartsem.edu/megachurch/definition.html.

Hick, S., & McNutt, J. G. (Eds.) (2002). *Advocacy and activism on the Internet: Perspectives from community organization and social policy.* Chicago, IL: Lyceum.

Hochman, G., Hochman, A., & Miller, J. (2004). *Foster care: Voices from the inside.* Washington, DC: The Pew Commission on Children in Foster Care.

Hoefer, R. (2000a). Human services interest groups in four states: Lessons for effective advocacy. *Journal of Community Practice, 7*(4), 77–94.

Hoefer, R. (2000b). Making a difference: Human service interest group influence on social welfare program regulations. *Journal of Sociology and Social Welfare, 27*(3), 21–38.

Hoefer, R. (2012a). *Advocacy practice for social justice* (2nd ed.). Chicago, IL: Lyceum.

Hoefer, R. (2012b). From website visitor to online contributor: Three Internet marketing strategies for nonprofits. *Social Work, 57*(4), 361–365.

Hoefer, R. (2012c). *Policy creation and evaluation.* New York, NY: Oxford.

Hoefer, R. (2016). *Advocacy practice for social justice* (3rd ed.). Chicago, IL: Lyceum.

Hoff, M., & McNutt, J. G. (Eds.) (1994). *The global environmental crisis: Implications for social welfare and social work.* Aldershot: Avebury.

Hoff, M., & McNutt, J. G. (2008) Social policy, health and the physical environment. In J. Midgley, M. Tracy, & M. Livermore (Eds.), *The handbook of social policy* (2nd ed.) (pp. 295–311). Beverly Hills, CA: Sage.

Holzer, M., Manoharan, A., Shick, R., & Stowers, G. (2009). *U.S. states e-governance survey (2008): A nationwide assessment of U.S. state websites.* Newark, NJ: National Center for Public Performance, E-Governance Institute, Rutgers University, Campus at Newark.

Hopps, J., Pinderhughes, E., & Shankar, R. (1995). *The power to care: Clinical practice effectiveness with overwhelmed clients.* New York, NY: Free Press.

Howe, N., & Strauss, W. (2000). *Millennials rising: The next great generation.* New York, NY: Vintage.

Huey, J. (1994). Waking up to the new economy. *Fortune, 129*(13), 36–46.

Iatridis, D. (1994). *Social policy.* Belmont, CA: Brooks/Cole.

Institute of Medicine (2008). *Retooling for an aging America: Building the health care workforce.* Washington, DC: National Academies Press.

Jansson, B. (2007). *Becoming an effective policy advocate: From policy practice to social justice.* Belmont, CA: Cengage.

Jenkins, M. (2011). *What's gotten into us? Staying healthy in a toxic world.* New York, NY: Random House.

Johnson, A., & Cnaan, R. (1998). Social work practice with homeless persons: State of the art. *Research on Social Work Practice, 8,* 172–199.

Kadushin, A. (1980). *Child welfare services* (3rd ed.). New York, NY: Macmillan.

Kahn, A., & Kammerman, S. (1976). *Social services in the United States.* Philadelphia, PA: Temple University Press.

Kaiser Family Foundation (n.d.). *Total Medicaid spending.* Retrieved from http://kff.org/medicaid/state-indicator/total-medicaid-spending/from.

Kaiser Family Foundation (2007). *The uninsured: A primer.* Retrieved from http://www.kff.org/uninsured/upload/7451-03.pdf.

Kammerman, S. B., & Kahn, A. J. (Eds.) (2014). *Privatization and the welfare state.* Princeton, NJ: Princeton University Press.

Karger, H., & Stoesz, D. (2009). *American social welfare policy.* Boston, MA: Allyn and Bacon.

Karl, T., Melillo, J., & Peterson, T. (2009). *Global climate change impacts in the United States.* New York, NY: Cambridge University Press.

Kennedy, R. F. (1964). A lawyer's responsibility redefined. *University of Chicago Magazine.* Retrieved from http://mag.uchicago.edu/robert-f-kennedy.

KidsCount (2015). *Data center.* Retrieved from http://datacenter.kidscount.org/.

Kingdon, J. (1995). *Agendas, alternatives and public policies* (2nd ed.). New York, NY: Longman.

Kirst-Ashman, K., & Hull, G. (2011). *Generalist practice with communities and organizations* (5th ed.). Belmont, CA: Brooks/Cole.

Kissick, D., Leibson, D., Kogul, M., Bachmann, J., Anderson, J., & Eckert, J. (2006). *Housing for all: Essential to economic, social, and civic development* (paper prepared for the World Urban Forum, III, Vancouver, British Columbia, Canada, June 19–23).

Kline, E. (2008). A limited health-care success in Massachusetts. *American Prospect*. Retrieved from http://www.prospect.org/cs/articles?article=a_limited_health_care_success_in_massachussetts.

Kristol, I. (2004). The conservative welfare state. In I. Stelzer (Ed.), *The neocon reader* (pp. 145–148). New York, NY: Grove.

Labor Party of Australia (2015a). *Fairness*. Retrieved from http://www.alp.org.au/fairness.

Labor Party of Australia (2015b). *Families*. Retrieved from http://www.alp.org.au/families.

Labor Party of Australia (2015c). *Growth and opportunity*. Retrieved from http://www.alp.org.au/growthandopportunity.

Labour Party of the United Kingdom (2015). *What is the Labour Party?* Retrieved from http://www.labour.org.uk/what_is_the_labour_party.

Laing, R. D. (1983). *The politics of experience*. New York, NY: Pantheon.

Laird, J., & Hartman, A. (Eds.) (1985). *A handbook of child welfare*. New York, NY: Free Press.

Lathrop, D., & Ruma, L. (Eds.) (2010). *Open government: Collaboration, transparency, and participation in practice*. Sevastopol, CA: O'Reilly.

Lauritsen, J. L. (2010). Advances and challenges in empirical studies of victimization. *Journal of Quantitative Criminology, 26*(4), 501–508.

Layne, K., & Lee, J. (2001). Developing fully functional e-government: A four stage model. *Government Information Quarterly, 18*(2), 122–136.

Lee, B. A., Tyler, K. A., & Wright, J. D. (2010). The new homelessness revisited. *Annual Review of Sociology, 36,* 501–521.

Lehti, M., & Aromaa, K. (2007). Trafficking in humans for sexual exploitation in Europe. *International Journal of Comparative and Applied Criminal Justice, 31*(2), 123–145.

Leiby, J. (1978). *A history of social welfare and social work in the United States*. New York, NY: Columbia University Press.

Lenski, G. E., & Lenski, J. (1982). *Human societies: An introduction to macro-sociology*. New York, NY: McGraw-Hill.

Leone, M., McCarthy, B., & MCarthy, B., Jr. (2007). *Community-based corrections* (6th ed.). Belmont, CA: Wadsworth.

Lewis, O. (1961). *The children of Sanchez*. New York, NY: Vintage.

Liberal Party of Australia (2014). *Our beliefs*. Retrieved from https://www.liberal.org.au/our-beliefs.

Liberal Party of Canada (n.d.). *Issues*. Retrieved from www.liberal.ca/issues.

Liberal Party of New York State (2011). *A liberal definition by John Kennedy*. Retrieved from http://www.liberalparty.org/JFKLPAcceptance.html.

Libertarian Party (2014, June). *Libertarian party platform*. Retrieved from https://www.lp.org/platform.

Logan, T. K., Walker, R., & Hunt, G. (2009).Understanding human trafficking in the United States. *Trauma, Violence, & Abuse: A Review Journal, 10*(1), 3–30.

Lohr, S. (2011, January 1). Computers that see you and keep watch over you. *New York Times*. Retrieved from http://www.nytimes.com/2011/01/02/science/02see.html?_r=1.

Louis, K., Thomas, E., Gordon, M., & Febey, K. (2008). State leadership for school improvement: An analysis of three states. *Educational Administration Quarterly, 44*(4), 562–592.

Lubove, R. (1965). *Professional altruist: The emergence of social work as a career, 1880–1930*. New York, NY: Macmillan.

Lucas, H. (2008). Information and communication technology for future health systems in developing countries. *Social Science and Medicine, 66*(10), 2122–2132.

Lucas, R. E. Jr. (2002). *Lectures on economic growth*. Cambridge, MA: Harvard University Press.

Luhby, T. (2011, November 8). *Global income inequality: Where the U.S. ranks*. Retrieved from http://money.cnn.com/2011/11/08/news/economy/global_income_inequality/index.htm.

Magalhaes, J. (2012). *Why do we age?* Retrieved from http://www.senescence.info/aging_theories.html.

Mallen, M. J., Vogel, D. L., Rochlen, A. B., & Day, S. X. (2005). Online counseling: Reviewing the literature from a counseling psychology framework. *Counseling Psychologist, 33*(6), 819–871.

Maluccio, A. N., & Anderson, G. R. (2000). Future challenges and opportunities in child welfare. *Child Welfare, 79*(1), 3–9.

Mary, N. (2008). *Social work in a sustainable world.* Chicago, IL: Lyceum.

Maslow, A. (1954). *Motivation and personality.* New York, NY: Harper.

McCafferty, J. T., & Travis, L. F. III (2014). History of probation and parole in the United States. In *Encyclopedia of criminology and criminal justice* (pp. 2217–2227). New York, NY: Springer.

McConnaughey, J., Everette, D. W., Reynolds, T., & Lader, W. (1999). *Falling through the net: Defining the digital divide.* Washington, DC: National Telecommunications and Information Administration, U.S. Department of Commerce.

McConnaughey, J., Nila, C. A., & Sloan, T. (1995). *Falling through the cracks: A survey of the "have-nots" in rural and urban America.* Washington, DC: U.S. Department of Commerce. Retrieved from http://www.ntia.doc.gov/ntiahome/fallingthru.html.

McConnell, C., Brue, S., & Flynn, S. (2011). *Economics* (19th ed.). New York, NY: McGraw-Hill.

McNutt, J. G. (1996a). National information infrastructure policy and the future of the American welfare state: Implications for the social welfare policy curriculum. *Journal of Social Work Education. 6*(3), 375–388.

McNutt, J. G. (1996b). Teaching social policy in the information age: Innovations in curriculum content and instructional methods. *Tulane University Studies in Social Welfare, 20,* 71–85.

McNutt, J. G. (1997). New communitarian thought and the future of social policy. *Journal of Sociology and Social Welfare, 24*(4), 45–56.

McNutt, J. G. (1998). Ensuring social justice for the new underclass: Community interventions to meet the needs of the new poor. In B. Ebo (Ed.), *The cyberghetto or cybertopia: Race, class, gender and marginalization in cyberspace* (pp. 33–47). New York, NY: Praeger.

McNutt, J. G. (2005). Social welfare policy in an information age: New visions or more of the same? *Advances in Social Work Practice, 6*(1), 60–67.

McNutt, J. G., & Austin, D. M. (1990). *Economics and social change: Implications for the social work curriculum* (paper prepared for the 36th Annual Program Meeting of the Council on Social Work Education, Reno, Nevada).

McNutt, J. G., & Menon, G. M. (2008). Cyberactivism and progressive human services. *Families and Society, 89*(1), 33–38.

McNutt, J. G., & Robinson, C. A. (2008). Policy research on housing and housing finance: Internet resources for studying a system in crisis. *Journal of Policy Practice, 7*(4), 314–319.

Mead, L. (2004). State political culture and welfare reform. *Policy Studies Journal, 32*(2), 271–296.

Medicaid.gov (n.d.). *Behavior health care.* Retrieved from http://www.medicaid .gov/medicaid-chip-program-information/by-topics/benefits/mental -health-services.html.

Michigan Department of Community Health (2011). *2011–2012 Michigan fish advisory: A family guide to eating Michigan fish.* Retrieved from http://www.michigan.gov/documents/FishAdvisory03_67354_7.pdf.

Mickelson, J. S. (1995). Advocacy. In R. L. Edwards (Ed.), *Encyclopedia of social work,* Vol. 1, pp. 95–100. Washington, DC: NASW Press.

Mills, C. W. (1956). *The power elite.* New York, NY: Oxford.

Mills, C. W. (1959). *The sociological imagination.* New York, NY: Oxford.

Miringoff, M., & Opdycke, S. (2008). *America's social health: Putting social issues back on the public agenda.* Armonk, NY: M. E. Sharpe.

Morris, D. (1976). The Physical Quality of Life Index (PQLI). *Development Digest, 1,* 95–109.

Mueller, E., & Tighe, R. (2007). Making the case for affordable housing: Connecting housing with health and education outcomes. *Journal of Planning Literature, 21*(4), 371–385.

Murray, C. (1984). *Losing ground: American social policy, 1950–1980.* New York, NY: Basic.

Murray, C. (1997). *What it means to be a Libertarian.* New York, NY: Broadway.

National Alliance to End Homelessness (2012). *Issues.* Retrieved from http://www.endhomelessness.org/section/issues.

National Center for Health Statistics (2014). *Health, United States, 2013: With special feature on prescription drugs.* Hyattsville, MD: Author.

National Center on Elder Abuse (2010). *Why should I care about elder abuse?* Retrieved from http://www.ncea.aoa.gov/Ncearoot/Main_Site/pdf/ publication/NCEA_WhatIsAbuse-2010.pdf.

National Center on Elder Abuse (2011). *About Adult Protective Services.* Retrieved from http://www.ncea.aoa.gov/ncearoot/Main_Site/Find_Help/ APS/About_APS.aspx.

National Clearinghouse for Long-term Care Information (n.d.). *Paying for LTC.* Retrieved from http://www.longtermcare.gov/LTC/Main_Site/Paying/Index.aspx.

National Conference of State Legislatures (2005). *Focusing on child welfare systems: Collaborating with state legislators on reform.* Retrieved from http://www.ncsl.org/print/cyf/collaborate.pdf.

National Council on Crime and Delinquency (2006, November). *U.S. rates of incarceration: A global perspective.* Retrieved from http://www.nccd-crc.org/nccd/pubs/2006nov_factsheet_incarceration.pdf.

National Public Radio (2013, December 27). *When memories never fade, the past can poison the present.* Retrieved from http://www.npr.org/blogs/health/2013/12/18/255285479/when-memories-never-fade-the-past-can-poison-the-present.

Nauert, R. (2011). *New way to measure societal impact of aging.* Retrieved from http://psychcentral.com/news/2011/12/21/new-way-to-measure-societal-impact-of-aging/32870.html.

Norris, P. (2001). *The digital divide.* New York, NY: Cambridge.

OECD (2002). *Understanding the digital divide.* Retrieved from www.oecd.org/dataoecd/38/57/1888451.pdf.

Offshoring your lawyer. *Economist* (2010, October 16). Retrieved from http://www.economist.com/node/17733545.

Olasky, M. (2000). *Compassionate conservatism: What it is, what it does and how it can transform America.* New York, NY: Free Press.

Oppel, R. (2011, May 23). Steady decline in major crime baffles experts. *New York Times.* Retrieved from http://www.nytimes.com/2011/05/24/us/24crime.html.

O'Toole, L. J. (1997). Treating networks seriously: Practical and research based agendas in public administration. *Public Administration Review, 57*(1), 43–52.

Patton, C. V., & Sawicki, D. S. (1993). *Basic methods of policy analysis and planning* (2nd ed.). Englewood Cliffs, NJ: Prentice Hall.

Pension Benefit Guaranty Corporation (2012). *About PBGC.* Retrieved from www.pbgc.gov.

Peters, B. G. (1994). Managing the hollow state. *International Journal of Public Administration, 17*(3/4), 739–756.

Pfeffer, F. T., Danziger, S., & Schoeni, R. F. (2013). Wealth disparities before and after the Great Recession. *The Annals of the American Academy of Political and Social Science, 650*(1), 98–123.

Pierce, D. (1984). *Policy for the social work practitioner.* New York, NY: Longman.

Piore, P. (1974). The dual labor market: Theory and implications. In D. Gordon (Ed.), *Problems in political economy: An urban perspective* (pp. 90–94). Lexington, MA: Heath.

Piven, F. F., & Cloward, R. (1971). *Regulating the poor: The functions of social welfare.* New York, NY: Vintage.

Platt, A. (1969). *The child savers: The invention of delinquency.* Chicago, IL: University of Chicago Press.

Pleis, J., & Lethbridge-Çejku, M. (2007). *Summary health statistics for U.S. adults: National Health Interview Survey, 2006.* National Center for Health Statistics. *Vital Health Statistics, 10*(235).

Polanyi, K. (1942). *The great transformation: The political and economic origins of our time.* Boston, MA: Beacon.

Pollack, A. (2010, February 27). Rising threat of infections unfazed by antibiotics. *New York Times.* Retrieved from http://www.nytimes.com/2010/02/27/business/27germ.html?em=&adxnnl=1&adxnnlx=1267412412-yP2bfl/3pu4+g34XVmluJA&_r=1.

Porat, M. (1977). *Information economy: Definition and measurement.* Washington, DC: U.S. Department of Commerce.

Posner, C. (2013). *House Republicans have collectively voted to repeal Obamacare over 7,000 times.* Retrieved from http://thinkprogress.org/health/2013/08/27/2533681/house-republicans-obamacare-repeal-votes/#.

Postel, M., de Haan, A., & De Jong, A. J. (2007). E-therapy for mental health problems: A systematic review. *Telemedicine and e-Health, 14*(7), 707–714.

Pratt, L. A., Brody, D. J., & Gu, Q. (2014). *Antidepressant use in persons aged 12 and over: United States, 2005–2008* (NCHS Data Brief No. 76). Washington, DC: CDC.

Prensky, M. (2001a). Digital natives, digital immigrants. *On the Horizon, 9*(5), 1–6.

Prensky, M. (2001b). Digital natives, digital immigrants, part 2: Do they really think differently? *On the Horizon, 9*(6), 1–6.

Price, T. (2005). Child welfare reform: Will recent changes make at-risk children safer? The *CQ Researcher, 15*(15), 345–368.

Prochaska, J., Norcross, J., & DiClemente, C. (1994). *Changing for good: The revolutionary program that explains the six stages of change and teaches you how to free yourself from bad habits*. New York, NY: Morrow.

Pronk, N. P. (2015). Fitness of the U.S. workforce. *Annual Review of Public Health, 36*, 131–149.

Putnam, R. D. (2000*). Bowling alone: The collapse and revival of American community*. New York, NY: Simon and Schuster.

Quinney, R. (1970). *The social reality of crime*. Boston, MA: Little Brown.

Randall, R. (2012). *Baby boomers' defining characteristics could help them redefine aging in America*. Retrieved from http://www.huffingtonpost.com/rhonda-l-randall-do/baby-boomers-redefining-aging_b_1448949.html.

Raskoff, S. (2009, February 4). Beyond bowling alone. *Everyday Sociology*. Retrieved from http://www.everydaysociologyblog.com/2009/02/beyond-bowling-alone.html.

Rawls, J. (1971). *A theory of justice*. Cambridge, MA: Harvard University Press.

Republican Party (2012). *2012 Republican Party platform*. Retrieved from https://cdn.gop.com/docs/2012GOPPlatform.pdf.

Rice, G. T. (1985). *The bold experiment: JFK's Peace Corps*. South Bend, IN: University of Notre Dame Press.

Rocha, C. (2007). *Essentials of social work policy practice*. New York, NY: Wiley.

Rogers, E. (2003). *Diffusion of innovations* (5th ed.). New York, NY: Free Press.

Rogge, M. E. (2000). Children, poverty, and environmental degradation: Protecting current and future generations. *Social Development Issues, 22*(2/3), 46–53.

Rostow, R. R. (1960). *The stages of economic growth: A non-communist manifesto*. London, England: Cambridge.

Ryan, W. (1976). *Blaming the victim* (2nd ed.). New York, NY: Vintage.

Sachs, J. (2008). *Common wealth: Economics for a crowded planet*. New York, NY: Penguin.

Salamon, L. (1994). The nonprofit sector and the evolution of the American welfare state. In R. Herman (Ed.), *The Jossey-Bass handbook of nonprofit leadership and management* (pp. 83–99). San Francisco, CA: Jossey-Bass.

Salamon, L. M., Sokolowski, S. W., & List, R. (2003). *Global civil society*. Baltimore, MD: Johns Hopkins Center for Civil Society Studies.

Santiago, A., & Galster, G. (2004). Moving from public housing to homeownership: Perceived barriers to program participation and success. *Journal of Urban Affairs, 26*(3), 297–324.

Sauter, M., & Stockdale, C. (2012, April 1). *Countries that spend the most on health care*. Retrieved from http://bottomline.msnbc.msn.com/_news/2012/04/01/10922752-countries-that-spend-the-most-on-health-care?chromedomain=worldnews.

Schneider, R. L., & Lester, L. (2001). *Social work advocacy: A new framework for action*. Belmont, CA: Brooks/Cole.

Schorr, L. B. (1997). *Common purpose: Strengthening families and neighborhoods to rebuild America*. New York, NY: Anchor.

Scriven, M. (1991). *Program evaluation thesaurus* (4th ed.). Thousand Oaks, CA: Sage.

Sentencing Project (n.d.-a). *Racial disparity*. Retrieved from http://www.sentencingproject.org/template/page.cfm?id=122.

Sentencing Project (n.d.-b). *Sentencing policy*. Retrieved from http://www.sentencingproject.org/template/page.cfm?id=92.

Shapiro, D. (2011). *Banking on bondage: Private prisons and mass incarceration*. Washington, DC: American Civil Liberties Union.

Shaw, C. R., & McKay, H. D. (1969). *Juvenile delinquency and urban areas: A study of rates of delinquency in relation to differential characteristics of local communities in American cities*. Chicago, IL: University of Chicago Press.

Shock, D. R. (2008). Securing a line on the ballot: Measuring and explaining the restrictiveness of ballot access laws for non-major party candidates in the United States. *Social Science Journal, 45*(1), 48–60.

Shur, E. M. (1973). *Radical nonintervention: Rethinking the delinquency problem*. Englewood Cliffs, NJ: Prentice-Hall.

Siegel, L. J. (2008). *Criminology* (10th ed.). Belmont, CA: Thomson-Wadsworth.

Siegel, L. J., & Welch, B. (2010). *Juvenile delinquency: The core* (4th ed.). Belmont, CA: Thomson-Wadsworth.

Silver, B. D., & Dowley, K. M. (2000). Measuring political culture in multiethnic societies: Reaggregating the world values survey. *Comparative Political Studies, 33*(4), 517–550.

Skocpol, T. (2003). *Diminished democracy: From membership to management in American civic life*. Oklahoma City, OK: University of Oklahoma Press.

Skocpol, T., & Ikenberry, J. (1983). The political formation of the American welfare state in historical and comparative perspective. In R. F. Tomasson (Ed.), *Comparative social research* (pp. 87–148). Greenwich, CT: JAI.

Slack, W. V. (1997). *Cybermedicine.* San Francisco, CA: Jossey-Bass.

Smart Communities Network (n.d.). *Welcome to NCAT's Smart Communities Network.* Retrieved from http://www.smartcommunities.ncat.org/welcome.shtml.

Smith, J. C., & Medalia, C. (2014). *Health insurance coverage in the United States: 2013.* Washington, DC: U.S. Department of Commerce, Economics and Statistics Administration, Bureau of the Census.

Smith, J. M. (2013, September 3). *U.S. Department of Education: Homeschooling continues to grow!* Retrieved from http://www.hslda.org/docs/news/2013/201309030.asp.

Smith, S. R., & Lipsky, M. (1995). *Nonprofits for hire: The welfare state in the age of contracting.* Cambridge, MA: Harvard University Press.

Sobolewski, J. (2012). *Startling new statistics reveal more baby boomers facing old age alone.* Retrieved from http://www.sott.net/articles/show/244204 -Startling-new-statistics-reveal-more-baby-boomers-facing-old-age-alone.

Social Security Administration (n.d.). *Life expectancy and social security.* Retrieved from http://www.ssa.gov/history/lifeexpect.html.

Social Security Administration (2012a). *Proposals addressing trust fund solvency.* Retrieved from http://www.ssa.gov/oact/solvency/index.html.

Social Security Administration (2012b). *Summary of the 2012 Annual Reports: A message to the public.* Retrieved from http://www.ssa.gov/oact/TRSUM/index.html.

Socialist International (1996). *XX Congress.* Retrieved from http://www.socialist international.org/viewArticle.cfm?ArticleID=126&ArticlePageID=51&ModuleID=18.

Socialist International (2009). *Advancing a global welfare statehood.* Retrieved from http://www.socialistinternational.org/viewArticle.cfm?ArticleID=1979.

Socialist Party U.S.A. (n.d.). *Statement of principles.* Retrieved from http://socialistparty-usa.net/principles.html.

Speth, J. G. (2004). *Red sky at morning: America and the global environmental crisis.* New Haven, CT: Yale University Press.

Starr, P. (1995). What happened to health care reform. *American Prospect,* Winter, 20–31.

Stein, T. J. (1998). *When do I go home? Child welfare and the law* (rev. ed.). New York, NY: Longman.

Sweden.se (2010, August 31). *Sweden's political parties: A quick guide.* Retrieved from http://www.sweden.se/eng/Home/Society/Government -politics/Reading/Swedens-political-parties—a-quick-guide/.

Szasz, T. (1974). *The myth of mental illness: Foundations of a theory of personal conduct.* New York, NY: Harper.

Tan, Y., & Weaver, D. (2009). Local media, public opinion and state legislative policies: Agenda setting at the state level. *International Journal of Press/ Politics, 14*(4), 454–476.

Tapscott, D. (1998). *Growing up digital: The rise of the net generation.* New York, NY: McGraw-Hill.

Tighe, R. (2010). Public opinion and affordable housing: A review of the literature. *Journal of Planning Literature, 25*(1), 3–17.

Titmuss, R. (1974). *Social policy: An introduction.* London, England: Allen and Unwin.

Tocqueville, A. D. (1945). *Democracy in America* (2 vols.). New York, NY: Vintage.

Todero, J. (1985). *Economic development for the third world.* New York, NY: Longman.

Tolan, P., Gorman-Smith, D., & Henry, D. (2006). Family violence. *Annual Review of Psychology, 57*, 557–583.

Trattner, W. I. (1998). *From poor law to welfare state* (6th ed.). New York, NY: Free Press.

Trumbull, M. (2007, December 10). Housing: A crisis with staying power. *Christian Science Monitor.* Retrieved from http://www.csmonitor.com/2007/ 1210/p01s01-usgn.html.

Turner, M. (2010). New life for U.S. housing and urban policy. *City and Community, 9*(1), 32–40.

United Nations (2002). *World population aging, 1950–2050.* Retrieved from http://www.un.org/esa/population/publications/worldageing19502050/.

United Nations Children's Fund (UNICEF) (n.d.). *A summary of the rights under the Convention on the Rights of the Child.* Retrieved from http://www.unicef .org/crc/files/Rights_overview.pdf.

United Nations Children's Fund (2012). *The state of the world's children 2012: Children in an urban world.* New York, NY: Author.

United Nations Development Program (n.d.). *About the MDGs: Basics.* Retrieved from http://www.undp.org/mdg/basics.shtml.

United Nations Habitat (n.d.). *Land and housing.* Retrieved from http://www.unhabitat.org/categories.asp?catid=277.

United States Census Bureau (2009). *Current population survey, Table 3.* Retrieved from http://www.census.gov/hhes/www/poverty/histpov/perindex.html.

United States Census Bureau (2011). *Income, poverty and health insurance coverage in the United States: 2010.* Retrieved from http://www.census.gov/newsroom/releases/archives/income_wealth/cb11-157.html.

United States Census Bureau (2012a). *Poverty threshold: 2011.* Retrieved from http://www.census.gov/hhes/www/poverty/data/threshld/index.html.

United States Census Bureau (2012b). *Statistical abstract of the United States: Expectation of life at birth, 1970–2008, and projections 2010 to 2020, Table 104.* Retrieved from http://www.census.gov/compendia/statab/2012/tables/12s0104.pdf.

United States Department of Health and Human Services, Administration for Children and Families (2010). *Child maltreatment, 2009.* Available from http://www.acf.hhs.gov/programs/cb/stats_research/index.htm#can.

United States Department of Health and Human Services, Office of the Assistant Secretary for Planning and Evaluation (2015). *U.S. federal poverty guidelines used to determine financial eligibility for certain federal programs.* Retrieved from http://aspe.hhs.gov/poverty/15poverty.cfm#thresholds.

United States Department of Housing and Urban Development (2011, December 5). Homeless emergency assistance and rapid transition to housing: Defining "homeless": Final rule (24 CFR Parts 91, 582, and 583). *Federal Register, 76*(233), 75994–76019. Retrieved from http://www.hudhre.info/documents/HEARTH_HomelessDefinition_FinalRule.pdf.

United States Department of Justice (2012). *Uniform crime reports.* Retrieved from http://bjs.ojp.usdoj.gov/ucrdata/Search/Crime/State/RunCrimeStatebyState.cfm.

United States Environmental Protection Agency (1989). *The potential effects of global climate change on the United States.* Washington, DC: EPA-230-05-89-050. Retrieved from http://www.epa.gov/climatechange/effects/downloads/potential_effects.pdf.

United States General Accounting Office (2003). *Child welfare: HHS could play a greater role in helping child welfare agencies recruit and retain staff.* Washington, DC: Author.

United States Veterans Administration (2011). *The National Center for Veterans Analysis and Statistics (NCVAS)*. Retrieved from http://www.va.gov/vetdata/.

van Deursen, A. J., & Van Dijk, J. A. (2014). The digital divide shifts to differences in usage. *New Media and Society, 16*(3), 507–526.

Varney, D., & van Vliet, W. (2008). Homelessness, children, and youth: Research in the United States and Canada. *American Behavioral Scientist, 51*(6), 715–720.

Verba, S., Schlozman, K., & Brady, H. (1995). *Voice and equality: Civic voluntarism in American politics.* Cambridge, MA: Harvard University Press.

Voice of America (2011, May 25). *Rising sea levels threaten island nations.* Retrieved from http://www.voanews.com/english/news/environment/Rising-Sea-Levels-Threaten-Island-Nations-122628579.html.

Von Drehle, D. (2010, February 22). What's behind America's falling crime rate? *Time.* Retrieved from http://www.time.com/time/magazine/article/0,9171,1963761,00.html.

Wakefield, S., & Uggen, C. (2010). Incarceration and stratification. *Annual Review of Sociology, 36,* 387–406.

Wall, D. (2007). *Cybercrime.* London, England: Polity.

Wallerstein, I. (1974). *The world system of capitalism.* New York, NY: Academic.

Walt, V. (2008, November 15). Why the energy crisis will outlast the credit crisis. *Time.* Retrieved from http://www.time.com/time/business/article/0,8599,1859236,00.html.

Warren, R. L. (1963). *The community in America.* Chicago, IL: Rand McNally.

Weber, M. (1956). *The Protestant ethic and the spirit of capitalism* (Talcott Parsons, Trans.). New York: Charles Scribner's Sons.

Weitzer, R. (2014). New directions in research on human trafficking. *Annals of the American Academy of Political and Social Science, 653*(1), 6–24.

Wellman, B., Haase, A., Witte, J., & Hampton, J. (2001). Does the Internet decrease, increase or supplement social capital? Social networks, participation and community commitment. *American Behavioral Scientist, 45*(3), 436–455.

West, D. M. (2001). *E-government and the transformation of public sector service delivery* (paper prepared for delivery at the 2001 Annual Meeting of the American Political Science Association, San Francisco, California, August 30–September 2, 2001).

West, D. M. (2005). *Digital government: Technology and public sector performance.* Princeton, NJ: Princeton University Press.

White, R. (2010). Prosecution and sentencing in relation to environmental crime: Recent socio-legal developments. *Crime, Law and Social Change, 53*(4), 365–381.

White House (2009, February 9). *Obama announces White House Office of Faith-based and Neighborhood Partnerships.* Retrieved from http://www.whitehouse.gov/the_press_office/ObamaAnnouncesWhiteHouseOffice ofFaith-basedandNeighborhoodPartnerships/.

Whittaker, J. K., & Maluccio, A. N. (2002). Rethinking "child placement": A reflective essay. *Social Service Review, 76*(1), 108–134.

Wilensky, H., & Lebeaux, F. (1958). *Industrial society and social welfare.* New York, NY: Russell Sage Foundation.

Wilhelm, A. G. (2004). *Digital nation: Toward an inclusive information society.* Cambridge, MA: MIT Press.

Wilkinson, R. G., & Pickett, K. E. (2006). Income inequality and population health: A review and explanation of the evidence. *Social Science and Medicine, 62,* 1768–1784.

Wilson, W. J. (1990). *The truly disadvantaged.* Chicago, IL: University of Chicago Press.

Wilson, W. J. (1996). *When work disappears: The world of the new urban poor.* New York, NY: Vintage.

Wineburg, R. (2007). *Faith based inefficiencies: The follies of Bush's initiatives.* Westport, CT: Greenwood.

Wolk, J. (1981). Are social workers politically active? *Social Work, 26*(4), 283–288.

Woolf, S. H., Purnell, J. Q., Simon, S. M., Zimmerman, E. B., Camberos, G. J., Haley, A., & Fields, R. P. (2015). Translating evidence into population health improvement: Strategies and barriers. *Annual Review of Public Health, 36,* 463–482.

Women's Health Center (n.d.). *Mental health concerns in the elderly.* Retrieved from http://www.womenshealth.org/a/elderly_mental_health.htm.

World Bank (n.d.-a). *Health expenditure, total (% of GDP).* Retrieved from http://data.worldbank.org/indicator/SH.XPD.TOTL.ZS).

World Bank (n.d.-b). *Poverty and equity data*. Retrieved from http://povertydata.worldbank.org/poverty/home.

World Bank (2011). *Measuring inequality*. Retrieved from http://web.worldbank.org/WBSITE/EXTERNAL/TOPICS/EXTPOVERTY/EXTPA/0,,contentMDK:20238991~menuPK:492138~pagePK:148956~piPK:216618~theSitePK:430367,00.html.

World Health Organization (WHO) (2007). *Core health indicators*. Retrieved from www3.who.int/whois/core/core_select_process.cfm.

Wright, K. (2010). Strange bedfellows? Reaffirming rehabilitation and prison privatization. *Journal of Offender Rehabilitation, 49*(1), 74–90.

Zerike, K. (2010). *Boiling mad: Inside Tea Party America*. New York, NY: Times.

Zimmerman, S. (1992). *Family policies and family well-being: The role of political culture*. Thousand Oaks, CA: Sage.

Zukin, C., Keeter, S., Andolina, M., Jenkins, K., & Delli Carpini, M. X. (2006*). A new engagement? Political participation, civic life, and the changing American citizen*. New York, NY: Oxford University Press.

Index

About the Authors

John McNutt is professor in the School of Public Policy and Administration at the University of Delaware. Prior to coming to the university in 2007, he was associate professor and coordinator of the Advanced Practice Concentration in Organizations and Communities at the University of South Carolina College of Social Work. He has more than thirty years of higher education experience, including posts at Boston College Graduate School of Social Work and Indiana University School of Social Work. McNutt's research efforts are in the areas of political use of the Internet and the use and adoption of technology by nonprofit organizations. His published works, more than one hundred, include five coauthored or coedited books and many articles, book chapters, reviews, and other works on advocacy, the digital divide, volunteerism, community development, technology and nonprofit organizations, and technology and public participation. His practice specialties are criminal justice and child welfare. He regularly presents at national and international conferences and is a member of the editorial boards of several scholarly journals.

Richard Hoefer is Roy E. Dulak Professor for Community Practice Research at the University of Texas at Arlington (UTA) School of Social Work, where he has been since 1992, publishing frequently and teaching how to conduct advocacy, evaluate programs, and administer and manage nonprofit organizations. His goal is to provide information to assist nonprofit leaders and social workers in becoming better at their jobs. Hoefer is an award-winning professor and a member of the National Association of Social Workers, the Council on Social Work Education, and the Association for Research on Nonprofit Organizations and Voluntary Action.